THE
COMPLETE GUIDE TO
DIVORCE LAW

THE
COMPLETE GUIDE TO
DIVORCE LAW

Nihara K. Choudhri, Esq.

CITADEL PRESS
Kensington Publishing Corp.
www.kensingtonbooks.com

DISCLAIMER

This book provides a general overview of divorce law for informational purposes only. This book is not designed to—and cannot—take the place of a legal professional. In order to ensure that your rights are protected, you should hire a lawyer to handle your divorce dispute. The author and publisher assume no liability for any inaccuracies contained in this book, whether as a result of changes in the law or otherwise.

CITADEL PRESS BOOKS are published by

Kensington Publishing Corp.
850 Third Avenue
New York, NY 10022

Copyright © 2004 Nihara K. Choudhri

All Kensington titles, imprints, and distributed lines are available at special quantity discounts for bulk purchases for sales promotions, premiums, fund-raising, educational, or institutional use. Special book excerpts or customized printings can also be created to fit specific needs. For details, write or phone the office of the Kensington special sales manager: Kensington Publishing Corp., 850 Third Avenue, New York, NY 10022, attn: Special Sales Department; phone 1-800-221-2647.

CITADEL PRESS and the Citadel logo are Reg. U.S. Pat. & TM Off.

First printing: June 2004

10 9 8 7 6 5 4 3 2 1

Printed in the United States of America

Book design by Leonard Telesca

Library of Congress Control Number: 2003112330

ISBN 0-8065-2528-2

Contents

Chapter Six
Pensions, Stock Options, and Other Special Categories of Property

Chapter Seven
Alimony

PART TWO
THE OUT-OF-COURT AGREEMENT: MINIMIZING THE COSTS AND UNCERTAINTY OF DIVORCE

Chapter Eleven

Chapter Twelve

Chapter Thirteen

Introduction:
Why You Need This Book

For a fraction of the cost of an hour with your divorce lawyer, this book will provide you with an easy-to-understand explanation of the divorce laws. It will teach you the requirements for filing for divorce, how divorce courts divide property, whether you or your soon-to-be ex-spouse may qualify for alimony, what factors courts take into account when making custody determinations, and how much child support will likely be required in your case. Although this book cannot take the place of a legal professional, it can help you understand the rules of the game and prepare you for what lies ahead. Perhaps more important, this book can save you thousands of dollars—if not more—in divorce-related legal fees.

There are several reasons why it is to your tremendous advantage to learn the divorce laws. First, because divorce lawyers generally bill by the hour, having your lawyer spend hours on end answering your basic divorce-related legal questions can become extraordinarily expensive. It is far more cost efficient for you to learn the basics of divorce law on your own and then to rely on your lawyer to explain the details of your state's divorce laws and how the law is likely to be applied to your case.

Second, learning the divorce laws will help you take an active and productive role in your divorce. A working knowledge of divorce law will help you focus your time—and consequently, your lawyer's expensive time—on the facts and issues that matter the most.

Third, understanding the divorce laws can help you reach a fair and comprehensive out-of-court divorce agreement with your spouse. Settling out of court is by far the least expensive, most efficient, and least traumatic way to divorce your spouse. Unlike litigated divorce disputes, which can take anywhere from months to years to resolve, out-of-court divorce settlements can often be reached within a matter of weeks. Because time is money when lawyers are involved, divorce disputes that are quickly resolved through out-of-court settlements usually cost tens of thousands of dollars less in legal fees than litigated cases.

The better informed you are about the divorce laws, the more likely it is that you and your spouse will be able to reach a reasonable out-of-court settlement. A good understanding of the divorce laws will help you appreciate what you stand to gain and lose by litigating your divorce dispute and to recognize when and on what terms you should settle out of court.

Part one of this book takes you step-by-step through the divorce laws, addressing everything from the basics—like the grounds for divorce—to complex topics like pensions, stock options, and professional licenses and degrees. Part two discusses out-of-court agreements in detail and provides valuable guidance on how to go about negotiating an out-of-court agreement with your spouse.

HOW TO USE THIS BOOK

As you probably already know, the divorce laws vary from state to state. To understand the law in your state, you should first read all of the general sections in part one of the book that apply to you. Feel free to skip any section that has absolutely no relevance to your case. For example, you should skip the custody, visitation, and child support sections if you and your spouse do not have children. Once you have read the applicable general sections, you should then turn to appendix A for a summary of the specific divorce laws of your state. Reading the state-specific rules set forth in appendix A will not be of much help to you unless you have first read the general sections of the book, because the concepts referred to in the state-specific appendix—such as "marital property" and "equitable distribution"—are only explained in the general sections of the book.

Part one relates how the majority of states address various divorce-related issues. You will notice that a state-specific rule is not provided in appendix A for every single concept discussed in part one. This is because the law in many states is still in flux on a number of issues. To ensure that the information provided in this book is as accurate as possible, state-specific rules are provided only if the law on a given issue is well settled. The information in appendix A is limited to the divorce statutes and well-established case law.

Once you have an understanding of the issues that are likely to be in dispute in your case, and a good sense of how courts tend to analyze those issues, you should then turn to your lawyer to learn how courts in your own state have recently addressed those issues. Ask your lawyer for an assessment of how the law in your state likely applies to the facts of your case.

Unfortunately, this book cannot replace your need for a lawyer or teach you how to be your own lawyer. To understand why you will need to consult a lawyer even after you have learned the basics of the divorce laws through reading this book, it helps to know how the divorce laws are made. The foundation for the divorce laws in any state is the *divorce statutes*—the rules enacted by your state legislature that dictate what constitutes marital property, how marital property is divided, when alimony may be awarded, how child custody determinations are made, and how child support is calculated. Some divorce statutes are relatively detailed; others are silent on many important issues. The divorce statutes are not designed to provide a specific formula for every possible divorce scenario. Rather, they set forth general principles that judges must bear in mind when deciding divorce cases.

The second layer of the divorce laws is *case law*—decisions issued by judges in divorce disputes. Divorce judges have the difficult task of applying the general principles set forth in the divorce statutes to the particular facts of the case at hand. Although judges often interpret the divorce statutes, they must just as often reach decisions on issues that are *not* covered by the statutes. In other words, judges must frequently make divorce law when there is no specific rule that addresses the issue in dispute.

To ensure that different judges will not reach opposite conclusions on the same issues in similar cases, the legal system is set up so that judges in the same state must generally follow previous decisions—or case law—involving the same issues and similar facts. Prior judicial decisions are known as *precedent*. Sometimes, however, judges in the same state will depart from precedent and reach a different decision, even when the case involves the same issues and similar facts. This may be because of the judge's own unique set of perspectives, ideas, and biases. Or it may be that a lawyer found a new way to present the question or came up with a novel legal argument.

Because the divorce statutes do not cover every possible scenario, and because judges are given a great deal of discretion when deciding divorce cases, it is impossible to predict with certainty how a judge will decide any given case. It is, however, possible to chart the general trends in the law and to evaluate how a judge in a given state would likely decide a particular issue. This book can only chart the general trends in the law. To determine how a judge is likely to decide the particular issues in your case, you will need the help of a lawyer in your own state. Your lawyer's job will be to research the most recent case law involving the issues in your case and to tell you how judges in your state have addressed cases with facts similar to yours. Your lawyer will also be able to tell you whether there have been any significant changes to the law in your state since this book was published.

To assist you in making the best use of your lawyer, part one of this book provides a preliminary list of questions to ask at the end of every chapter. You should ask your lawyer only the questions that are relevant to your case.

Together with your lawyer, part one of this book will help you understand how your divorce dispute would likely be resolved if you were to go to trial. Part two of this book then invites you to consider whether and on what terms you should settle out of court and takes you step by step through the process of negotiating an out-of-court settlement.

Though this book encourages out-of-court settlements, there are some couples for whom litigation is inevitable. This book will be useful even if you expect a contentious divorce battle, as it will serve as an invaluable guide to the many different issues that can arise in heated divorce disputes.

PART ONE

UNDERSTANDING DIVORCE LAW

Chapter One

Where Can You File for Divorce?

In order to file for divorce in any given state, you must meet that state's residency requirements. The specific residency requirements vary from state to state; however, certain general principles are common to all. First, either you or your spouse must currently live in the state where you wish to file for divorce. It is not enough that you were married in that state or that you lived there together at one time. In some states, the rules specifically require that the *petitioner*—the individual filing for divorce—be a resident of the state.

Second, the resident spouse must generally have been living in the state for a certain minimum amount of time. For example, in order to file for divorce in Rhode Island, either you or your spouse must have resided in Rhode Island for at least one year prior to filing for divorce.

Third, the state court must have *personal jurisdiction* over both you and your spouse. Personal jurisdiction is a court's authority to make legal decisions with respect to someone. In general, a court will have personal jurisdiction over you and your spouse only if you both have some connection with the state. The personal jurisdiction requirement ensures that people cannot be sued in faraway states that they have never even visited. For example, you cannot move to Hawaii and file for divorce there if your spouse lives in North Carolina, has never visited Hawaii, and does not wish to litigate a divorce dispute thousands of miles away.

There are three ways in which a court can have personal jurisdiction over someone. First, a court has personal jurisdiction over anyone who has a significant connection to the state. Under this rule, a court has personal jurisdiction over anyone who lives in the state. A court also has personal jurisdiction over anyone who maintains a vacation home in the state or runs a business with an office in the state. It gets tricky, however, when a person has only some very small connection to the state. For example, if Susan was married in Ohio twenty years ago, but has never visited nor had any connection to Ohio since then, an Ohio court would not have personal jurisdiction over her. This is because Susan does not have any present connection to Ohio.

Second, a court has personal jurisdiction over anyone who is served with divorce papers while physically in the state. By visiting a state, a person takes advantage of what that state has to offer and therefore becomes subject to the authority of courts in that state. For example, if Arthur lives in Arizona but is served with divorce papers while visiting Oregon, an Oregon court would have personal jurisdiction over him.

Third, a court generally has personal jurisdiction over anyone who agrees to litigate a case in that state. For example, Donald could simply agree to have his divorce dispute heard in his wife's home state of Oklahoma, even though he resides in New Mexico and has never even set foot in Oklahoma. An Oklahoma court would have personal jurisdiction over Donald because he consented to the court's jurisdiction.

WHY IT MATTERS WHERE YOU FILE FOR DIVORCE

Depending on the facts of your case, you may qualify to file for divorce in more than one state. For example, suppose that Ellen lives in New York, but her husband, Bruce, has been living in California since their separation one year ago. Ellen and Bruce both have sufficient contacts with California and New York, such that courts in both states would have personal jurisdiction over Ellen and Bruce. In this case, Ellen would have her choice of filing for divorce in New York or California.

The question of where to file for divorce is extremely important because the laws of the state in which you file for divorce will generally govern the terms of your divorce. Instead of filing for divorce in the state that is most convenient, it is critical that you file for divorce in the state with the most favorable divorce laws pertaining to the facts of your case. When evaluating which state's divorce laws are better for you, you should consider the available grounds for divorce, how each state defines and divides marital property, the factors each state considers in awarding alimony, how each state determines custody, and how each state calculates child support. Because the laws can vary a great deal from state to state, where you file for divorce may have a dramatic impact on the outcome of your case.

If you are considering moving to another state before filing for divorce, you should take into account the effect of that move on your ability to file for divorce in your current home state. In addition, you should determine whether it would be more advantageous for you to file for divorce in your current home state or in the state where you plan to move. If you plan to file for divorce in your new home state, bear in mind that you will have to meet that state's residency requirements before filing for divorce.

It is possible that your spouse will file for divorce before you have a chance to do so. In that case, your spouse will get to choose the state in which to file for divorce. Because of this advantage of being the first to file, you may want to file for divorce as soon as you have made the decision to do so.

QUESTIONS TO ASK YOUR LAWYER

- Given the facts of my case, where can I file for divorce?
- If I have the option of filing for divorce in more than one state, which state's divorce laws are more favorable for me, given the facts of my case?
- If I plan to move to another state:
  - Would I still be able to file for divorce in my current home state?
  - Would I be able to file for divorce in the state to which I plan to move?
  - How long would I have to wait to file for divorce in the state to which I plan to move?

Chapter Two

Grounds for Divorce

In order to obtain a divorce, you must demonstrate to the court that you have good reasons—or *grounds*—for divorce. At one time, you could only divorce your spouse on fault-based grounds, such as adultery. You had to point the finger of blame at your spouse, and air some of the "dirty laundry" of your marriage, just to have the legal freedom to go your separate ways. Those days are over. Courts now allow unhappy couples to divorce on a "no-fault" basis. If the marriage has broken down beyond the point of repair, or if a couple has been separated for a specified period of time, courts will grant a divorce. In a number of states, the only grounds for divorce are no-fault.

There are several reasons for the shift toward no-fault divorces. First, fault-based divorces assume that one spouse is solely to blame for the failure of the marriage. Courts increasingly consider both spouses to share some responsibility for the marital breakdown. Second, requiring spouses to demonstrate fault in order to obtain a divorce only adds to the anger and bitterness of the divorce process. No spouse, however blameworthy, tends to react well to accusations of adultery, cruelty, or any other type of marital fault in divorce papers. The result is often nasty and endless litigation. Third, the old fault-based system encouraged spouses to hire private investigators, publicize compromising photographs, and so forth. Taking fault out of the equation has cleaned up the divorce process and enabled courts to focus on the important issues of economics and children. One result of the shift toward no-fault divorces is that many courts are now reluctant to consider fault when dividing marital property and awarding alimony. A substantial number of states prohibit courts from considering marital fault for such purposes.

Although the no-fault divorce system has many benefits, not everyone is pleased with the results. Divorce opponents argue that no-fault divorces have made it easier for couples to divorce and that the no-fault system is responsible for the growing number of divorces in America. Advocates of women contend that no-fault divorces have resulted in a lower post-divorce standard of living for many women who have received smaller property allocations and less alimony and child support than they would have under the previous fault-based system.

THE NO-FAULT GROUNDS FOR DIVORCE

All states now offer no-fault grounds for divorce. Many states allow couples to divorce if there has been an "irretrievable breakdown of the marriage relationship." Different states use different terminologies—such as "irreconcilable differences" or "incompatibility of temperament"—to describe this ground for divorce. Regardless of the specific language used, all of these states essentially allow a couple to divorce if their marriage has broken down and there is no chance of reconciliation. In order to obtain a divorce on grounds of irretrievable marital breakdown, all that is usually required is that one spouse state under oath that the marriage is irreparably broken. Alternatively, both spouses can simply agree in writing that their marriage is broken beyond repair.

The other, more restrictive, no-fault ground for divorce is living separate and apart for a specified period of time. Depending on the state, you and your spouse must live separately for anywhere from six months to five years in order to divorce on this basis. Some states offer the separation ground in addition to the marital breakdown ground. In other states, such as New York, living separate and apart for a set period of time is the only no-fault divorce option. To determine the no-fault grounds for divorce available in your state, please turn to appendix A.

THE FAULT GROUNDS FOR DIVORCE

The most common fault grounds for divorce are

- Adultery
- Cruelty
- Abandonment
- Mental illness
- Criminal conviction

A discussion of these grounds follows.

Adultery

In order to obtain a divorce on grounds of adultery, you must demonstrate that your spouse voluntarily engaged in sexual relations with someone else. Sexual relations with someone of the same sex qualifies as adultery, and activities that fall short of intercourse—such as oral sex—can also constitute adultery.

To prove adultery, you will not have to produce a videotape of your spouse in the act or any other such direct evidence. Rather, you just need to provide the court with circumstantial evidence of your spouse's adultery. For example, a court may consider it sufficient if Jane presents testimony that her husband, Sean, has an unusually close relationship with one of his more attractive female coworkers—the two have often been sent off on business trips together and the coworker has answered the telephone in Sean's hotel room late at night on numerous occasions. Because adultery is still a crime in many states, it is unlikely that one spouse would simply admit his or her unfaithfulness to the court.

Cruelty

To obtain a divorce on grounds of cruelty (sometimes called "cruel and inhuman treatment"), you must demonstrate that it would be physically, mentally, or emotionally dangerous for you to continue living with your spouse because of his or her behavior. Occasional temper tantrums or outbursts of unkindness are generally not enough to warrant a divorce based on cruelty. Rather, your spouse's cruelty must somehow be outside the bounds of normally tolerable behavior.

A related ground for divorce is "indignities," which consists of emotional or mental abuse by your spouse. If your spouse regularly speaks to you in a vulgar manner, or criticizes you endlessly, a court may grant you a divorce on grounds of indignities.

Abandonment

To obtain a divorce on grounds of abandonment, you must demonstrate that your spouse has abandoned you and your marriage for a specified period of time (usually one year). The period of abandonment must be continuous. If you and your spouse reconcile at some point after one of you leaves the other, one of you must again abandon the other for the entire specified period before either of you can obtain a divorce on grounds of abandonment.

Leaving one's spouse for reasons unrelated to the marriage does not count as abandonment. For example, suppose that Michael left his wife, Marcia, for two years in order to complete his active military duty. He would not be deemed to have abandoned his wife because he was away for reasons unrelated to their marriage.

Leaving the marital home with the consent of the other spouse—as in the case of spouses who make a mutual decision to separate—also does not count as abandonment. Moreover, a spouse who is forced to leave the marital home by the other spouse—as in the case of a spouse who leaves in order to escape domestic violence—will not be considered "guilty" of abandonment.

Physically leaving the marital home is not the only way in which one spouse can abandon the other. Refusing to engage in sexual relations with one's spouse can also constitute abandonment. If sexual relations are impossible because of one spouse's impotency, or if the decision to cease sexual relations is a mutual one, neither spouse will be considered "guilty" of abandoning the other.

Mental Illness

In order to file for divorce on the grounds that your spouse is mentally ill, you must generally demonstrate that your spouse has suffered from a serious mental illness for a specified number of years. Some states require that your spouse must have been committed to an institution or declared incurable before you can obtain a divorce on the grounds of your spouse's mental illness. In no state is minor mental illness—such as a bout of depression—grounds for divorce.

Criminal Conviction

In most states, you do not have to remain married to your spouse if he or she has been convicted of a serious crime—such as rape or robbery. Some states will allow you to divorce your spouse the moment that he or she is convicted of a serious crime. Other states require that your spouse be imprisoned for a specified period of time before you can file for divorce on this basis.

Other Grounds for Divorce

Other common grounds for divorce are

- Alcohol or drug abuse
- Impotency beginning from the time of the marriage and continuing until the time of the divorce, such that the marriage was never consummated
- Failure to support one's spouse even though one has the ability to do so

Some states also offer unusual grounds for divorce, such as joining a religious sect that destroys the marriage (New Hampshire), and infecting one's spouse with a venereal disease (Illinois). To determine the specific fault grounds for divorce available in your state, please turn to appendix A.

DEFENSES TO A DIVORCE PETITION

One spouse may be able to defeat the other's petition for divorce, or obtain a divorce on different grounds, if he or she can establish a defense to the grounds set forth in the petition. Because courts are now generally inclined to grant divorces even when one spouse opposes the divorce, courts do not pay nearly as much attention to divorce defenses as they once did.

For the no-fault divorce ground of irretrievable marital breakdown, the only real defense is a claim that there is still a chance of reconciliation. If one spouse asserts that the marriage is irretrievably broken, however, a court is unlikely to place much weight on the other spouse's claim that the marriage can be saved.

For the no-fault divorce ground of separation for a specified period of time, the only defense is that the spouses were not actually separated for the requisite period of time. If the spouses temporarily reconciled or resumed sexual relations during their separation, a court may conclude that the couple was not in fact living separate and apart for the required amount of time.

With respect to the fault grounds, the main defense is that the accused spouse was not actually at fault. For example, if one spouse files for divorce on grounds of adultery, the other spouse can defend him- or herself by proving that he or she did not commit adultery. Legal defenses to the fault grounds include recrimination, reconciliation (also known as con-donation), and insanity.

The defense of *recrimination* prevents one spouse from obtaining a divorce on fault grounds when he or she is also guilty of some kind of marital fault. For example, a husband who has himself committed adultery may be barred from obtaining a divorce on the grounds of his wife's adultery.

The defense of *reconciliation* (also known as *condonation)* prevents one spouse from obtaining a divorce on fault grounds after he or she has already forgiven the other spouse for the conduct at issue. For example, a wife will not be able to obtain a divorce on the grounds of her husband's abandonment if the couple reconciled after the abandonment. This is because she had already forgiven her husband for leaving her.

Finally, the defense of *insanity* prevents one spouse from obtaining a divorce on fault grounds—such as cruelty—when the other spouse was insane at the time of the acts in question. The theory behind this defense is that people should not be held as accountable for conduct outside of their control as for conduct that is intentional.

DETERMINING WHETHER TO DIVORCE ON NO-FAULT OR FAULT GROUNDS

The most important consideration in determining the grounds for divorce is whether your state takes marital fault into account for the purposes of property division and alimony. If your state factors in marital fault when making such economic determinations, it may be to your advantage to file for divorce on fault-based grounds. If, on the other hand, your state does not take fault into account for property division and alimony purposes, it may not make sense to file for divorce on fault-based grounds. Doing so will only serve to anger your spouse and make it more difficult to reach an out-of-court settlement.

An additional consideration in determining the grounds for divorce is whether you anticipate a custody battle. If a custody dispute is likely, it may be in your best interests to file for divorce on fault-based grounds. Provided that your allegations of fault are well founded, filing for divorce on fault-based grounds such as cruelty or alcohol abuse may bolster your claims that your spouse is less fit than you are to be the children's primary custodian. Filing for divorce based on adultery, however, is unlikely to have much of an impact on your custody case. This is because most courts do not consider adulterous behavior to be directly related to one's parenting skills.

You should discuss with your lawyer the pros and cons of filing for divorce based on fault versus no-fault grounds before making a final decision. In no event should you file for divorce based on fault grounds simply to establish that your spouse is to blame for the breakdown of your marriage. You are likely to derive little consolation from doing so, and you may unleash a fury on your spouse's part that ultimately results in a less favorable divorce settlement for you.

QUESTIONS TO ASK YOUR LAWYER

- Given the facts of my case, on what grounds can I file for divorce?
- What are the proof requirements for the fault-based grounds for which I qualify?
- Does my state take marital fault into account for the purposes of property division and alimony?
- Does my state take extramarital affairs into account when awarding custody? If so, to what extent?
- Is there any other advantage to filing for divorce on one ground rather than another?

Chapter Three

An Overview of Property Division

Property division is often the most complex and contentious aspect of any divorce. Even in simple cases, property division is a multistep process. First, divorce courts must determine what property is subject to division, a process so involved that this book devotes an entire chapter to it. The property subject to division in a divorce is called "community property" in some states and "marital property" in others. For the sake of convenience, this book will use the term "marital property." When referring to the entire pot of marital property, this book will use the term "marital estate."

Second, divorce courts must value each piece of marital property. Though valuation is relatively simple in the case of stocks and bonds, it can be very complicated in the case of businesses, pensions, and other assets. The use of accountants or other financial experts is often required when complex assets are involved.

Third, divorce courts must determine each spouse's share of marital property. Some states divide marital property equally between the spouses; others divide marital property equitably, according to what is fair under the circumstances. As you might expect, husbands and wives tend to have very different views of what would be equitable in any given case.

Finally, divorce courts must allocate the marital property. This is easier said than done. Even if the law provides for equal division of marital property, it is generally impractical simply to divide each piece of marital property in half. Instead, divorce courts must apportion marital property in such a way that each spouse gets his or her appropriate share, which may mean that one spouse gets the house and the other spouse gets the mutual fund account. In some cases, it may be impossible for one spouse to receive his or her full share of the marital property right away. This may be because much of the marital property is tied up in an asset that is not liquid—such as a business or a pension—and there are insufficient funds for the other spouse to "buy out" his or her share. In such cases, divorce courts may provide for payment plans or other methods of ensuring that each spouse ultimately receives his or her fair share.

COMMON LAW VERSUS COMMUNITY PROPERTY

You may be aware that there are two different systems in the United States for property ownership and management during a marriage: the *common law system* and the *community property system*. Under the common law system, each spouse has the sole right to property owned in his or her name. In common law states, title dictates ownership and property rights during the marriage. For example, suppose Jack purchased a house during his marriage to Jill using money he earned during their marriage. He put only his name on the title. In a common law state such as New York, Jill would have no right to that house during her marriage to Jack. Thus, Jack would be free to sell the house and keep the proceeds, or do anything he pleased with respect to the house during his marriage to Jill.

Under the community property system, however, each spouse has a present one-half interest in any property acquired during the marriage. In community property states, title is irrelevant to ownership and property rights during the marriage. Thus, if Jack and Jill lived in a community property state such as California, Jill would own one-half of the house that Jack bought even though he did not put her name on the title. Depending on the particular rules of the community property state, Jack would no longer be free to do what he wished with respect to the house, because half of the house would belong to Jill.

These particular differences between the common law system and the community property system disappear in the event of divorce. Neither common law states nor community property states consider title determinative of ownership when spouses divorce. If divorce courts distributed property according to title, you could ensure that your spouse had no claim to property you acquired during your marriage simply by keeping property in your own name—for example, by depositing your paychecks into a separate account in your name only. Because this would lead to tremendously unfair results, divorce courts do not consider title when dividing property. Rather, divorce courts focus on whether the property constitutes marital property. The issue of whether or not property counts as marital property is discussed in detail in chapter four.

MARRIAGE AS AN ECONOMIC PARTNERSHIP

A key to understanding how the divorce laws work with respect to property division is the economic partnership theory of marriage. Divorce courts view failed marriages as failed economic partnerships and use this as the starting point in their analysis of any divorce case. Divorce courts assume that husbands and wives, like business partners, work together to better their financial situation. Courts recognize that husbands and wives may contribute to the family finances in different ways—one spouse may work outside the home to earn a living; the other may stay at home or accept a less demanding, less lucrative position in order to raise a family. Divorce courts understand that raising a family, providing emotional support to one's spouse, and engaging in other homemaking activities positively impact the family finances. This is because one spouse's work in the home arena allows the other spouse to devote more time and energy to income-producing activities.

Why is the economic partnership theory of marriage important? Because divorce courts rely on this theory to justify giving each spouse an equal or at least equitable share of marital property, even if only one spouse earned most or all of the marital property. It may come as a surprise that divorce courts never divide marital property solely according to who earned it, nor do they automatically grant a larger share of marital property to the spouse who earned the most during the marriage. The economic partnership theory of marriage is also important in defining marital property. Under this theory, virtually all property acquired by either spouse during the marriage counts as marital property, irrespective of which spouse actually earned the property in question.

The economic partnership theory of marriage may not make a great deal of sense to you at first. But consider this: If divorce courts applied a keep-what-you-earned rule instead of treating spouses as business partners working for their mutual benefit, stay-at-home parents and parents who make career sacrifices for their children would invariably emerge from a divorce with a disproportionately smaller share of marital property than their spouses. Husbands and wives would effectively be penalized for making decisions that put their children before their careers or their personal happiness before their bank accounts.

If you keep the economic partnership theory of marriage in mind as you read through the property division chapters, the divorce laws will make much more sense to you. You will better understand why certain property is classified as separate property and why other property is classified as marital property, and you will better understand why property is divided in certain ways in some cases and in other ways in other cases.

WHAT COUNTS AS "PROPERTY"?

An important though perhaps not obvious concept in property division is the issue of what counts as "property." You probably already know that cash, real estate, stocks, bonds, automobiles, art, jewelry, furs, and furniture count as property, but you may be surprised to learn what else counts as property. The following generally count as property for the purposes of property division in a divorce:

- Pensions
- Stock options
- Businesses
- Closely held corporations
- Professional practices
- Inventions
- Books authored by you or your spouse
- Songs written by you or your spouse
- Contingency fees (depending on the state)
- Accounts receivable
- Disability pay
- Lottery winnings
- Accrued vacation time that has a cash value
- Frequent flier miles
- Goodwill
- Income tax refunds

One important exception to the definition of property for the purposes of a divorce action is *expectancies*. Expectancies are funds or property that you expect to receive in the future but have not yet received and have no vested right to receive. A classic example is an expected inheritance. Even if your grandmother has already prepared her will and plans to bequeath $1 million to you upon her death, a divorce court will not consider that $1 million to be property for the purposes of your divorce. This is because you would simply expect to receive an inheritance but have no vested right to such an inheritance and no guarantee that you will actually receive it. After all, your grandmother could always reconsider and redraft her will.

Apart from this exception, the general rule to bear in mind is that virtually anything of value counts as property in the context of a divorce. When you try to determine what your spouse and you own, remember to include anything that has any value of any kind. Chances are that it counts as property and thus could potentially be marital property subject to division in your divorce.

When considering what counts as property, don't forget to consider "negative property" in the form of debts and liabilities. Divorce courts tend to divide debt using the same rules that they apply when dividing property. Depending on your financial situation, the division of debts and liabilities may be a key aspect of property division in your divorce.

PROPERTY DIVISION IS FINAL

All property division decisions are final. This is true irrespective of whether a judge decides the terms of your property division or whether you and your spouse reach agreement on the property division issues out of court. In general, a judge will reevaluate a divorce judgment or settlement agreement only if one spouse engaged in fraud—for example, by concealing assets during the property division process—or if both spouses made a substantial mistake in the course of property division. In one Illinois case, for example, the husband did not inform his wife that he had won more than $5 million just days before filing for divorce. When the husband's concealment came to the court's attention, the court nullified its divorce judgment.

Mistakes regarding the value of property are another potential basis for having property division decisions nullified. Suppose for example that neither you nor your spouse realized that the painting you had purchased for $5 at a garage sale was by a now-famous artist and worth $40,000. In such a case, a divorce court would consider nullifying its previous decision because it failed to take into account an asset worth a substantial amount of money when dividing your marital property.

If your case involves neither fraud nor mistake, but you still want to challenge the court's division of marital property, your only option is to file an appeal. Appellate courts are very reluctant to overturn trial court decisions in divorce cases. In general, an appellate court will not overturn a divorce judgment unless the trial court committed an *abuse of dis-*

cretion—an extremely high standard. Appeals are also extremely expensive. In the event that you successfully appeal your divorce judgment, the appellate court may very well remand the case to the trial court for reconsideration in light of the appellate court's guidelines. This would mean that you win the opportunity to litigate your case once more—hardly an appealing result.

If your case does not proceed to trial, and you and your spouse simply settle out of court, you will have no right to appeal your case. You will generally be able to challenge your property division agreement only if your spouse engaged in fraud during the settlement process or forced you to sign the agreement against your will.

THE EFFECTS OF DEATH AND BANKRUPTCY

Both death and bankruptcy pose serious problems in the context of divorce. If your spouse dies during the course of your divorce proceedings, you probably will not be allowed to continue your divorce proceedings for the perhaps obvious reason that your opponent is dead. Decisions relating to the division of marital property will then be made according to the laws of probate, rather than the laws of divorce. Thus, a court would look to the terms of your spouse's will to determine property division issues.

In many states, courts will nullify any will provisions bequeathing property to a spouse if divorce proceedings had already been commenced by the time of that individual's death. If your spouse dies during the course of your divorce proceedings, and your state nullifies any will provisions bequeathing property to you, you could be left with virtually no marital property. You would then receive only the property that you and your spouse held jointly, such as the funds in your joint bank account.

If there is a reasonable likelihood that your spouse could die during the course of your divorce proceedings, you should consult with your lawyer about your property rights in that event. You may even want to consider having your spouse draft a temporary will, designed to be in effect only during the course of your divorce proceedings, that acknowledges the existence of the divorce proceedings and provides you with a reasonable share of all marital property. Even if the terms of the temporary will are quite different from what you would ideally like to receive at the end of your divorce proceedings, the temporary will may prove critical in the event that your spouse dies prematurely.

Bankruptcy is almost equally disruptive to property division. Generally speaking, bankruptcy wipes out any obligations associated with property division. For example, suppose that your spouse was obligated to pay you your share of his or her medical practice using an installment plan, pursuant to which he or she paid a certain sum to you every month. If your spouse then filed for bankruptcy, a bankruptcy court may very well find that he or she is no longer obligated to make those payments to you. This is not the case with alimony and child support. If your spouse were required to make alimony and child support payments to you before filing for bankruptcy, he or she would have to continue making those payments to you even after filing for bankruptcy. This is because alimony and child support payments are not dischargeable in bankruptcy.

If your spouse has high amounts of debt and you believe that bankruptcy is a reasonable possibility, be certain to discuss this with your lawyer as soon as possible. Your lawyer may advise you to file for bankruptcy together with your spouse before filing for divorce, as this often leads to a more favorable result. If you live in a community property state, all community property gets swept into the bankruptcy estate when one spouse files for divorce. Thus, when one spouse files for bankruptcy, it is almost as if both spouses are filing for bankruptcy together. Regardless of whether you would consider filing for bankruptcy jointly with your spouse, it is critical that your lawyer is aware of the possibility of bankruptcy and provides for protections in the event of bankruptcy in your settlement agreement.

QUESTIONS TO ASK YOUR LAWYER

- On what grounds would a court in my state nullify a divorce judgment?
- On what grounds would a court in my state nullify a settlement agreement?
- What are the grounds for appeal in my state?
- Should I consider asking my spouse to draft a temporary will providing me with certain assets, pending the finalization of the divorce?
- Should I consider filing for bankruptcy together with my spouse prior to filing for divorce?
- What kinds of bankruptcy protections should be included in my settlement agreement?

Chapter Four

Marital Property Versus Separate Property

The starting point for property division is determining what constitutes marital property. Only marital property is divisible in a divorce, so the question of whether property counts as marital property or separate property is an important threshold issue. The three different systems for classifying property as marital property are the "dual property" system, the "hybrid" system, and the "kitchen sink" system.

Most states use the "dual property" system. Under this system, marital property consists of all property earned or acquired during the marriage. Property acquired prior to marriage is considered separate property, as is property received by one spouse as a gift or inheritance during the marriage.

Under the "hybrid" system, courts adhere to the dual property system unless doing so would lead to an unjust or unfair result. Courts in hybrid states have the power to classify all property as marital property in appropriate cases. Let us consider an example. Suppose that Justin and Jessica have property worth $500,000, of which $475,000 came from Justin's inheritance. This would normally be considered Justin's separate property. If a court were to apply a strict separate property–marital property distinction, Jessica would leave the marriage with at most $25,000, while Justin would leave the marriage with at least $475,000. Depending on the circumstances of the case, this may be a tremendously unfair result. In Justin and Jessica's case, a divorce court in a hybrid state would be allowed to sweep Justin's inheritance into the marital estate to provide Jessica with a larger share of the property.

Finally, the "kitchen sink" system considers all property owned by a couple to constitute marital property, regardless of how or when the property was acquired. Even if property was acquired prior to marriage or through an inheritance, courts in kitchen sink states will consider that property to be marital property. The rationale behind the kitchen sink system is that putting all property into the marital estate provides the courts with the most flexibility to reach a property division that is fair and just.

To learn which system applies in your state, please turn to appendix A. If you happen to live in a state that follows the kitchen sink system, don't skip the rest of this chapter just yet. While divorce courts in kitchen sink states count all property as marital property, they take into account many of the same factors that other states use for classifying property as separate property when dividing marital property. For example, the kitchen sink states classify inheritances as marital property but will generally consider the fact that one spouse inherited that property when dividing marital property. The end result is often the same: the inherited property goes to the spouse who inherited it. So continue reading, because it will be very helpful for you to understand the general principles that other states use in distinguishing marital property from separate property.

MARITAL PROPERTY

In the dual property and hybrid states, marital property consists of all property earned or acquired during the marriage, subject to certain exceptions. Property earned or acquired by either spouse during the marriage is considered marital property because it was earned through marital labor (the work of either spouse during the marriage), the investment of marital funds (any money earned by either spouse during the marriage), or marital luck (for example, winning a lottery during the marriage). Property acquired during the marriage counts as marital property irrespective of the manner in which title is held.

Marital property consists not only of property acquired during the marriage, but also property earned during the marriage even if that property is not actually received until after the marriage has ended. For example, Wall Street bonuses constitute marital property to the extent that they were earned during the marriage, even if the bonuses are not actually paid until after the marriage had ended. If property earned during the marriage but actually received after the marriage were counted as separate property, you could deprive your spouse of marital property simply by arranging to receive your compensation after your marriage has ended. For example, a lawyer would be able to keep his fees all to himself simply by asking his clients to postpone their payments until after his divorce was final. To avoid such a result, divorce courts consider all property earned during the marriage to be marital property.

Often, property is received for work that was done in part during the marriage and in part after the marriage has ended. In such cases, the property is considered part marital property and part separate property. For example, suppose that Patricia spent three years working on a successful class action lawsuit on a contingency fee basis. Suppose further that Patricia was married to Peter for only two of those three years. In Patricia's case, only two-thirds of her contingency fee would count as marital property because only two-thirds of her fee was earned during her marriage to Peter.

Property Acquired After the Marriage Has Ended

Although property earned or acquired during the marriage counts as marital property, property earned or acquired after the marriage has ended counts as separate property. Different states have different rules on what constitutes the end of a marriage. The various cutoff dates for the acquisition of marital property used by the states include:

- The date of the divorce decree
- The date of the decree of legal separation
- The date the spouses execute a separation agreement
- The date either spouse files for divorce
- The date of the spouses' final physical separation

In some states, the rules do not specify a cutoff date for the acquisition of marital property.

Because of the importance of the cutoff date for the acquisition of marital property, you should immediately learn the cutoff date that applies in your state (see appendix A). Be aware that courts strictly enforce the cutoff dates. If you don't keep the cutoff dates in mind as you proceed with your divorce, you could be in for quite a surprise. In one Hawaii case, for example, the husband started a business after separating from his wife but before obtaining a divorce. The husband did not use any marital funds to start the business, and the wife strongly objected to her husband's starting the business. Because Hawaii uses the date of the divorce decree as the cutoff date for the acquisition of marital property, however, the divorce court held that the husband's business constituted marital property and awarded the wife half of the business.

Property Acquired When Living Together

An increasingly common issue in divorces is whether property acquired while a couple was living together constitutes marital property. Courts around the country are still grappling with how to handle this situation. Some courts have held that because such property was not acquired during the marriage, the property does not constitute marital property. Other courts have taken a more progressive view, reasoning that property acquired before the marriage but in contemplation of marriage should count as marital property. Still other courts have held that such property should not count as marital property, but that courts should provide for some kind of compensation outside of the divorce context to ensure that property acquired while a couple was living together is distributed fairly.

Because couples these days tend to live together for a number of years before finally tying the knot, excluding property acquired during those years from the marital estate can lead to tremendously unfair results. If the status of property acquired while you and your spouse were living together is an issue in your case, you should consult with your lawyer about how courts in your state have recently addressed the issue. It may be best if you and your spouse could simply agree that property acquired while you were living together counts as marital property.

SEPARATE PROPERTY

Though marital property is subject to division in a divorce, separate property is completely separate and not divisible upon divorce. In the dual property and hybrid states, the most common categories of separate property are:

- Property acquired prior to marriage
- Inherited property
- Property received as a gift
- Property received as compensation for a personal injury
- Property earned or acquired after the marriage has ended

These categories of property are not classified as marital property because neither marital funds (any money earned by either spouse during the marriage) nor marital labor (the work of either spouse during the marriage) was involved in obtaining or earning such property. Each of the categories of separate property is discussed in turn next, with the exception of the last category, which has already been discussed.

Property Acquired Prior to Marriage

Divorce courts in dual property and hybrid states generally consider property either spouse earned or acquired prior to marriage to constitute that spouse's separate property. This is because this property was obtained before the marital partnership came into existence.

In some cases, determining whether property was earned or acquired before the marriage can be a tricky question. For example, Henry may have paid a $10,000 down payment and purchased a $100,000 cottage before his marriage to Eliza, but he may have paid down the $90,000 mortgage on that cottage during his marriage to Eliza. Some states would consider the cottage to constitute Henry's separate property because he purchased the cottage before his marriage to Eliza. Other states would consider the cottage to be part marital property and part separate property, because the purchase price was paid using both separate and marital funds.

Inherited Property

Divorce courts in dual property and hybrid states generally consider inherited property to constitute the recipient's separate property. This is because it was acquired through the generosity of a deceased relative or friend, rather than as a result of marital labor or marital funds.

Only property that is left to one spouse alone—rather than to both spouses together—constitutes separate property. Property left to both spouses jointly is considered marital property. To determine whether an inheritance was left to one spouse alone or to both spouses jointly, you need only look to the provisions of the will bequeathing that property.

Gifted Property

As is the case with inherited property, divorce courts in dual property and hybrid states generally consider property received by one spouse as a gift to constitute that spouse's separate property. Gifts made to both spouses jointly are classified as marital property.

Unlike inheritances, gifts are usually not accompanied by a formal legal document indicating the intended recipient. It is therefore not always easy to determine whether a gift was made to one spouse alone or to both spouses jointly. The question of whether property was gifted to one spouse alone or to both spouses jointly is an important one, as this determines whether the gift counts as marital property or separate property.

Let us consider an example. Suppose that Philip and Maria were married for fifteen years and had two children. On the occasion of their tenth anniversary, Philip's parents presented the couple with a brand new Mercedes. Philip and Maria both drove the Mercedes regularly until Philip filed for divorce. Philip argued that the Mercedes constituted his separate property because it was a gift to him from his parents. Maria, on the other hand, claimed that the Mercedes was marital property because it was an anniversary gift to both Philip and Maria. If they were unable to settle their differences on this issue, it would be up to a divorce court to determine whether Philip's parents gifted the Mercedes to Philip alone or to Philip and Maria jointly. Whether or not the Mercedes constituted marital property would turn on this determination.

Notably, gifts only count as separate property if they were received from someone other than one's spouse. It may come as quite a surprise that all of the gifts you and your spouse have given to each other over the years—from jewelry to fur coats to automobiles—all constitute marital property.

An important exception to this general rule is the engagement ring. Unlike gifts given during the marriage, an engagement ring is traditionally given before the marriage. In legal-speak, an engagement ring is a conditional gift, with the condition being that the recipient of the ring wed the bearer of the ring. Once the wedding has taken place and this condition is satisfied, the engagement ring belongs to the wife as her separate property.

Property Received as Compensation for a Personal Injury

Divorce courts in many states consider property received as compensation for a personal injury—such as the injuries caused by an automobile accident—to constitute separate property. However, when part of the compensation for the personal injury is a reimbursement for medical expenses and lost wages, that part of the award may count as marital property.

Let us consider an example. Suppose that Chris was badly injured in a rollover accident involving a sports utility vehicle. He and his wife, Jeanne, spent $10,000 out-of-pocket for Chris's medical expenses. He lost $40,000 in wages during the six months that he was out of work as a result of the injury. Chris sued the manufacturer of the sports utility vehicle and recovered $150,000 as a personal injury award for pain and suffering, medical expenses, and lost wages. A divorce court would likely hold that $50,000 of Chris's personal injury award constitutes marital property, because marital funds were used to pay $10,000 of Chris's medical expenses and the marital partnership suffered $40,000 in lost wages. A divorce court would likely classify the remaining $100,000 of Chris's personal injury award as his separate property, paid to compensate him for the pain and suffering that he alone experienced.

Workers' compensation and disability payments are similar to personal injury awards because such payments are also received in connection with a personal injury. Some divorce courts treat workers' compensation and disability payments as the injured spouse's separate property, just as they would treat a personal injury award. Other courts treat workers' compensation and disability payments as marital property, because these payments are designed to replace the wages that the worker would have earned had he or she not been injured. Because different states vary as to how workers' compensation and disability payments are treated, be certain to ask your lawyer about your state's position if either is an issue in your case.

PROPERTY ACQUIRED IN EXCHANGE FOR SEPARATE PROPERTY

Property acquired in exchange for separate property is generally treated as separate property. For example, if inheritance money is used to purchase a yacht, the yacht would be classified as separate property because the yacht was bought using separate property funds. Notably, it would be up to the owner of the yacht to prove that the yacht was in fact purchased using inheritance money. Depending on how long it has been since the original acquisition of the separate property, it may be very difficult to demonstrate that certain property was acquired in exchange for separate property or purchased using separate property funds.

Let us consider an example. Suppose that Melissa held $100,000 in IBM shares before her marriage to Benjamin. After her marriage to Benjamin, Melissa sold her IBM shares for $200,000 and purchased a small studio apartment. Several years later, she sold the small studio apartment for $300,000 to purchase shares in a technology sector mutual fund. Suppose finally that Melissa sold her shares in the technology sector mutual fund for the healthy sum of $500,000, which she then used to buy a luxury condominium overlooking the river. A divorce court would ordinarily assume that the luxury condominium constituted marital property because it was acquired during the marriage. In order for a divorce court to classify the luxury condominium as Melissa's separate property, Melissa would have to trace that purchase back to her original separate property in the form of $100,000 worth of IBM shares. If Melissa could not produce the necessary receipts and paperwork to trace the luxury condominium back to her original IBM shares, and if Benjamin did not agree that the condominium constituted Melissa's separate property, a divorce court may very well classify Melissa's luxury condominium as marital property.

THE APPRECIATION OF SEPARATE PROPERTY

The increase in value of separate property during the marriage is generally classified as separate property. However, when separate property appreciates as a result of the efforts of either spouse during the marriage, or through the use of marital funds, courts tend to classify that appreciation as marital property. In determining whether the appreciation of separate property constitutes marital property or separate property, divorce courts will consider whether the separate property required the active management of either spouse or whether marital funds were spent in improving, maintaining, or reducing indebtedness on separate property.

Let us consider two different examples. Suppose that Jonathan inherited $50,000 of Cisco stock. Thanks to a bull market, Jonathan's Cisco stock appreciated by $25,000 during his marriage to Lynn. Because Jonathan's separate property appreciated as a result of market forces rather than marital labor or the investment of marital funds, most divorce courts would classify Jonathan's $25,000 worth of stock appreciation as his separate property.

Now suppose that Jonathan received a ramschackle old country house worth $75,000 as a gift from his great uncle, and Jonathan and Lynn spent every weekend for two summers fixing up the cottage and successfully restored the house to its original charm. When Jonathan and Lynn finally filed for divorce, the country house was worth $150,000. A divorce court would likely hold that while the $75,000 representing the original value of the country house constitutes Jonathan's separate property, the $75,000 of appreciation counts as marital property. This is because the property appreciated as a result of marital labor: the hard work of both Jonathan and Lynn during their marriage.

Even if only Jonathan worked to fix up the ramshackle old cottage, most divorce courts would consider the appreciation of Jonathan's cottage to constitute marital property. This is because under the economic partnership theory of marriage, any property earned by either spouse during the marriage constitutes marital property.

One exception to this rule is if the spouse whose efforts resulted in the appreciation of separate property was adequately compensated for those efforts during the marriage. Suppose for example that Jennifer owned a florist shop prior to her marriage to Tyler. During her marriage to Tyler, Jennifer drew a salary of $50,000 a year from her florist shop, reinvested the remainder of her profits into her business, and as a result, the florist shop appreciated by $150,000. In determining whether the $150,000 of appreciation constitutes marital property or Jennifer's separate property, a divorce court would likely consider whether Jennifer's salary of $50,000 adequately compensated the marital partnership for her work at the florist shop.

Another exception to this rule is if only a minor amount of marital labor or marital funds was involved in the separate property appreciation. For example, suppose that Carlos's $10,000 worth of investment holdings appreciated to $15,000 during his marriage and that his only involvement in the appreciation of his investment holdings was spending a few minutes a week chatting with his stockbroker about the management of his account. Because Carlos's investment holdings appreciated primarily as a result of market forces and his stockbroker's efforts, a divorce court would probably conclude that the appreciation of Carlos's investment holdings constitutes his separate property.

INCOME FROM SEPARATE PROPERTY

Divorce courts in many states count income from separate property as marital property to the extent that the income was earned during the marriage. For example, courts in these states would classify rental income from a separate property building as marital property, provided that the income was earned during the marriage.

Some states, such as Nevada, consider income from separate property to constitute separate property, even if it was earned during the marriage.

In other states, the issue of how to classify income from separate property remains unresolved.

TRANSMUTATION: WHEN SEPARATE PROPERTY BECOMES MARITAL PROPERTY

A very tricky concept to understand is that, depending on how property is managed during the marriage, separate property can become marital property, a process known as *transmutation*. Separate property can be transmuted into marital property when separate property is *commingled*—or mixed—with marital property during the marriage and can also be transmuted into marital property when one spouse changes the title from separate ownership to joint ownership.

If separate property is commingled with marital property during the marriage, such that it is impossible to distinguish the separate property from marital property, divorce courts will generally consider the separate property to have been transmuted into marital property. A common example is when husbands and wives maintain one joint bank account, and deposit all funds—including inheritances, gifts, and money earned prior to marriage—into the joint bank account. Commingling can also occur when a couple purchases property with a mix of marital funds and separate funds or uses separate property to improve, maintain, or reduce indebtedness on marital property—for example, by using separate property funds to pay down a mortgage on the marital home.

If it is possible to trace the separate property, many divorce courts will consider the separate property to remain separate property despite the commingling. Let us consider an example. Suppose that Dennis inherited $4,000 from his grandmother, which he deposited into a rainy-day savings account held jointly with his wife, Victoria. No withdrawals were ever made from the savings account during their marriage. In such a case, Dennis could easily trace his separate property inheritance to the savings account and would likely succeed in arguing that the $4,000 still remains his separate property. Unfortunately, not all commingling cases are as simple as the case of Dennis's inheritance. Tracing separate property can be quite challenging, and it is up to the owner of the separate property to demonstrate that the separate property is traceable.

Changing title of separate property to joint ownership is another way in which separate property can be transmuted into separate property. Many divorce courts presume that when one spouse changes the title of separate property to joint ownership—for example, by changing the title of a separate property house to include his or her spouse on the title—that spouse intends to make a gift of the separate property to the marital estate.

When title to separate property is changed purely for administrative convenience or for tax or estate planning purposes, divorce courts will generally conclude that the separate property remains separate. For example, physicians often transfer virtually all of their property to their spouses in order to place their assets beyond the reach of patients suing for medical malpractice. In such cases, the physicians do not intend to make a gift of all of their property to their spouses. Rather, the property is transferred to their spouses' names for strategic reasons.

If a divorce court considers separate property to have been transmuted into marital property, the court may simply treat the separate property as marital property. Alternatively, the court may consider the property as part marital property and part separate property, according to the proportions of marital and separate property that were contributed. Finally, the court may count the separate property as marital property but reimburse the former owner of the separate property for the value of that property.

At the end of the day, the issue of transmutation boils down to how you managed family finances during your marriage. Did you maintain a strict "mine" versus "yours" distinction? Or did you pool your resources together and treat all of your assets as "ours"? If you were rigorous about treating your assets as your own separate property during your marriage, chances are that a divorce court will hold that such property remains your separate property in the event of a divorce. If, on the other hand, you shared and shared alike with your spouse, you may face an uphill battle in seeking to classify your assets as separate property. The moral of the story—and a helpful concept to bear in mind if you remarry—is that most states require you to treat separate property separately during your marriage to avoid having it become marital property. The only other option is to enter into a prenuptial agreement that clearly delineates what counts as marital property and what counts as separate property, and the conditions under which transmutation can occur, if ever.

FRAUDULENT TRANSFERS

In any state—even kitchen sink states—property that does not belong either to you or to your spouse at the end of your marriage does not count as marital property. To take advantage of this rule, your spouse may attempt to "gift" property or "sell" property for a bargain price to friends or relatives shortly before filing for divorce in order to reduce the size of the marital estate. Generally, these gifts or bargain-price sales are made with the tacit understanding that the property will be returned once the divorce is final. Such gifts or bargain-price sales are called *fraudulent transfers,* and divorce courts look very harshly on such attempts to reduce the size of the marital estate. If a divorce court finds that property was gifted or sold at a bargain price shortly before a divorce with the primary purpose of reducing the size of the marital estate, the court may reverse the fraudulent transfer and bring the property back into the marital estate.

Let us consider the following. Suppose that George made a $500,000 gift to his parents just two weeks before filing for divorce. He did not consult his wife, Amanda, before making the gift. The total value of all of the property owned by George and Amanda—including the $500,000 gifted to George's parents—is $650,000. In such a case, a divorce court would likely find that George's half a million dollar gift to his parents was in fact a fraudulent transfer, designed to deprive Amanda of her right to her share of those funds. The divorce court may therefore reverse George's gift to his parents and include the $500,000 gift in the marital estate.

When one spouse has children from a previous marriage, it is not too uncommon for that spouse to make a sizeable gift to his or her children shortly before filing for divorce. If the gift meets the requirements of either the Uniform Gifts to Minors Act (UGMA) or the Uniform Transfers to Minors Act (UTMA), a divorce court may presume that the gift was a valid one and not a fraudulent transfer. If, however, a gift to children from a previous marriage does not meet the requirements of either UTMA or UGMA, a divorce court may consider the gift a fraudulent transfer and include the gift in the marital estate. If this is an issue in your case, you should check with your lawyer to see whether the requirements of UTMA or UGMA were met with respect to the gift.

QUESTIONS TO ASK YOUR LAWYER

- Given the facts of my case, what property will be deemed marital property and what property will be deemed separate property?
- What is the cutoff date for the acquisition of marital property in my state?

- What date is used for the valuation of marital property?
- If I live in a kitchen sink state, will the court take into account the source of the property for the purposes of property division?
- How do courts in my state classify the appreciation of separate property?
- How do courts in my state classify income from separate property?
- Given the facts of my case, will a court consider any of my separate property to have been transmuted into marital property?
- How do courts in my state treat property acquired while a couple was living together?
- How do courts in my state treat workers' compensation, disability payments, and personal injury awards?
- How do courts in my state handle fraudulent transfers?
- Given the facts of my case, is a court likely to find that either I or my spouse fraudulently transferred property?

Chapter Five

The Division of Marital Property

Determining what counts as marital property is only the first step in property division. The marital property at issue must then be valued, a process that may require the assistance of appraisers, experts, certified public accountants, or other financial professionals. Divorce courts must then determine how much marital property each spouse is to receive and allocate it between the spouses.

The three systems for dividing marital property in the United States are as follows. The first provides for a simple 50-50 division of all marital property, irrespective of the particular circumstances of each case. In these states, determining what counts as marital property is the most critical issue.

The second and most common system divides marital property according to what is *equitable*—or most fair and appropriate—in any given case. Equitable division is not the same as equal division. Depending on the circumstances of the case, equitable division may mean a 60-40 split, a 70-30 split, or a 50-50 split. In arriving at an equitable division of marital property, divorce courts consider a number of different factors. These *equitable distribution factors* are discussed in more detail later in this chapter.

The third system divides marital property equally between the spouses unless an equal division would be inequitable—or unfair and inappropriate—in any particular case. In determining whether an equal division of marital property would be inequitable, divorce courts in these states consider the same equitable distribution factors used in states that always divide marital property equitably rather than equally.

To determine which system of property division applies in your state, please turn to appendix A.

THE EQUITABLE DISTRIBUTION FACTORS

The factors that courts consider most often when arriving at an equitable distribution of marital property are:

- Each spouse's contributions to the marriage
- Each spouse's contributions to the other's career and earning potential
- Financial misconduct
- The present and future economic circumstances of each spouse
- The length of the marriage
- The needs of each spouse
- The age and health of each spouse

What may surprise you is that marital fault—such as adultery or abandonment—is generally not taken into account for the purposes of equitable distribution.

The advantage of equitable distribution is that it allows courts to tailor property division to the specific circumstances of each case, with due consideration given to each spouse's behavior and contributions during the marriage. A key drawback of equitable distribution, however, is its tremendous unpredictability. Even though courts must take certain equitable distribution factors into account when dividing marital property, they are not provided with mathematical formulas dictating how much weight must be given to each factor or how property should be divided in different cases. Thus, it can be very difficult for divorcing spouses in equitable distribution states to anticipate how a judge will rule on their property division issues.

The Role of Marital Fault in Equitable Distribution

In most states, divorce courts do not consider marital fault when dividing marital property. Courts are increasingly uncomfortable with using the property division process to punish spouses who behave badly. This is due in part to the fact that both spouses are generally able to dredge up examples of egregious behavior on the part of the other spouse, and it may be difficult for a court to determine who was more at fault. Courts also recognize that marital fault may simply be the manifestation of a sick marriage. One spouse's adultery, for example, may signify that the marital relationship is already so irreparably damaged that the spouse had to look outside the marriage for physical and emotional comfort. Finally, the elimination of marital fault as a determining factor in the division of marital property "sanitizes" divorce proceedings. Taking marital fault out of the equation reduces the need for courts to hear the sordid details of each spouse's bad behavior and enables courts to focus their attention on the economic issues at hand.

The overwhelming trend leans toward eliminating the role of marital fault in property division; however, a few states still officially take marital fault into account when dividing marital property. The consideration of marital fault in these states can lead to dramatically unequal property divisions. As noted by one Connecticut court, "[i]t has not been unusual for courts to award a wife virtually all the marital assets as well as child support when a husband has broken up a marriage by committing adultery." *Charpentier v. Charpentier,* 206 Conn. 150, 154 (Ct. 1988).

The elimination of fault from marital property division can lead to tremendously unfair results when one spouse has been physically, sexually, or emotionally abused by the other during the marriage. If abuse is an issue in your case, you should be particularly careful about where you file for divorce if you have a choice of more than one state and the laws differ. You should also consider consulting your lawyer about seeking relief outside of the divorce context. For example, you may be able to file a marital tort action if your spouse has been physically abusive but your state does not consider marital fault in property division.

Each Spouse's Contributions to the Marriage

In arriving at an equitable division of marital property, divorce courts place great emphasis on each spouse's contributions to the marriage and the family finances, including a spouse's non-economic contributions as a homemaker and parent. Divorce courts reason that one spouse's non-economic contributions enable the other spouse to devote more time and energy to the acquisition of marital property. The rationale for considering non-economic contributions as well as economic contributions was explained by one New York court as follows:

> The [equitable distribution] statute is a reflection of the awareness that marriage is, among other things, an economic partnership, the success of which depends not only on the respective

economic contributions of the parties, but also on a wide range
of unremunerated services to the joint enterprise, such as homemaking, raising children, and providing the emotional and moral
support necessary to sustain the other spouse in coping with life
outside the home.
Mele v. Mele, A.D.2d 685, 686 (N.Y. App. Div. 1989).

Divorce courts place little weight on non-economic contributions in
short marriages. In lengthy marriages, however, divorce courts take non-
economic contributions quite seriously. When evaluating non-economic
contributions, divorce courts do not generally place a dollar value on
such contributions because it is impossible to put a price tag on love and
emotional support. Thus, if you attempt to demonstrate that your homemaker spouse's non-economic contributions should be valued at no more
than the cost of a nanny and a part-time housekeeper, a court is unlikely
to be impressed with the analogy and your soon-to-be ex-spouse will
probably never again entertain the possibility of an out-of-court divorce
settlement.

Still, divorce courts do not completely disregard economic realities
when considering non-economic contributions. If it is clear that one
spouse's non-economic contributions could not possibly have had any effect on the acquisition of marital property, courts will take that fact into
account when dividing marital property. For example, suppose that
Karen worked long hours as an investment banker and earned all of the
marital property at issue in her case. Her husband, Nelson, was not
employed outside of the home and did not make any significant contributions to the family or the household. Suppose further that Karen employed
a full-time nanny and housekeeper to take care of the house and the children. In Karen's case, a divorce court would be unlikely to place much
weight on Nelson's non-economic contributions when dividing marital
property because Nelson did very little to benefit the marital partnership.

The fact that one spouse was responsible for the acquisition of the
vast majority of marital property is not determinative of property division questions. Divorce courts do, however, somewhat favor the spouse
who actually earned the marital property. For example, in one high-profile
Connecticut case, the wife of a top General Electric executive claimed
that she was entitled to half of the couple's multi-million-dollar fortune
based on her non-economic contributions as a corporate wife and mother.
The court awarded the wife substantially less than half of the marital assets on the grounds that her husband was primarily responsible for the
growth of the family fortune.

This is not to say that a homemaker spouse inevitably receives less than half of all marital property in equitable distribution states. Depending on the circumstances of the case, the homemaker spouse can emerge from a divorce with more than half of the marital property. For example, one Nevada court has noted that it is entirely appropriate to award more than half of the marital property to a wife and mother in a long-term marriage who has given up career opportunities to devote herself to her family.

In considering each spouse's contributions to the marriage, divorce courts will take into account the fact that one spouse used his or her separate property for marital purposes. For example, if one spouse used his or her inheritance to pay down the mortgage on the marital home, a divorce court would keep that contribution in mind when deciding how to distribute the marital home.

Each Spouse's Contributions to the Other's Career or Earning Potential

Divorce courts will consider each spouse's contributions to the education or training of the other spouse when dividing marital property. If one spouse worked two jobs in order to support the other spouse's graduate school education, a court will certainly take that sacrifice into account when dividing marital property. As explained by the Iowa Supreme Court, it would be tremendously unfair to disregard those contributions when dividing marital property:

> During the years of this marriage, the parties undertook the long-range project of transforming Joe from a largely uneducated man of modest means into a practicing physician with great earning potential. Joe's radically improved situation was undoubtedly achieved with considerable effort and sacrifice on his own part, but the effort and sacrifice cannot be isolated from the marriage. It does not strike us as fair . . . to simply add up the family assets, subtract the liabilities (including those for student loans and bonding obligations for a clinic), and divide the net by two.
> *In re Marriage of McNemey,* 417 N.W.2d 205, 209 (Iowa 1987).

Divorce courts will also consider the career opportunities that one spouse had to forgo in order to provide the other spouse with opportunities to advance his or her career. A common scenario is when a couple moves to a state that offers one spouse more professional opportunities but decreases the other spouse's chances of career growth. Divorce courts will also factor in any unpaid work that one spouse did in the other spouse's business or professional practice, such as assisting a physician-spouse with medical billing.

Financial Misconduct

Though divorce courts are increasingly reluctant to consider marital fault when dividing marital property, they uniformly take financial fault into account. The most commonly considered type of financial fault in a divorce is *dissipation,* which is defined as wasting marital property. Classic examples of dissipation are gambling losses and luxurious gifts to lovers. In one Illinois case, for example, the appellate court found that the husband had dissipated marital assets by spending more than $116,000 on gifts for his mistress.

A spouse will not be deemed to have dissipated marital property if the other spouse either approved of or did not object to the expenditures in question. For example, suppose that Allison regularly withdrew money to purchase cocaine from the joint checking account she held with her husband, Dylan. Dylan was aware that Allison regularly withdrew money from their account to support her addiction but did nothing to stop her. Because Dylan did not object to Allison's misuse of the funds in their joint checking account, a divorce court would probably find that she did not dissipate marital assets.

In addition to dissipation, some divorce courts will consider one spouse's extraordinary financial mismanagement during the marriage when dividing marital property. One Illinois court, for example, took into account the fact that the value of a couple's stock holdings declined from $2 million to $15,000 under the husband's supervision, and the husband's only explanation was that he had made poor investments.

The problem with holding spouses accountable for poor financial decisions during the marriage is that virtually every divorcing spouse could theoretically be found guilty of financial mismanagement, whether by excessive spending on one's wardrobe, making poor career decisions, or loaning marital funds to irresponsible relatives. The South Carolina Court of Appeals summed up the issue neatly as follows:

> One spouse or the other may have spent marital funds foolishly or selfishly or may have invested them unprofitably. The [equitable distribution] statute wisely prevents the other spouse from resurrecting these transactions at the end of the marriage to gain

> an advantage in the equitable distribution. Were it . . . otherwise, human greed and vindictiveness would transform the courts into "auditing agencies" for every marriage that falters.
> *Panhorst v. Panhorst,* 301 S.C. 100, 105 (S.C. Ct. App.1990).

Unless your spouse's financial mismanagement during your marriage was somehow extreme and outside of your control, a court is unlikely to consider such behavior when dividing marital property. A divorce court would be more concerned if your spouse engaged in financial misman-agement of marital property after your marriage had effectively ended, however. This is because post-marriage financial mismanagement may be a vindictive act on the part of one spouse, and the other spouse may have very little control over such behavior.

If you live in a community property state, your chances of success on a financial mismanagement claim may be somewhat higher because a number of community property states have statutes providing that each spouse owes the other a duty of good faith in the management of com-munity property. You should be certain to consult with your lawyer if financial mismanagement is an issue and you live in a community prop-erty state.

The Economic Circumstances of Each Spouse

In dividing marital property, divorce courts place great weight on the economic circumstances of each spouse at the time of the divorce. Addi-tionally, courts will take into account each spouse's income, separate property, and separate debts and liabilities. Additionally, courts will con-sider each spouse's future economic circumstances, including his or her employment history, job prospects, and opportunities to acquire property in the future.

Part of the reason divorce courts take each spouse's economic cir-cumstances into account when dividing marital property is that they would prefer to provide the less well-off spouse with adequate resources through property division rather than through alimony. This is because property division is a one-time, final event that cuts off the ties between the spouses. Alimony, on the other hand, requires the spouses to maintain an ongoing financial relationship of sorts. Alimony is also far more likely to result in future litigation than property division.

When evaluating each spouse's present and future economic circum-stances, divorce courts recognize that spouses who have been full-time parents and homemakers for many years are going to be at a significant economic disadvantage after their divorce. As explained by the Utah Supreme Court:

> It is entirely unrealistic to assume that a woman in her mid-50's with no substantial work experience or training will be able to enter the job market and support herself in anything even resembling the style in which the couple had been living.
> *Jones v. Jones,* 700 P.2d 1072, 1075 (Utah 1985).

Divorce courts may provide the less well-off spouse with a larger share of marital property to enable him or her to maintain an adequate standard of living after the divorce. In one New York case, for example, the court granted the wife 80 percent of the marital assets because of her lack of education, the unlikelihood of her ever achieving a reasonable measure of financial independence, and her husband's relatively strong economic position.

Depending on the circumstances of the case, however, the fact that one spouse has a substantial amount of separate property may not necessarily warrant an unequal distribution of marital property. For example, another New York court divided marital property worth $500,000 equally between the spouses even though the husband had $4,500,000 worth of separate property.

The Length of the Marriage

Divorce courts take different approaches to dividing marital property depending on the length of the marriage. In short-term marriages, divorce courts are usually inclined to restore each spouse to the financial condition that he or she was in prior to the marriage. This is usually easier said than done, because couples often take out mortgages, purchase assets together, or make other joint financial decisions even in short-term marriages.

In long-term marriages, divorce courts are far more likely to award a substantial share of marital property to the less well-off spouse. Divorce courts tend to presume that the spouses' contributions equal out, more or less, in long-term marriages. As a result, a stay-at-home parent and homemaker has a much stronger marital property claim in a marriage of twenty-five years than in a marriage of four years.

Classifying marriages as either long- or short-term can be tricky if the spouses lived together for an extended period of time prior to their mar-

riage. In modern times, it is not unusual for a couple to have lived together for six years and then to have been married for four. Should such
a couple be treated the same as a couple who was married for ten years,
or as a couple who was married for only four years? Because the length
of the marriage is very relevant to property division, this could prove to
be an important issue.

The Needs of Each Spouse

When dividing marital property, divorce courts will take into account the
needs of each spouse, including the standard of living to which each
spouse is accustomed, the financial needs arising out of one spouse's custody of the couple's children, and any financial obligations to children or
ex-spouses from previous marriages. Divorce courts consider the marital
standard of living when deciding property division issues, but they recognize that maintaining an identical standard of living for both spouses
after the divorce may not always be possible or desirable. Because two
households cost substantially more than one, divorcing spouses often
suffer a decline in their standard of living following their divorce. This is
particularly true for couples that lived well beyond their means during
their marriage, with heavy reliance on credit cards and other loans.

Divorce courts understand that property division impacts the children's post-divorce standard of living. Whenever possible, divorce courts
prefer that the children continue living at a standard comparable with the
one to which they were accustomed. Child support is one method for ensuring this, but divorce courts may also use the property division process
as a means to provide children (through their custodial parents) with adequate resources. Property division is more secure and immediate than
child support, which is usually paid in monthly installments and is entirely dependent on the paying spouse's compliance. In one Missouri
case, for example, the court decided that property division was a better
means to provide for the child's needs than a child support order because
the father had very modest earnings but substantial capital holdings.

The Age and Health of Each Spouse

Divorce courts factor in the age and health of each spouse when dividing
marital property for two reasons. First, a consideration of each spouse's
age and health may be necessary to evaluate his or her contributions to
the marriage. A cancer patient undergoing extensive chemotherapy, for
example, may not have been able to hold down a steady job or contribute
much as a homemaker. Divorce courts recognize that such individuals

should not be penalized for the fact that they were unable to contribute to the marriage in the same way as their spouses. Second, a spouse's age and health is very relevant to his or her future economic needs. A thirty-two-year-old in perfect health, for example, would have very different future financial needs than a seventy-four-year-old suffering from Alzheimer's disease.

When one spouse is in poor health and needs additional resources to sustain him- or herself, divorce courts may award that spouse with a disproportionate share of marital property. In one Indiana case, for example, the court awarded a quadriplegic wife with assets worth more than $4 million—or twenty times what the husband received. A key factor in the court's decision was the wife's disability.

The Catch-All Factor

Divorce courts in equitable distribution states are generally not limited to the specific equitable distribution factors listed in the statutes or discussed in the case law. Rather, divorce courts are free to consider any other factor they deem relevant for the purposes of property division. For example, a divorce court may take into account the fact that one spouse voluntarily supported the other spouse's child from a previous marriage when arriving at an equitable division of marital property.

THE MECHANICS OF PROPERTY DIVISION

Once a divorce court determines the share of marital property to which each spouse is entitled—a straightforward determination in states with a 50-50 division of marital property, a more complex analysis in equitable distribution states—the divorce court must then address the mechanics of property division. It is generally impossible simply to split each marital asset to provide each spouse with his or her appropriate share of marital property. Rather, divorce courts must usually give one spouse certain assets and the other spouse the remaining assets to achieve the correct distribution of marital property. For example, suppose a divorce court in an equitable distribution state determined that Robert was to receive 40 percent of the marital property and Sara was to receive 60 percent. The marital estate consisted of a home worth $600,000, a mutual fund account worth $200,000, and government bonds worth $200,000. In such a case, the court could award Sara with the home (worth 60 percent of the marital estate) and Robert with the mutual fund account and the government bonds (together worth 40 percent of the marital estate).

Divorce courts can allocate marital assets in several ways. The easiest method is *in-kind division*—or dividing the marital asset itself between the spouses. In-kind division is very well suited for cash, stocks, and bonds. As discussed in more detail in chapter six, in-kind division can also be used for dividing pensions and stock options. The advantage of in-kind division is that it eliminates the necessity of valuation and divides the risks and rewards associated with any given asset between the spouses. For example, when stocks are divided in-kind, both spouses share the risk that the stock will plummet and the potential for gain if the stock rises.

In-kind division may be the only option in the case of speculative assets, such as unvested pensions or a lawyer's yet-unearned contingency fee. In such cases, a divorce court may determine each spouse's share of the asset and then direct that the asset be divided if and when it is actually received. For example, a divorce court may decide that Gwendolyn is entitled to 20 percent of her husband, David's, contingency fees for the class action lawsuit that he worked on during their marriage. If David is ultimately successful and actually earns his contingency fees at some point after his divorce, he will then have to turn over 20 percent of those fees to Gwendolyn.

Although in-kind division has many advantages, it is not practical or appropriate for all marital assets. For example, it is impossible to divide a diamond choker in-kind between two spouses. In-kind division is particularly unsuited for closely held corporations, partnerships, and small businesses, because this would leave divorcing spouses as business partners after their divorce—a generally undesirable result. In such cases, the usual form of division is for one spouse to buy out the other spouse's share of the marital asset.

A second method for dividing marital property is to sell the marital asset and divide the proceeds. This may be a wise option if there is a ready market for the marital asset in question, and neither spouse has the desire and financial capability to buy out the other's interest in the asset. For example, a couple may decide to sell their vacation home and divide the proceeds upon their divorce. If a forced sale of a particular marital asset would result in a dramatically lower price for the asset, a divorce court would be very reluctant to order a couple to sell the asset and divide the proceeds. Moreover, when one spouse has a continued need for a particular marital asset, a divorce court may provide for the asset to be sold at some point in the future, rather than immediately following the divorce. For example, courts frequently postpone the sale of the marital home in order to allow the custodial parent and the children of the marriage to continue living there until the children reach the age of majority (usually eighteen).

For income-producing assets such as small businesses, selling the marital asset and dividing the proceeds is generally not an appropriate method of division. Selling an income-producing asset would eliminate an important source of income that could be used to provide for one spouse's living expenses, as well as spousal and child support obligations arising out of the divorce.

A third method for dividing marital property is for one spouse to buy out the other's interest in a particular marital asset. For example, a physician may provide his soon-to-be ex-wife with additional marital assets equal to the amount of her share in his medical practice in order to enable him to keep his medical practice free and clear of any claim by her after their divorce. A key problem with the buyout method is that it hinges on a correct valuation of the marital asset in question. In the case of a medical practice, for example, experts could arrive at wildly differing valuations of the practice. The fairness of the buyout amount would depend on the accuracy of the valuation. Not only is valuation a somewhat imprecise art, but also potentially expensive and contentious. Where the value of an asset is easily determinable—as in the case of real estate or a piece of fine jewelry—the buyout method poses far fewer problems.

When a couple wishes to use the buyout method with respect to a particular marital asset but there are insufficient assets to allow one spouse to buy out the other's share immediately, divorce courts often prescribe an installment payment plan. This is sometimes the only possible method of division in cases involving professional practices, small businesses, and closely held corporations. Using the buyout method with an installment payment plan suffers from all of the problems posed by the buyout method alone, coupled with the additional risk of nonpayment. If your interest in a particular marital asset will be bought out using an installment payment plan, consult with your lawyer about obtaining appropriate security for these payments. For example, you may want to obtain a lien on real estate owned by your spouse to allow you recourse to other assets in the event that your spouse is either unwilling or unable to make payments in accordance with the terms of the installment plan.

In dividing marital assets, divorce courts prefer methods that separate the financial relationship of the parties. Divorce courts assume—usually correctly—that divorcing spouses are unlikely to make the best business partners. Divorce courts are therefore very reluctant to divide marital assets in such a way that the ex-spouses remain as co-owners. In rare cases, a divorce court may find it has no choice but to allow the divorcing spouses to continue as co-owners of a particular marital asset. For example, suppose that Paul and Barbara together had built up a small Internet company. They are very attached to the business and want to continue being involved in the business in the future. There are insufficient other assets to allow either Paul or Barbara to buy out the other's interest in the business. In such a case, a divorce court would probably have to order Paul and Barbara to continue as co-owners of the Internet company even after their divorce.

Divorce courts try to divide marital property in a manner that provides each spouse with some liquid assets—in other words, assets that can be easily accessed for immediate cash needs. Divorce courts recognize that individuals often face a number of expenses soon after their divorces and understand that nonliquid assets, however valuable, can generally not be used for such expenses. A property division arrangement in which one spouse receives only nonliquid marital assets may be very unfair unless that spouse has separate liquid assets. In one New York case, for example, the appellate court reversed a property division decision that gave the wife all of the liquid assets and gave the husband only his nonliquid pension.

Divorce courts also take tax consequences into account in dividing marital assets, provided that the tax consequences are not speculative. For example, a divorce court may consider the capital gains impact of redeeming stock options in the near future when dividing such options. A divorce court might be more reluctant to take into account the potential tax consequences of selling the marital home if there is no indication that the marital home will be sold in the relatively near future. Divorce courts limit their consideration of tax consequences because doing so requires courts to engage in guesswork regarding the government tax structure in effect at some point in the future, the future financial condition of the divorcing spouses, and so forth.

Other factors divorce courts take into account when dividing marital assets include the difficulty of valuing a particular marital asset and the risks associated with a given marital asset. When a marital asset is very difficult to value accurately, divorce courts may be hesitant to allow one spouse to buy out the other's interest in the marital asset because of the risk that the asset could be undervalued. In addition, divorce courts try to avoid giving one spouse all the risky marital assets and the other spouse all the stable marital assets, because that one spouse could be left holding nearly worthless assets. For example, a divorce court would be hesitant to award one spouse the shares of a nonpublicly traded biotechnology company while giving the other spouse the marital home and the couple's government bond holdings.

THE TAX ASPECTS OF DIVIDING MARITAL PROPERTY

All transfers of property between spouses incident to a divorce are nontaxable events, and neither gain nor loss is recognized. For example, suppose that Serena held Microsoft stock that had appreciated by $100,000 since her original purchase. She transferred this Microsoft stock to her husband, Matt, pursuant to their divorce settlement agreement. In this case, Serena would not have to pay any taxes on her $100,000 of capital gains.

Property transfers between spouses incident to a divorce are nontaxable events only if:

- The property is transferred either within one year of the divorce or within six years of the divorce and pursuant to a divorce or separation agreement.
- The property is transferred directly to the other spouse.

When property is transferred between spouses in connection with a divorce, the property retains its original basis. In other words, the spouse who receives the property must use the original purchase price when ultimately calculating his or her capital gains. Let us consider an example. Suppose that Kevin purchased one thousand shares of Widget stock for $20 a share. The stock had appreciated to $40 a share by the time of his divorce from his wife, Annette. Because Kevin transferred all of his Widget stock to Annette pursuant to their divorce settlement, he paid no capital gains on the transfer. Suppose finally that Annette decided to sell the Widget stock one year later, when the price hit $50 a share. She would then have to pay $30 a share (the sale price of $50 per share minus the basis of $20 per share) in capital gains instead of $10 a share. This is because she took on the Widget stock with Kevin's original basis of $20 a share.

This original basis rule is critical to bear in mind when deciding how to divide marital property. For example, suppose that Don and his wife Angela own $10,000 worth of Company A stock and $10,000 worth of Company B stock. Both stocks are now trading at $50 a share. Given these facts, it may seem like an easy solution for Don to take the Company A stock and for Angela to take the Company B stock. Before deciding how to divide the stock, however, Don and Angela should consider the original purchase price of the Company A and the Company B stock. Let's assume that the Company A stock was purchased for $10 a share, while the Company B stock was purchased for $40 a share. The Company A stock would therefore have $40 of latent tax liability per share, while the Company B stock would have only $10 of latent tax liability per share. Giving one spouse all of the Company A stock and the other spouse all of the Company B stock would lead to a tremendously unfair result, because the spouse receiving the Company A stock would ultimately have to pay far more in capital gains taxes than the spouse receiving the Company B stock. If Don and Angela truly wished to divide their stock equally, they should each take one-half of both the Company A holdings and the Company B holdings.

This original basis rule applies not only to stock but also to all property that is transferred incident to a divorce. You should remember to consider the original purchase price of all of your marital property—including art and real estate—when deciding how to allocate the property. This will keep you from facing unexpected tax liabilities years after your divorce is complete.

Assignment of Income Rule

The general rule is that whoever earns income must pay tax on that income, even if the income earner has assigned his or her income to someone else. This "assignment of income" rule is designed to prevent individuals from achieving a lower tax rate simply by assigning part or all of their income to someone eligible for a lower tax rate—such as a small child with no other income. In the context of a divorce, however, assigning income to one's former spouse may simply be a means to achieve proper property division. For example, the author of a best-seller may have to assign part of his book royalties to his wife to compensate her for her interest in the best-seller.

Unfortunately, the IRS has yet to resolve conclusively the question of whether the usual assignment of income rule applies in the context of divorce. If your property division arrangement calls for you to assign future income to your spouse, you should be aware that you may nevertheless be held liable to pay the taxes on that income. Be sure to consult with your lawyer about this issue if the assignment of income rule could potentially be applicable in your case.

SPECIAL ISSUES INVOLVED IN DIVIDING THE MARITAL HOME

If there are young children of the marriage, divorce courts will strongly consider awarding the marital home to the custodial parent in order to provide the children with stability in the post-divorce years. Divorce courts will take into account the age of the children and the children's ties to the home and neighborhood in determining whether an award of the marital home to the custodial parent is warranted. If the children have lived in the marital home for only a short period of time, or if the children are simply too young to have developed any substantial ties to the home and neighborhood, the chances of a court awarding the marital home to the custodial parent on the basis of the children's needs are relatively slim.

Rather than awarding the marital home to the custodial parent outright, divorce courts generally provide the custodial parent with *exclusive use and occupancy* of the marital home until the time that the children reach the age of majority (usually age eighteen). Once the children have grown, the marital home must then be sold and the proceeds divided between the former spouses according to their appropriate shares.

When deciding whether to award the custodial parent with exclusive use and occupancy of the marital home, divorce courts will weigh the couple's financial condition against the children's need to remain in the marital home. In many cases, it may not be financially possible for the custodial parent to retain exclusive use and occupancy of the marital home until the children are grown. The marital home is often the most substantial marital asset, and postponing the sale of the marital home may deprive the non-custodial parent of much of his or her share of the marital estate for many years to come.

Mortgage Liability

Both spouses will continue to be liable on an outstanding mortgage on the marital home until it is paid in full if both spouses signed the mortgage note. This is true even if one spouse is awarded exclusive use and occupancy of the marital home. Significantly, the continued existence of a mortgage on the marital home may make it impossible for either spouse to purchase another home. This is because each spouse may have already maximized his or her credit capacity through the first mortgage.

When considering whether to allow one spouse to retain exclusive use and occupancy of the marital home in your case, remember to think about the mortgage issues before making a final decision.

The Tax Consequences of Selling the Marital Home

If you and your spouse decide to sell your marital home immediately and divide the proceeds, you will not have to pay any taxes on the first $500,000 of capital gains provided that the home was used as a primary residence by both you and your spouse for two of the five preceding years. If only one of you lived in the home for two of the five preceding years, only that individual can exclude $250,000 of gains on the sale of the marital home. This capital gains exclusion can generally be used only once every two years.

Let us consider an example. Suppose that Harry and Samantha purchased a home in Silicon Valley for $200,000. They lived in the home for the next fifteen years. The house had appreciated to $700,000 by the time they decided to sell it. In this case, Harry and Samantha would not have to pay any taxes on the $500,000 of capital gains on their home because both of them had lived in the home for the years preceding the sale of the home.

Now suppose that Samantha lived in the house right up until their divorce, but Harry had moved out four years prior. In this case, only Samantha would be able to exclude $250,000 of capital gains on the sale of the house because only she lived in the house for at least two of the five years immediately preceding the sale. Since Harry lived in the house for only one of the five years preceding the sale, he would not qualify for the capital gains exclusion. Harry would therefore have to pay taxes on $250,000 of the capital gains on the house because he did not meet the requirements of the primary residence capital gains exclusion.

These rules become more flexible if the marital home is not sold until after a couple has divorced. If you and your spouse decide to postpone the sale of your marital home until some years following your divorce, you can each exclude $250,000 of capital gains on the sale of the home even if only one of you was living in the home for two of the five years immediately preceding the sale. In other words, both of you need not have been living in the home for two of the five years immediately preceding the sale in order to qualify for the capital gains exclusion.

For example, suppose that after her divorce from William, Rhonda and the children lived in the marital home for the next ten years. By the time that Rhonda was ready to sell the home, it had appreciated by $500,000 from its original price. Because she lived in the home for more than two of the five years immediately preceding the sale of the home, Rhonda and William could each exclude $250,000 of capital gains on the home. Thus, neither Rhonda nor William would have to pay any capital gains taxes upon the sale of the home.

If you purchased any property prior to May 7, 1997, you may have taken advantage of the old rollover rules that applied then. Under the old rollover rules, individuals were not taxed on any capital gains on their primary residences provided that they purchased another primary residence for at least as much as the sale price of their original home within two years of the sale. The catch was that the basis—or the purchase price as considered for capital gains purposes—of their new home would be the purchase price less any unrealized gains on the old home. Let us consider an example. Suppose that Myra purchased a home for $100,000 in 1994. In 1996, she sold the house for $300,000 and immediately purchased another house for $400,000, thus avoiding any capital gains taxes. Pursuant to the old rollover rules, the basis for Myra's second house would be the purchase price of $400,000 minus the $200,000 of capital gains on her first house—or $200,000.

Be very careful to bear in mind the rollover rules if you or your spouse rolled over capital gains from a previous home when purchasing the home you currently own. Because of the reduced basis that results from doing so, you and your spouse could be facing far more capital gains than you might have anticipated. For example, suppose that Jason and Colleen purchased a home in 1992 for $200,000, sold the home in 1996 for $450,000, and purchased another home for the same amount. Finally, Jason and Colleen sold that home for $950,000 when they divorced. In this case, the basis of Jason and Colleen's second home would be $200,000 (the purchase price of $450,000 less the unrealized capital gains of $250,000 on their first home). The capital gains on the sale of Jason and Colleen's second home would therefore be $750,000 (the sale price of $950,000 less the basis of $200,000). Only $500,000 of these capital gains would be tax-free; Jason and Colleen would still be liable for the taxes on the remaining $250,000 of capital gains.

The capital gains rules with respect to the sale of the marital home can be confusing, but it is worth the time it takes to understand them. With a little careful planning, you and your spouse may be able to save thousands of valuable tax dollars by learning and applying these rules.

DIVIDING DEBTS

Divorce courts generally characterize debt as marital or separate according to the same criteria used to classify property. After determining what debt counts as marital debt, many courts will deduct the value of marital debt from the value of marital property, then divide the difference. For example, suppose that Mark and Julie have $10,000 in credit card debt, $90,000 in mortgage debt, and $400,000 in marital assets. A court may simply subtract the credit card debt and mortgage debt from the $400,000 in marital assets and divide the net marital property—$300,000—between Mark and Julie.

Other courts will divide the marital assets and the marital liabilities separately, instead of merging them into one pot. In the case of Mark and Julie, a divorce court may determine that they are each entitled to 50 percent of the marital assets but that Mark should be responsible for 75 percent of the marital debt because he was primarily responsible for incurring it. Finally, some courts will simply factor in debts and liabilities when dividing marital property.

Even if a judge assigns all of the debts and liabilities in your case to your spouse, you may still be held responsible for the full amount of any debt that was taken out in both of your names. For example, suppose that Shelly and her husband, Kyle, maintained a joint credit card account throughout their ten years of marriage. A divorce court assigned their $35,000 in credit card debt to Kyle because he incurred the debt as a result of his gambling habit. In this case, the credit card company could still go after Shelly for the full sum of $35,000 in the event that Kyle did not pay his bills. The same would hold true in the case of jointly held mortgage debt. This is because a divorce court cannot alter the terms of a preexisting contract between you and a credit or lending agency.

Consider taking the following steps to protect yourself if jointly held debt is an issue in your case. First, cancel each and every joint credit card account once one of you files for divorce. You should discuss this step with your spouse and ensure that each of you has access to adequate funds for living expenses before doing so. Second, request that your spouse pay off all jointly held debt assigned to him or her before releasing marital assets. If this is not an option, you may wish to consult your lawyer about obtaining some security—such as a lien on your spouse's separate property—to provide you with some recourse in the event that your spouse does not pay down jointly held debt in accordance with the terms of your divorce.

TAX LIABILITIES

If you and your spouse filed joint returns during your marriage, you are completely responsible along with your spouse for any tax liability—as well as interest and penalties—arising out of an underpayment of taxes on those joint returns. For example, suppose that Greg and his wife, Alexis, filed joint returns for ten years. Alexis is a hairdresser and runs a substantial portion of her business "off the books," so her total under-reporting of income for those ten years amounted to $500,000. In this case, both Greg and Alexis would be liable for the underpayment of taxes, as well as any interest and penalties assessed.

Tax liability is perhaps the most tenacious form of debt in existence. It is virtually inescapable and can haunt you for years to come. Particularly problematic is the fact that there is no time limit on tax liability. The IRS can come after you for a tax deficiency arising out of a tax fraud any time after you file your joint return—even five, ten, or twenty years later.

If tax liability is an issue in your case, you may be able to free yourself of any responsibility if you were genuinely unaware that you and your spouse had underpaid your taxes on your joint tax returns, whether as a result of underreported income or inappropriate deductions. The IRS has established Innocent Spouse Relief to address situations in which one spouse was innocent of a tax understatement. To qualify for Innocent Spouse Relief, you must meet the following requirements:

- You and your spouse filed a joint return containing an understatement of taxes.
- You can establish that you did not know, and had no reason to know, that there was a tax understatement on your joint tax return.
- It would be unfair to hold you liable for the tax deficiency (along with interest and penalties) given all the facts and circumstances of your case.
- You applied for Innocent Spouse Relief within two years of the time when the IRS began collection activities against you.

Significantly, Innocent Spouse Relief is available even if you were aware of part of the tax understatement but unaware of the rest.

In determining whether you had reason to know of the tax understatement on your joint tax return, the IRS will consider whether a reasonably prudent person like you would have known that the return contained an understatement. Factors the IRS will look to in determining whether you had reason to know of the tax understatement are:

- Your level of education
- Your involvement in the family business and/or the family's financial activities
- Any substantial unexplained increase in the family's standard of living
- Your spouse's evasiveness about family finances

If you had reason to be suspicious of a tax understatement on your joint returns, you would have had an obligation to look into the situation and confirm that you and your spouse are reporting your income and claiming deductions accurately.

In determining whether it would be unfair to hold you liable for the tax deficiency given the facts and circumstances of your case, the IRS will consider whether you benefited significantly from the tax understatement. Suppose for example that Maurice and Ivana reported only $100,000 of income every year. Maurice was a businessman, but Ivana earned no income from any source. She lived on Fifth Avenue, received gifts of diamonds from her husband every year, and indulged in a new mink coat each fall. In this case, the IRS would likely conclude that it is perfectly fair to hold Ivana liable for the tax deficiency because of the extent to which she benefited from the tax understatement.

Another option for relief from your spouse's tax liability is the filing of a separate return election. This option is available only if:

- You and your spouse are no longer married or have been physically separated for at least twelve months.
- The IRS cannot demonstrate that you had actual knowledge of the tax understatement at issue.

When you file a separate return election, it is as if you had filed your tax returns separately instead of jointly during your marriage. The amount you must report as income on your separate return election is your income alone, even if you live in a community property state. This option works best when only one spouse earned the income that was underreported. For example, suppose that in 1999, Margaret earned $50,000 and her husband, Andrew, earned $150,000. Andrew reported only $50,000 on his 1999 joint tax return with Margaret, and she truly believed that he earned only $50,000 a year. If Margaret were later to file a separate return election, she would only have to report her $50,000 of income on her tax return. She would thus no longer have any liability for Andrew's dramatic underreporting of his income.

The IRS has the authority to relieve you from liability for the tax deficiency even if you do not qualify for Innocent Spouse Relief or any other relief, provided it would be inequitable to hold you liable for the tax deficiency, given the facts and circumstances of your case.

For more information on tax liability and the available avenues for relief, log on to www.irs.gov.

ATTORNEY'S FEES

Some of your divorce-related legal costs are tax deductible to the extent they exceed 2 percent of your adjusted gross income. You can deduct any legal costs incurred to obtain taxable income or assets—such as an interest in your spouse's pension if those pension payments will be taxable to you when received. You can also deduct any fees associated with tax planning. For example, you can deduct the costs of determining the adjusted basis of the assets awarded to each spouse.

In addition, legal fees incurred to assert or defend title to an asset can be added to the basis of the asset. For example, Simon incurred $5,000 in legal fees to obtain the marital home as part of his divorce settlement. The actual basis of the marital home is $350,000. Because of the legal fees Simon incurred, the basis of the marital home would become $355,000. Additions to the basis of any asset can be very helpful in reducing taxes later when the asset is sold.

To take advantage of these tax breaks, make certain that your lawyer provides you with an itemized bill detailing the costs that can be allocated to producing taxable income or assets; the costs that can be considered tax planning or advice; and the costs that are related to obtaining or defending title to property. Your lawyer should also indicate which costs are non-deductible.

QUESTIONS TO ASK YOUR LAWYER

- How is a court likely to divide the marital property in my case?
- If I live in a "hybrid" state, is it likely that a court will consider it inequitable to divide marital property equally given the facts of my case?

- If I live in an equitable distribution state, what factors is a court going to consider most relevant in dividing marital property given the facts of my case?
- Does my state consider marital fault for the purposes of property division, and to what extent?
- Is marital fault likely to be a significant factor in the division of marital property in my case?
- Is a court likely to conclude that either I or my spouse dissipated marital assets? If so, how will the court likely remedy the situation?
- How do you, as my lawyer, recommend that I divide my various marital assets: in-kind, selling the assets and dividing the proceeds, or using the buyout method?
- What tax consequences are associated with the division of marital property in my case?
- Can you recommend any tax-advantageous methods of dividing my marital property?
- Is a court in my state likely to award either me or my spouse exclusive use and occupancy of the marital home?
- What are the tax consequences of selling my marital home?
- Do I need to adjust my plans with respect to the marital home to ensure that I will qualify for the most favorable tax treatment possible?
- How is a court in my state likely to classify the debt at issue in my case?
- How is a court in my state likely to allocate the debt at issue in my case?
- If tax liability is an issue in my case, do I qualify for Innocent Spouse Relief or any other form of relief from liability? How do you recommend that I proceed with respect to such tax liability?
- Which of your fees, if any, will be tax deductible?
- Which of your fees, if any, can you add on to the basis of an asset?

Chapter Six

Pensions, Stock Options, and Other Special Categories of Property

Certain categories of property pose unique classification and valuation issues in the context of a divorce. This chapter addresses:

- Pensions and other retirement benefits
- Stock options
- Professional licenses and degrees
- Closely held corporations and other businesses
- Professional goodwill

If any of these categories of property are at issue in your case, you will need a great deal of help from your lawyer to classify, value, and divide the property. You will almost certainly also need the services of a financial professional—such as a valuation expert—to determine the market value of the property.

PENSIONS AND OTHER RETIREMENT BENEFITS

Pensions and other retirement benefits constitute marital property to the extent that they were earned during the marriage, because they are a form of deferred compensation.

There are a wide variety of pensions and retirement benefits. Some pensions are funded solely by the employer; others are funded solely by the employee. Some pensions provide a defined benefit upon retirement, the amount of which is determined by the number of years of employment and the employee's highest pre-retirement salary, others consist of defined contribution plans, in which the employee, the employer, or both contribute a set amount of money every year. Regardless of the type of pension plan at issue in your case, the pension will count as marital property to the extent that it was earned during your marriage. If you live in a "kitchen sink" state, the entire pension will count as marital property even if part of it was earned prior to your marriage.

Pensions may be *vested,* which means that the employee is guaranteed to receive the pension upon his or her retirement. Pensions may also be *unvested,* which means that the employee must satisfy certain conditions—such as remaining with the company for a specified number of additional years—in order to be guaranteed the pension upon his or her retirement. Unvested pensions may never vest because the employee may · fail to meet some condition for vesting. For example, an employee may leave the company before the number of years required for his or her pension to vest. Despite the fact that unvested pensions are much less of a "sure thing" than vested pensions, the majority of divorce courts nevertheless consider unvested pensions to constitute property subject to division upon divorce for the amount earned during the marriage.

Determining the Marital Property Share of a Pension

Most states consider pensions and other retirement benefits as marital property only for the amount earned during the marriage. To determine the percentage of the earned pension, courts often use the "time rule." The time rule is a fraction in which the numerator is the number of pension-qualifying years the employee worked during the marriage. The denominator is the total years that the employee worked or will work to earn the pension. This time rule fraction is then multiplied by the total amount of pension benefits to arrive at the marital property share. The time rule equation looks like this:

$$\frac{\text{The number of pension-qualifying years that the employee worked to earn the pension during the marriage}}{\text{The total number of years that the employee worked to earn the pension}} \times \text{The total amount of pension benefits} = \text{The marital property share}$$

Let us consider an example. Suppose that Mark began working at a telephone company in January of 1990. Mark married Katie in January of 1995 and filed for divorce from Katie in January of 2000. He must work until January of 2010 to qualify for his pension, and all of his years of employment with the telephone company were pension-qualifying years.

In Mark's case, the numerator for the time rule fraction would be five years—the number of pension-qualifying years that he worked while married to Katie. The denominator for the time rule fraction would be twenty years—the total number of years that Mark would have to work at the telephone company in order to qualify for his pension. According to the time rule, $\frac{5}{20}$ of Mark's pension—or 20 percent—would constitute marital property subject to division upon divorce.

Divorce courts like the time rule for its ease and simplicity and apply the rule to both defined benefit plans and defined contribution plans. Some have argued that the time rule does not make sense for defined contribution plans because larger contributions are usually made later in one's career, after the spouses have divorced. Divorce courts have nevertheless applied the time rule to defined contribution plans, reasoning that earlier contributions are compounded for a longer period of time, making them roughly equal to larger contributions made later.

Others have argued that the time rule is inappropriate for defined benefit plans wherein the pension benefits are based on the employee's highest pre-retirement salary. Because marital property does not include property earned or acquired after the marriage has ended, it is arguably unfair for a spouse to benefit from post-divorce pension increases. Divorce courts have generally rejected these arguments as well because the time rule is simple to administer and provides rough justice.

The Mechanics of Dividing a Pension

The two main ways of dividing a pension or other retirement benefit are the "buyout" method and the "wait and see" method. In the buyout method, the pension holder effectively purchases his or her spouse's interest in the pension. This is accomplished either by a lump-sum cash payment upon divorce or by giving the non-pension holder spouse marital assets equal to his or her share of the pension. The buyout method can be used only if the pension has been valued—a task that almost always requires the assistance of a financial professional. A key advantage of the buyout method is that it enables divorcing spouses to make a clean financial break from each other.

The wait and see method divides the pension between the spouses as and when the pension benefits are actually received. It is not necessary to value the pension in order to use the wait and see method. All that is required is that the non-pension holder's share of the pension benefits be known in advance. For example, suppose that the marital property share of Art's pension is 60 percent. Art and his wife, Isabelle, have agreed that Isabelle is entitled to half of all marital property, including the marital property share of Art's pension. Under the wait and see method, Isabelle would receive half of the marital property share of Art's pension—or 30 percent of each pension check that Art receives.

Isabelle would be able to receive her 30 percent share of his pension checks directly from his pension plan administrator by using a Qualified Domestic Relations Order (QDRO). A QDRO is a document served on a pension-plan administrator that specifies the share of the pension that the non-pension-holder spouse must receive when the pension holder reaches retirement age. Without a QDRO in place, Isabelle would have to rely on Art to write her a check for 30 percent of his retirement benefits every month—hardly a promising concept.

Using a QDRO would also benefit Art by reducing his pension-related tax liability. When pension benefits are paid directly to one's former spouse pursuant to a QDRO, the pension holder is not responsible for any taxes due on his or her spouse's share of the retirement benefits. This shifting of tax liability can save the pension holder valuable tax dollars.

There are several advantages to the wait and see method of dividing a pension. First, the wait and see method forces both spouses to assume the risks associated with a pension. A pension may decline in value due to market performance, or the pension holder may die before reaching retirement age. In unvested pensions, the pension holder may fail to meet a condition necessary for the pension to vest. With the wait and see method, the non-pension-holder spouse shares these risks equally with the pension holder.

Second, the wait and see method eliminates any uncertainty about the value of the pension. Rather than having to estimate the value of the pension in advance—as is required for the buyout method—the spouses simply receive their appropriate shares of the pension as and when it is paid.

Third, the pension holder does not need to make an immediate payment to his or her spouse for an asset that cannot be accessed for years to come. The wait and see method is particularly useful when one spouse cannot afford to buy out the other's interest in the pension.

Although the wait and see method offers many benefits, it also entails some risks. One risk is that the pension holder may take out loans that dramatically reduce the ultimate value of the pension. To reduce this risk, the non-pension-holder spouse should ensure that there are strict controls on the pension holder's ability to take out pension loans. If you are the non-pension-holder spouse, you should consult with your lawyer about the possibility of placing a hold or a block on your spouse's pension account and directing the pension plan administrator to deny any requests for pension loans.

Another risk is that the pension holder may simply refuse to retire, thereby delaying the non-pension-holder's receipt of his or her share of the pension benefits. If you are the non-pension-holder spouse, you should consult with your lawyer about drafting your QDRO to provide that the pension plan administrator must begin paying your share of the pension benefits when your spouse reaches the earliest retirement age under the plan.

Military Pensions

Just like any other pension, a military pension is considered marital property to the extent that it was earned during a marriage. However, there are restrictions on when and how a state court can divide a military pension in the context of a divorce. The Uniformed Services Former Spouse's Protection Act (USFSPA) provides that a state court may only divide a military pension if:

- The military employee resides in the state and is not simply stationed there.
- The military employee is domiciled in the state—in other words, he or she intends to reside permanently in the state.
- The military employee consents to have his or her divorce dispute heard by the state court.

If you are the spouse of a current or former military employee, you may be able to have your share of your spouse's pension paid directly to you by the military. This is a significant benefit because you will not have to rely on your spouse to obtain your fair share of his or her retirement pay. You will only be able to obtain direct pension payments from the military if two conditions are met:

1. You were married to your military employee spouse for at least ten years.

2. Your share of your spouse's retirement pay does not exceed 50 percent.

Some state courts have interpreted these restrictions on the direct payment mechanism as an overall restriction on when courts can divide military pensions. In other words, some state courts have held that a former spouse cannot share in military retirement pay unless the couple was married for at least ten years. Some state courts have also held that a former spouse's share of the military retirement pay cannot exceed 50 percent.

One problem with military pensions is that military personnel have the option of waiving their retirement benefits to obtain disability benefits, provided they qualify for disability benefits. Even though military disability payments effectively replace military retirement benefits, courts are prohibited from dividing military disability payments in the event of a divorce. If your spouse elects to receive disability payments instead of retirement pay, you will unfortunately be shortchanged of your share of his or her pension.

Because dividing a military pension is far more complicated than dividing a standard private pension, you should consult a lawyer with experience in military pensions if this is a factor. For more information, a good resource is www.militarydivorceonline.com.

Government Pensions

Special rules sometimes apply with respect to government pensions, such as railroad pensions and civil and foreign service pensions. In some states, for example, the pensions of public school teachers cannot be divided during a divorce. If a government pension of any kind is at issue in your case, you should be certain to ask your lawyer whether any special rules govern the division of that pension.

Social Security Benefits

Courts are prohibited from dividing social security benefits in the event of a divorce. However, you may qualify for spousal social security benefits based on your spouse's social security contributions if:

- You were married to your spouse for at least ten years.
- You are at least sixty-two years old.
- You have not remarried.
- Your marriage has been dissolved for at least two years or your former spouse is already receiving social security benefits.

- Your former spouse is eligible to receive social security benefits (the current eligibility age is sixty-two).

Any benefits you receive will not reduce the benefits paid to your former spouse.

You will only qualify for spousal social security benefits if your spouse is eligible for social security. If you are the spouse of a government employee, you may not qualify for spousal social security benefits. This is because some government employees do not contribute to social security and are therefore not entitled to social security benefits.

To determine your eligibility for spousal social security benefits or for more information, go to www.ssa.gov or call 1-800-772-1213.

STOCK OPTIONS

More and more Americans receive stock options as part of their compensation packages. Stock options provide employees with the opportunity to purchase or sell company stock at a predetermined price—known as the *strike price*—after a certain period of time. The strike price is generally tremendously favorable compared with prevailing market conditions. If the market and the company both perform well, stock options offer employees the opportunity to realize substantial wealth. Because stock options can be very valuable, virtually all divorce courts consider vested—or immediately exercisable—stock options to constitute marital property for the amount earned during the marriage.

Stock options may also be unvested, or not yet exercisable. Before an employee can exercise unvested stock options, he or she must generally remain with the company for a certain number of additional years. Even though unvested stock options are not immediately exercisable, most divorce courts consider unvested stock options to constitute marital property for the amount earned during the marriage. This is because employees who receive stock options often earn lower salaries than they otherwise would. In other words, stock options are a form of alternative compensation.

Determining the Marital Property Share of Stock Options

Stock options pose unique problems in the context of a divorce because unlike other forms of property, it can be very difficult to determine whether the stock options were earned during the marriage. This is because some stock options are granted mainly as a bonus for work well done in the past, while other stock options are granted primarily to provide an incentive for workers to perform well in the future. Some stock options are even granted in part as a "thank you" for past work, and in part as "golden handcuffs" to ensure that the employee will continue working for the company for a number of years to come.

Before a court can assess whether or not a particular set of stock options was earned during the marriage, the court must first determine whether the stock options were granted primarily as compensation for past work or as an incentive for future work. Divorce courts have considered the following factors in making this determination:

- Whether the stock options were offered as a bonus or as an alternative to a fixed salary
- Whether the value or the quantity of the employee's stock options is tied to future performance
- Whether the plan is used to attract key personnel from other companies
- What the stock option contract specifies with respect to the reason for the granting of the stock options

If a court concludes that the stock options at issue were granted primarily as compensation for past work performed during the marriage, the court will consider the stock options to constitute marital property. In one New Jersey case, for example, the court held that stock options granted ten days after the wife filed for divorce constituted marital property because the stock options were compensation for work performed by the wife during the marriage.

If a court determines that the stock options were granted in part or in whole as an incentive for future services, and the stock options are not exercisable at the end of the marriage, the marital property analysis becomes considerably more complicated. Since the employee must perform additional work on behalf of the company before he or she can exercise the options, at least part of the stock options should constitute separate property. This is because all property earned or acquired after the marriage has ended generally counts as that spouse's separate property.

To calculate the marital property share of unvested stock options, courts usually apply a "time rule" formula. Different courts use different time rule formulas, depending on the nature of the stock options at issue.

Perhaps the most well-known time rule formula for dividing stock options that are not exercisable at the end of a marriage is the one developed by a California court in the case of *Hug*.

The *Hug* time rule is a fraction in which the numerator is the period between the date the employee began working for the company and the date of the end of the marriage. The denominator is the period between the date the employee began working for the company and the date when the stock options become exercisable. The *Hug* time rule fraction is then multiplied by the total value of the stock options (or the total number of stock options) to arrive at the marital property share. The *Hug* time rule formula looks like this:

$$\frac{\text{The period between when the employee began working for the company and when the marriage ended}}{\text{The period between when the employee began working for the company and when the stock options become exercisable}} \times \text{The total value or number of stock options} = \text{The marital property share}$$

Let us consider an example. Suppose that Frederick married Anita in June of 1993 and began work for IBM in June of 1994. He divorced Anita in June of 1999. In June of 1997, Frederick received stock options exercisable in June of 2001. Using the *Hug* time rule fraction, the marital property share of Frederick's stock options would be derived as follows: the numerator would be 5 (the number of years between when Frederick began work for IBM and when Frederick divorced Anita), and the denominator would be 7 (the number of years between when Frederick began work for IBM and when Frederick's stock options become exercisable). Thus, 5/7—or approximately 71 percent—of Frederick's stock options would constitute marital property subject to division upon divorce under the *Hug* rule.

The *Hug* rule is just one possible formula that a court may use to determine the marital property share of stock options. Depending on the law of your state and the nature of the stock options at issue in your case, an entirely different formula may apply. As explained by the court in *Hug,* "no single rule or formula is applicable to every dissolution case involving employee stock options."

The Mechanics of Dividing Stock Options

Two methods are used for dividing stock options: the options themselves can be divided between the spouses (in-kind division) or the holder of the stock options can buy out his or her spouse's interest in the options. The buyout method can be used only if the stock options have been valued. As discussed in the next section, valuing stock options is an inherently uncertain and complicated task. Moreover, the buyout method carries with it the risk that the stock options could dramatically change in value between the date of the divorce and the exercise date. If the stock price declines, the pension holder will have paid his or her spouse far more than the options are ultimately worth. If the stock price rises, the non-option-holder spouse could end up shortchanged of his of her share of the full value of the stock options.

Dividing stock options in-kind avoids all of the problems associated with valuation. However, in-kind division poses other issues. One problem with in-kind division is that stock options are typically non-transferable and non-assignable. The option holder therefore remains in complete control of when, if ever, to exercise the options. If the option holder decides not to exercise the options, the other spouse receives nothing because no value was realized. This potential problem can be addressed in advance in a settlement agreement. Divorcing spouses can agree that the option holder must provide the other spouse with the opportunity to purchase his or her share of the options within a certain period of time (say thirty days) after the date that the options are first exercisable. Alternatively, divorcing spouses can agree that the non-option-holder spouse will receive a predetermined cash payout within a certain period of time after the date that the options are first exercisable, so that the non-option-holder spouse is protected in the event that the option holder decides never to exercise the options.

Another problem with in-kind division is that the option holder remains liable for any capital gains taxes associated with the exercise of the options, even if the non-option-holder actually pays to exercise a certain number of the options. Divorcing spouses should be very careful to factor in the tax consequences of exercising the options when dividing the options. To offset the tax impact to the option holder, the non-option-holder spouse might agree to receive a smaller proportion of the stock options than his or her true fair share. Alternatively, the non-option-holder spouse might agree to pay any capital gains taxes associated with his or her share of the options by paying that amount in after-tax dollars to the option holder.

The Valuation of Stock Options

The two main ways to value stock options are the intrinsic value method and the Black-Scholes formula. Under the intrinsic value method, a court must simply subtract the strike price—the price at which the stock option can be exercised—from the current price of the stock to arrive at a value for the options. For example, suppose that Nelson holds 2,000 stock options to purchase the Double Digit Company's stock at $10 per share. At the time of Nelson's divorce from Clara, the Double Digit Company's stock is trading at $35 per share. To value Nelson's stock options, a court would subtract the strike price of $10 from the current trading price of $35 to determine that each option is worth $25. A court would therefore conclude that Nelson's 2,000 stock options are worth $50,000 ($25 x 2,000).

Though the intrinsic value method is simple, it is problematic because it does not take into account stock volatility. Suppose for example that five years after Nelson's divorce, the value of the Double Digit Company's stock plummeted from $35 per share to $10 per share. Exercising the stock options at that point would leave Nelson with no profit, because the options' strike price would be the same as the trading price of the stock. Nelson would then be in the unfortunate position of having paid his wife, Clara, her share of the stock options based on a dramatically higher valuation of the stock.

Because the Black-Scholes method factors in stock volatility when valuing stock options, it is generally considered far more accurate than the intrinsic value method. Unfortunately, it is also far more involved. As explained by one Connecticut judge, "[i]t appears to a layman to be one of the most complicated formulas ever devised by mankind." *Wendt v. Wendt,* 1998 WL 161165, *184 (Conn. Super. Ct. 1998). The Black-Scholes formula takes into account, among other things, the value and market price of the underlying stock, the exercise price of the option, the volatility of the underlying stock, the amount of time before the option can be exercised, and current interest rates. A financial professional trained in the Black-Scholes methodology will consider all of these factors together to arrive at an appropriate valuation for the stock options.

The Black-Scholes method yields more accurate valuations of stock options than the intrinsic value method, but no formula can predict all of the potential ups and downs of a given stock. Choosing the buyout method for the division of stock options carries with it the risk that the stock price could experience a dramatic and unexpected decline at some point after your divorce, thus dramatically affecting the value of the options.

Significantly, stock options are not valueless even if the strike price is above the current trading price, because the price of the stock could go up at any time and the options could become quite valuable. When the strike price exceeds the current trading price, in-kind division may be the most appropriate solution.

PROFESSIONAL LICENSES AND DEGREES

Virtually all states agree that professional licenses and degrees are not property subject to division upon divorce. This is because professional licenses and degrees have no independent market value. Unlike other types of property, professional licenses and degree cannot be bought, sold, or transferred.

In long-term marriages, it usually does not matter that a professional license or degree does not count as property subject to division in a divorce, because the marital partnership would already have benefited from the professional spouse's credentials. For example, suppose that James was a medical student when he met Miranda, whom he later married. Miranda worked long hours as a nurse to help pay for James's medical school education and to supplement the family income while James was in his surgery residency. James and Miranda remained married for fifteen years after James graduated from his surgical residency and James's $250,000 a year annual salary allowed the couple to acquire a beautiful home, a healthy retirement savings account, and substantial stock holdings. In this case, it would be perfectly fair for a divorce court to conclude that James's medical license is not property subject to division in the couple's divorce. This is because Miranda would receive her fair share of the house, the healthy retirement savings account, and substantial stock holdings—all property acquired as a result of James's salary as a practicing surgeon.

If a marriage ends shortly after one spouse earns a professional license or degree, however, the nonprofessional spouse can end up short-changed. For example, suppose that Dan married Adele when Adele was in her first month of law school. For the next three years, Dan put his own aspirations to attend medical school on the back burner in order to support the couple and help pay Adele's tuition. Just one week after her graduation from law school, Adele informed Dan that she had fallen in love with a partner at the law firm where she had interned and planned to file for divorce. In this case, Dan would be in a tremendously unfair position. While he sacrificed his career ambitions to help pay for Adele's law school tuition and their living expenses, his marriage ended before he could benefit financially in any way from Adele's valuable degree.

Recognizing the fact that there are often cases like Dan's, divorce courts have devised creative ways to achieve a fair result without classifying professional licenses and degrees as property subject to division upon divorce. Courts in many states will reimburse the nonprofessional spouse for any out-of-pocket costs—such as tuition, books, and living expenses—incurred to enable the other spouse to acquire a professional license or degree. This is called *cost reimbursement* or *reimbursement alimony,* depending on the state.

Some states also reimburse the nonprofessional spouse for costs that are more difficult to quantify in pure economic terms, such as lost opportunities, a lower marital standard of living, and other intangible sacrifices. In Dan's case, for example, a divorce court might provide him with additional compensation over and above his out-of-pocket costs for Adele's educational expenses because he postponed his dream of attending medical school in order to help her pursue her legal education.

Instead of directly compensating the nonprofessional spouse, some states simply factor in contributions to the other spouse's education and training in arriving at an equitable division of marital property. Courts in these states might award the nonprofessional spouse with a greater share of marital property than he or she would otherwise receive as compensation for his or her contributions to the other spouse's career and earning potential.

Courts will only reimburse the nonprofessional spouse if he or she actually made financial sacrifices to enable the other spouse to pursue his or her education or training. If the professional spouse bore all the financial burdens of his or her education or training and contributed to household finances during the marriage—for example, by relying on student loans or parental assistance—no reimbursement will be warranted.

The Minority Approach to Professional Licenses and Degrees

In a tiny minority of states, the most notable of which is New York, professional licenses and degrees are considered property subject to division upon divorce. Courts in these states count professional licenses and degrees as marital property because they confer upon their holders the ability to earn far more than they otherwise would. In essence, these courts consider the *enhanced earning capacity* that professional licenses and degrees represent to constitute property subject to division upon divorce.

In the landmark case of *O'Brien,* New York's highest court determined that a surgical resident's medical license was a marital asset. The court explained its rationale as follows:

> Working spouses are often required to contribute substantial income as wage earners, sacrifice their own educational or career goals and opportunities for child rearing, perform the bulk of household duties and responsibilities and forego the acquisition of marital assets that could have been accumulated if the professional spouse had been employed rather than occupied with the study and training necessary to acquire a professional license. *O'Brien v. O'Brien,* 66 N.Y.2d 567, 585 (N.Y. 1985).

In *O'Brien,* the husband had worked toward his goal of becoming a physician throughout the couple's nine-year marriage. The wife had made career sacrifices to help him achieve his dream, and she had provided much of the household income during their marriage. At the end of the couple's marriage, the only asset of any real value was the husband's medical license.

The *O'Brien* court valued the husband's medical license by comparing the income of the average college graduate with the income of the average surgeon. The court assumed that the husband would work as a surgeon from the time he graduated from his residency until he retired and made some adjustments for taxes, inflation, and interest. Based on the assessment of an expert, the court concluded that the present value of the husband's medical degree was $472,000. The court further concluded that the wife's equitable share of this marital asset was $188,000, to be paid by the husband in eleven annual installments.

As the case of *O'Brien* demonstrates, the present value of many professional licenses and degrees can run to the hundreds of thousands of dollars. The nonprofessional spouse therefore receives substantially more in states like New York than he or she would in states that do not consider professional licenses and degrees to constitute property subject to division in a divorce.

One problem with counting professional licenses and degrees as marital property is that doing so usually compels the professional spouse to continue practicing his or her profession until his or her spouse's share is paid. In *O'Brien,* for example, the husband had no choice but to practice surgery (or find some very lucrative alternative) for the next eleven years in order to meet his installment payment obligations to his wife.

Another problem with including professional licenses and degrees as marital property is that the methods for valuing professional licenses and degrees generally assume that the professional spouse will continue earning at a particular rate for the duration of his or her career. These methods usually do not take into account the possibility that the professional spouse may suffer a disability, encounter career troubles, or die prematurely—all of which would affect the present value of the professional license or degree.

CLOSELY HELD CORPORATIONS AND OTHER BUSINESSES

Closely held corporations and other businesses constitute marital property to the extent that they were built during the marriage. The increase in value of a business that was developed before the marriage that can also constitute marital property for the amount of the appreciation resulted from marital labor (the efforts of either spouse during the marriage) or the investment of marital funds (money earned or acquired during the marriage).

Business interests can pose serious problems in the context of a divorce. Because courts recognize that divorcing spouses rarely make the best business partners, courts prefer that one spouse—usually the spouse who has been most involved in the business—retain his or her interest in the business free and clear from any claim by the other spouse. In other words, courts do not like to see businesses divided in-kind upon divorce. Rather, courts will value the business and then require one spouse to buy out the other's interest.

Valuing a Closely Held Corporation: Revenue Ruling 59-60

Closely held corporations are quite difficult to value because such corporations are, by definition, entities in which the shares are owned by a relatively limited number of stockholders—often just the members of one family. Because little if any trading takes place, there is no established market for the shares of a closely held corporation. A court therefore cannot value the shares of a closely held corporation simply by reference to their current trading price.

Instead, the valuation of a closely held corporation requires a sweeping evaluation of the entire business. Not only is such a valuation complicated, but it can also be very costly because it requires the services of a valuation expert. An expert must consider a number of different factors set forth in the IRS Ruling No. 59-60 when valuing a closely held corporation:

- *The nature and history of the business.* An expert must take into account the corporation's assets and capital structure, any growth or stagnation in earnings, whether the business' earnings have been stable, and whether the business is diverse or focused on just one product or service line.
- *The economic outlook in general and the outlook of the specific industry.* An expert must consider how a corporation rates among its competitors and the prospective economic conditions for the industry.
- *The book value of the stock and the financial condition of the business.* An expert should review the balance sheets for at least two years, an interim statement from the previous month, the charter and certificates of incorporation, and supplementary schedules listing working capital, liquid liabilities, long-term indebtedness, and other relevant financial data.
- *The earning capacity of the company.* An expert should review a detailed profit and loss statement and consider whether any line of business is operating at a loss.
- *The company's dividend-paying capacity.* An expert should consider the dividends that a corporation could have paid, not simply the dividends that were in fact paid. Corporations generally limit dividends for a variety of reasons, often paying more in salaries instead of dividends because salaries reduce taxable earnings.
- *The company's goodwill value.* An expert should consider whether a corporation has prestige or reputation value. For example, Hallmark has significant goodwill value because people recognize the brand name and many associate it with quality greeting cards.
- *The sales of the stock and the size of the block to be valued.* An expert should bear in mind that stock sales of closely held corporations often do not represent arm's length transactions. In terms of the size of the block to be valued, an expert will discount a minority stake in a corporation. Because minority stakes in closely held corporations lack the key element of control over the business, they are generally worth less per share than a controlling stake.

• *The market price of actively traded stocks of corporations engaged in the same line of business.* An expert should consider whether there are any truly comparable businesses whose stocks are actively traded on a public exchange or over the counter.

Revenue Ruling 59-60 provides only a starting point for the valuation of a closely held corporation. Depending on the situation, an expert may consider other factors as well.

Revenue Ruling 59-60 specifies certain factors that an expert must consider in valuing a closely held corporation, but it does not dictate the use of a particular valuation method. The various methods of business valuation are discussed in the next section.

Methods of Business Valuation

Many methods are available for valuing a business. Because an expert's valuation of a business can vary dramatically depending on the valuation method used, divorcing spouses often end up in heated battles over competing valuations of the same business.

One valuation method is the book value method. This method considers the net value of the assets of the business—the business assets minus the liabilities. If a closely held corporation is at issue, the net value will then be divided by the number of shares to yield a value per share. The book value method does not take goodwill into account when valuing a business; moreover, it is vulnerable to manipulation because a business owner may overstate business liabilities or undervalue business assets.

Another valuation method is the comparable sales method. This method considers the sales of businesses of the same size, in the same location and line of business, and with similar ownership structures and growth rates. The accuracy of the comparable sales method will turn on whether or not a truly similar business can be identified. If the only business similar to a closely held corporation is a publicly traded company, the analysis may be inherently flawed because closely held corporations do not have access to the same type of market for their shares.

Perhaps the most widely accepted business valuation method is the capitalization of earnings method. This method values a business according to its ability to generate income. An expert using this method will take the normal annual earnings of the business, then multiply those earnings by an appropriate capitalization factor to arrive at a valuation. The net annual earnings of the business would generally be determined after an examination of a five-year business history. The appropriate capitalization rate would be determined by considering the nature of the business, the risk involved, and the stability of earnings. A very old established business with substantial capital assets and much in the way of goodwill is usually valued at a capitalization rate of 12.5 to 10 percent—amounting to eight to ten times net earnings. Small businesses, on the other hand, are generally valued at a capitalization rate of between 100 and 25 percent—amounting to between one and four times net earnings.

In valuing a business, courts will consider the terms of any applicable buy-sell agreement. For partnerships, buy-sell agreements generally set forth the amount that a partner would receive in the event that he or she decides to leave the partnership. For closely held corporations, buy-sell agreements usually provide a formula for valuing the stock of the corporation. Buy-sell agreements often place a relatively low value on business interests as compared with the true market value. Some courts adopt the business value set forth in buy-sell agreements; others will simply take the terms of these agreements into account as one of many factors when valuing business interests.

If a business of any kind is at issue in your case, a good source for valuation experts is the American Society of Appraisers. Check their website, www.appraisers.org, for contact and other information.

Professional Goodwill

Unlike other businesses, most professional practices have very little in the way of tangible assets. The assets of a doctor's office, for example, might consist simply of an examining table, several filing cabinets, and the waiting room chairs. The real value of professional practices lies not in their tangible assets but in their goodwill value—the reputation and prestige that brings in new clients or patients every day.

Not all courts consider professional goodwill to constitute property subject to division in a divorce; this is because professional goodwill is often nothing more than the reputation of the individual physician, lawyer, or other professional. For example, suppose that Dr. Swanson was the most well-known ophthalmologist in his hometown of Buffalo. His one-man practice earned more than the three competing ophthalmology practices combined. Dr. Swanson's practice clearly has tremendous goodwill value. However, the goodwill is personal to Dr. Swanson. If he were to retire and his newly trained son were to take over his practice, it is entirely possible that Dr. Swanson's patients would switch over to one of the competing ophthalmology practices. Their loyalty was probably to Dr. Swanson himself—not to his practice.

Now let us consider a different example. Suppose that Dr. Wexel was an oncologist whose practice was affiliated with Memorial-Sloan Kettering Hospital. There are eight other oncologists in his group, and they all earn nearly double what other oncologists in their area make. Dr. Wexel's practice has tremendous goodwill value, but in this case it is probably not personal to Dr. Wexel. Rather, the practice itself has goodwill because of its affiliation with a prestigious cancer hospital and the patients' reasonable expectation that only top-notch oncologists would be invited to join such a practice. If Dr. Wexel were to retire, chances are his former patients would simply switch over to one of the eight other oncologists in the practice because the practice's goodwill is probably separate from Dr. Wexel's own reputation.

Some courts consider professional goodwill to constitute property subject to division upon divorce only to the extent that the goodwill is independent from the professional. The strongest evidence that goodwill is independent of the professional's personal reputation is a recent offer to purchase the practice for more than the value of the practice's tangible assets. A third party would only be willing to pay a premium for the goodwill value of the practice if the goodwill could be transferred—in other words, if the goodwill was independent of the professional.

The courts that consider professional goodwill to constitute property subject to division upon divorce use several different methods to value the goodwill. The fair market value method values goodwill together with the rest of the practice. A court relying on the fair market value method would consider what a willing buyer would pay to purchase the practice in an open and competitive market. A problem with the fair market value method is that there may not have been any recent offers to purchase the practice or any comparable practice. Another problem is that there are ethical prohibitions against selling law practices in some states, so it may be impossible to determine what a buyer would be willing to pay for a legal practice.

The capitalization of excess earnings method considers how much more the professional is earning than the average individual in his or her field. The first step is to determine what a professional with comparable experience, expertise, education, and age would be earning in the same geographic area. The second step is to determine the professional's average net income, taking into account his or her income for the preceding five years to arrive at an appropriate average. The third step is to subtract from the professional's net income the income of a comparable professional. The fourth step is to multiply this difference by a capitalization factor—usually between one and three. It would be up to an expert to determine which capitalization factor applied given the nature of the practice and other relevant considerations.

Let us consider a brief example. Suppose that Jackson, an accountant, earns an average of $250,000 per year in his accounting practice. An expert determines that an average accountant with Jackson's training and experience would be earning around $180,000 per year in Jackson's hometown. Finally, an expert determines that 50 percent—or two times earnings—would be an appropriate capitalization factor for valuing the goodwill of Jackson's professional practice. Jackson's goodwill would therefore be valued as follows: his excess earnings ($250,000 - $180,000 = $70,000) multiplied by two ($70,000 x 2 = $140,000) to yield a goodwill value of $140,000.

As this simple example illustrates, a problem with the excess earnings method of valuing goodwill is that it can result in rather high valuation figures. When there are insufficient marital assets to provide the nonprofessional spouse with his or her share of the professional goodwill immediately, the excess earnings method effectively requires the professional spouse to continue working at his or profession in order to pay off the nonprofessional spouse's share of goodwill.

In valuing goodwill, courts will consider the goodwill value set forth in a buy-sell agreement. Buy-sell agreements typically set forth a formula to value the professional's interest in the practice in the event that he or she leaves the partnership for any reason. Buy-sell agreements usually provide a valuation for the practice goodwill. Some courts will accept the goodwill value set forth in these agreements to ensure that the nonprofessional spouse does not receive more compensation for the professional's goodwill than the professional would be able to obtain if he or she left the practice. Other courts will simply take the terms of these agreements into account as one of many factors when valuing professional goodwill.

QUESTIONS TO ASK YOUR LAWYER

Pensions

- Is the pension at issue in my case likely to be considered marital property in whole or in part?

- How will the marital property share of the pension at issue in my case be determined?
- Should the pension at issue in my case be divided in kind using a QDRO or through the buyout method?
- If the pension is to be divided using the buyout method, how will the pension be valued?
- If a military pension is relative in my case, do I meet the jurisdictional and other requirements for a court in my state to divide the military pension? How will the marital property share of the military pension be calculated?
- If a government pension is at issue in my case, do any special rules apply with respect to the division of that pension? How will the marital property share of that pension be calculated?
- Do I qualify for spousal social security benefits?

Stock Options

- Does my state consider vested and/or unvested stock options to constitute property subject to division upon divorce?
- Are the stock options at issue in my case likely to be considered marital property in whole or in part?
- How will the marital property share of the stock options at stake in my case be determined?
- How do you recommend that the stock options at issue in my case be divided—in kind or using the buyout method?
- If stock options are to be divided using the buyout method, what method do you recommend for valuing the stock options?
- If stock options are to be divided in-kind, what protections should be included in a settlement agreement for the benefit of the non-option-holder spouse?

Professional Licenses and Degrees

- How does my state treat professional licenses and degrees?
- Given the facts of my case, will I or my spouse be entitled to some form of reimbursement for contributions to the other's career and education? What will such a reimbursement cover?
- If my state considers professional licenses and degrees to be property subject to division in a divorce, what method is a court likely to use for valuing the professional license or degree?

Closely Held Corporations and Other Businesses

- Is the business at issue in my case likely to be considered marital property in whole or in part?
- How will the marital property share of the business be determined?
- Which spouse is likely to be awarded the interest in the business at issue?
- What method is preferred in my state for valuing business interests?
- Regarding the facts of my case, what is the most advantageous business valuation method for my position?
- Do you recommend that my spouse and I appoint a valuation expert together, to arrive at one agreed-upon valuation of the business?
- Can you suggest any tax-advantageous or creative options for dividing the business interest at issue?

Professional Goodwill

- Does my state consider professional goodwill to constitute property subject to division upon divorce?
- Is a court likely to consider the professional goodwill in my case to constitute marital property in whole or in part?
- What method is preferred in my state for valuing professional goodwill?
- After reviewing the facts of my case, what is the most advantageous goodwill valuation method for my position?
- Do you recommend that my spouse and I appoint a valuation expert together, to arrive at one agreed-upon valuation of the professional goodwill?

Chapter Seven

Alimony

When one spouse lacks sufficient income and assets to meet his or her reasonable needs, courts may require the other spouse to pay spousal support—or alimony—for a set period of time. Alimony was once paid only by husbands to wives. Now, either spouse may be required to pay alimony, depending on who is in the better economic position.

Courts award alimony only in a small percentage of divorces. Even though husbands and wives face vastly different post-divorce economic prospects in many cases, more and more courts are taking the view that each spouse must provide for his or her own financial needs after the marriage has ended.

Courts are also increasingly uncomfortable with having alimony continue for an indefinite period of time. Instead, courts prefer to award alimony for a limited period of time, if at all. Courts expect the financially dependent spouse to use the time that he or she receives alimony to acquire the job skills, education, and training that will enable him or her to become self-sufficient. Such short-term alimony is called *rehabilitative alimony*.

FACTORS CONSIDERED IN AWARDING ALIMONY

Courts have complete discretion over the amount and duration of alimony. In considering whether one spouse lacks sufficient income and assets to meet his or her reasonable needs, courts will take into account:

- The length of the marriage
- The economic circumstances of each spouse

- The standard of living established during the marriage
- The age and health of each spouse
- The needs of each spouse
- Each spouse's contributions to the marriage
- The time necessary for the financially dependent spouse to acquire sufficient education or training to allow him or her to find appropriate employment

While marital fault was once a key factor in awarding alimony, courts are now much less likely to take marital fault into account for alimony purposes. A substantial number of states prohibit courts from considering marital fault in determining alimony. However, a few states are still holding on to the old rules and bar alimony entirely when the financially dependent spouse is guilty of marital misconduct.

The Length of the Marriage

Courts generally do not award alimony in marriages of relatively short duration, such as marriages lasting less than five years, because courts prefer to see spouses end short-term marriages with no financial obligations to one another and with roughly the same proportion of resources that they each had when they entered the marriage. In short-term marriages, courts simply like to return each spouse to his or her pre-marital financial position.

In long-term marriages of fifteen to twenty years, however, courts are much more open to awarding alimony. Courts recognize that spouses in long-term marriages contribute tremendously to one another's lives, both financially and emotionally. Spouses in long-term marriages also tend to make financial decisions based on one another. For example, a wife may decide to give up her career in order to raise her children, with the expectation that her financial needs will be provided for by her husband. A husband may decide to spend long hours helping his wife build her graphic design business, with the expectation that he will always profit from her success. In such cases, alimony may be the only means to ensure that the financially dependent spouse's needs are taken care of in an appropriate manner.

The Economic Circumstances of Each Spouse

Before ordering either spouse to pay alimony, courts will consider the income, financial resources, and earning capacity of both spouses. A spouse who is the beneficiary of a sizeable trust fund is far less likely to be awarded alimony than a spouse who has virtually no resources of his own and a salary of only $20,000 per year. Similarly, a Wall Street millionaire is more likely to be required to pay alimony than a tailor who makes only $35,000 a year and will have to struggle just to meet her child support obligations.

Courts will also take into account each spouse's earning capacity when determining alimony. A spouse will generally not be able to escape an alimony obligation by voluntarily exchanging a high-paying job for a low-paying job. For example, a spouse who gives up a lucrative surgery practice to pursue a career as a painter may still be credited with having a surgeon's salary for alimony purposes. A spouse will also not be able to obtain alimony if he or she has the capacity to obtain a high-paying job but simply does not wish to work that hard.

Finally, courts will consider the amount of marital property that was awarded to each spouse. Wherever possible, courts prefer to address each spouse's need for support through property division rather than alimony. This is because continuing obligations between spouses often eventually cause disputes, many of which make their way back to the courthouse.

The Marital Standard of Living

To the extent possible, courts like to see both spouses enjoy the same standard of living after the divorce that they enjoyed during the marriage. As a practical matter, this is often impossible because many couples simply lack adequate funds to support two households at the same standard that they enjoyed during the marriage. Nevertheless, courts will consider a couple's lifestyle in determining the need for and the amount of alimony.

If a couple lived in a large house in an affluent suburb, had the assistance of household help, and indulged regularly in luxurious vacations during the marriage, a court may be more likely to award a significant amount of alimony to the financially dependent spouse to enable him or her to enjoy a similar lifestyle after the divorce. If, on the other hand, a couple lived in a small apartment, handled all of the household tasks on their own, and shopped at discount stores during their marriage, a court might conclude that less alimony is required to enable the financially dependent spouse to maintain that same standard of living.

The Age and Health of Each Spouse

Courts will take into account the age and health of the less well-off spouse when evaluating his or her reasonable needs and considering whether he or she has the capacity to meet those needs. While courts may expect a healthy thirty-year-old to meet his or her own reasonable needs, courts recognize that older individuals who have been out of the workforce for an extended period of time may find it very difficult to support themselves. The same holds true for individuals with serious physical or mental health issues.

Courts also consider the age and health of the wealthier spouse when determining his or her ability to pay alimony. A spouse on the verge of retirement, or one who has been forced to cut back on job responsibilities because of a debilitating disease, may not be in a position to pay alimony at all or may have only a limited ability to support the other spouse.

The Needs of Each Spouse

Courts limit alimony to the amount necessary for the financially dependent spouse to meet his or her reasonable needs. If a spouse's living expenses amount to only $2,500 per month, a court will generally not award more than $2,500 per month in alimony. A court will also be very careful to ensure that the financially dependent spouse is not overstating his or her needs in order to obtain more alimony. For example, a woman who spent her married years living in a two-bedroom apartment and driving a second-hand car will not be able to claim that she now requires enough alimony to enable her to afford a four-bedroom townhouse and a brand new car.

Courts will also take into account the needs of the wealthier spouse in determining how much alimony he or she can afford to pay. For example, a man who makes $200,000 a year but spends approximately $40,000 before taxes on preexisting spousal and child support obligations will be considered to have only $160,000 of available income for alimony purposes.

Each Spouse's Contributions to the Marriage

Courts will factor in each spouse's contributions to the marriage and to the other spouse's career and earning potential when determining whether an award of alimony is appropriate. A spouse who shouldered the burden of raising children and homemaking is more likely to receive alimony than a spouse who neither worked outside the home nor handled the tasks of homemaking and child rearing. Economic contributions are also important. For example, a spouse who contributed his or her separate property savings to provide the family with living expenses during difficult times will be viewed more favorably than a spendthrift spouse whose main economic contribution to the marriage was the accumulation of a substantial amount of credit card debt.

Courts will also consider whether either spouse was guilty of economic fault when awarding alimony. If one spouse gambled away tens of thousands of dollars during the marriage, or spent the family's retirement savings on a luxury vacation, a court might view alimony as the only means for reimbursing the other spouse.

The Time Necessary for the Spouse to Acquire Sufficient Education and Training to Secure Appropriate Employment

In general, courts now prefer to award alimony only for the limited period of time necessary for the financially dependent spouse to become financially independent. Because courts are not particularly comfortable with ordering one spouse to support the other indefinitely, courts like to see that the financially dependent spouse has a logical and reasonable plan for becoming financially self-sufficient. A court is likely to look far more favorably on a spouse who has obtained admission to law school and requires alimony for only three years than a spouse who has no tangible plans for becoming self-sufficient. Courts will often provide that alimony will terminate when the dependent spouse's income has reached or should have reached a suitable level.

In some cases, it would be virtually impossible for the financially dependent spouse to secure employment at a level that would provide for his or her reasonable needs. For example, if the spouse has been out of the workforce for over thirty years, spending that time raising a family and taking care of the family home, it is simply not realistic to expect him or her to go to school and find a job that will enable him or her to live at even a fraction of the level to which he or she was accustomed. In cases like this, courts recognize that permanent alimony is the only fair and reasonable option.

WHEN ALIMONY ENDS

Unless the spouses agree otherwise, alimony generally ends upon the death of either spouse or the remarriage of the supported spouse. Alimony terminates upon the recipient's remarriage because courts expect the recipient's new husband or wife to take care of the recipient's reasonable needs. In some states, alimony also ends if the recipient begins living with someone in a marriage-like relationship.

HOW ALIMONY IS PAID

Alimony is generally paid in monthly or weekly installments; however, it can also be paid as a lump sum amount. Lump sum alimony may be preferable if the wealthier spouse is unlikely to make regular alimony payments or if the spouses wish to sever their financial relationship completely upon divorce and adequate resources enable them to do so. One disadvantage of lump sum alimony is that it cannot be modified later to account for the increased needs of the supported spouse or changes in the wealthier spouse's ability to pay alimony.

MODIFICATION OF ALIMONY

Except in cases of lump sum alimony, alimony can be increased or decreased when there has been a relevant change of circumstances. If the alimony recipient's financial circumstances change for the better, such as through a lucrative job promotion, the alimony payer may be able to petition the court successfully for a reduction in alimony obligations. If the needs of the alimony recipient rise—for example, as the result of an accident that left him or her completely unable to work—a court might consider increasing alimony. Similarly, if the alimony payer loses a job, or experiences a sizeable downturn in business, the court may reduce alimony. However, a court would not reduce alimony payments if the alimony payer voluntarily left a high-paying job for a low-paying job.

Courts will usually not reduce alimony as a result of the alimony-paying spouse's new family obligations. Even if the alimony payer were to remarry and become the parent of triplets, a court would generally not consider these new family expenses to be grounds for decreasing alimony. Courts agree that you cannot reduce or eliminate your obligations to your first family due to the needs of your second family. If the alimony recipient were to petition for an increase in alimony, however, a court would take the alimony payer's new family obligations into account when determining whether he or she could afford to pay more alimony.

When the alimony payer petitions the court for an alimony reduction at a time when he or she is already behind on alimony payments, a court could retroactively modify the amount of alimony due. Let us consider an example. Suppose that Michelle was required to pay Eliot $800 per month in alimony. Michelle had not paid Eliot alimony for six months— amounting to arrears of $4,800—when she petitioned the court for a reduction in alimony due to her changed financial circumstances. The court granted her request and reduced her alimony obligation to $500 per month. In this case, the court could apply the modification retroactively to Michelle's $4,800 in alimony arrears. Michelle may then owe Eliot only $3,000 ($500 x 6 months) in unpaid alimony rather than $4,800 ($800 x 6 months).

Because of the risk that the alimony-paying spouse may be able to obtain a retroactive reduction in alimony at some later time, it is in the best interests of the alimony recipient to take steps to ensure that alimony is paid in full and on time. If you are the financially dependent spouse, consider discussing with your lawyer the possibility of obtaining some security for your spouse's alimony payments, such as a lien on his or her property, to protect you in the event your spouse falls behind on his or her payments.

TEMPORARY ALIMONY

Courts may award the financially dependent spouse with temporary alimony pending the outcome of the divorce. Temporary alimony is designed to provide for the financially dependent spouse's needs during the course of the divorce, before final alimony arrangements are made. If the financially dependent spouse does not request temporary alimony, and the divorce dispute drags on for many months, the wealthier spouse is likely to argue that the financially dependent spouse obviously has no need for alimony since he or she managed to live without any support for such a long time. For this reason, it is usually in the best interests of the financially dependent spouse to petition the court for temporary alimony as soon as the action for divorce is commenced.

In awarding temporary alimony, courts will consider the same factors relied on to determine whether alimony is finally necessary. Because the case has usually just begun and the court does not have all of the facts at its disposal, the temporary alimony award will often turn on the disparity in the spouses' economic circumstances and the financially dependent spouse's needs.

One potential disadvantage of temporary alimony is that the temporary alimony amount may become the amount of alimony that is finally awarded. This is because a court may reason that if the amount of temporary alimony was sufficient to enable the financially dependent spouse to meet his or her reasonable needs, there is no reason to change that amount when making a final alimony award. It is therefore in the financially dependent spouse's best interests to obtain the highest amount of temporary alimony possible.

ATTORNEY'S FEES

Courts may require one spouse to pay the other's attorney's fees, either early on in the case or as part of the final divorce "package." Having one spouse pay the other's legal fees may be the only way that both spouses can have access to counsel of comparable skill and experience. Courts do not like to see one spouse forced to hire an inexperienced clinic attorney while the other spouse can afford to hire the most expensive, most aggressive legal team in town. Courts recognize that the quality of one's lawyers can make a dramatic difference in the ultimate outcome of any dispute and that a spouse who lacks proper legal assistance may end up with undesirable results in the divorce process.

In determining whether an award of attorney's fees is appropriate, courts will consider the relative financial circumstances of each spouse and the issues in dispute. If one spouse's income is disproportionately higher than the other's, and the less well-off spouse does not have savings or other resources that would help him or her make up the difference, an award of attorneys' fees may be warranted. The complexity of the divorce dispute is also relevant to the need for and amount of an attorney's fee award. For example, when spouses have virtually no property to divide and no children, a court is likely to award much less in attorney's fees than in a complex case involving a custody dispute and the division of a pension and a professional practice.

If an award of attorney's fees is made after the lawyer has already commenced work on the case, the court will review the lawyer's bills to determine the appropriate amount of an attorney's fee award. Courts will not reimburse the financially dependent spouse for duplicative legal costs or for unnecessary legal work. Courts will also not reimburse the financially dependent spouse for costs representing excessive time spent by the lawyer on any given matter. Finally, courts will consider the reasonableness of the lawyer's hourly rate when making a fee award. Because courts will take into account a lawyer's skill and his or her standing in the community when determining whether a given hourly rate is appropriate, a court may find the same hourly rate to be reasonable for one lawyer and entirely unreasonable for another.

Irrespective of who ultimately pays the legal bills, a spouse can deduct legal fees incurred to obtain alimony or an increase in alimony, or to fight a decrease in alimony, to the extent that such fees exceed 2 percent of his or her adjusted gross income. This deduction is particularly helpful if attorney's fees are paid in the form of taxable alimony, as the less well-off spouse can then offset some of the tax burden by taking a deduction for alimony-related legal fees. The tax aspects of alimony are discussed in more detail below.

Health Insurance

A very important issue in many cases is health insurance for the financially dependent spouse. If one spouse does not work outside the home and has always relied on the other spouse's employee benefits for his or her health insurance benefits, that spouse may face the prospect of becoming uninsured after the divorce. This is because he or she will no longer qualify as a "beneficiary" on the other spouse's health insurance plan.

To address this problem, the federal government now requires health insurance companies to provide health insurance for former spouses of primary beneficiaries at the same rate as before the divorce plus a small additional charge to cover administrative costs. These extended health insurance benefits—known as COBRA benefits—continue for only thirty-six months from the date of the divorce.

If you are the financially dependent spouse and you are concerned about health insurance after your divorce, be certain to ask your lawyer about COBRA benefits. You may also wish to have part or all of your alimony paid in the form of health insurance premiums.

If you are the spouse of a current or former military employee, you may be able to qualify for military health insurance if you meet certain rather stringent criteria. First, you must have been married to a military employee for at least twenty years, and your spouse must have been working for the military for at least twenty of the years that you were married. Second, you must not be enrolled in an employer-sponsored health plan. Third, you must not have remarried. If you meet these criteria, you should contact your local military benefits office about applying for health insurance benefits.

LIFE INSURANCE

If you are the financially dependent spouse and will be relying on alimony to help meet your day-to-day expenses after your divorce, you should strongly consider having your spouse purchase a life insurance policy with the proceeds made payable to you. An insurance policy will protect you in the event that your spouse dies before he or she has completed all of his or her alimony obligations to you.

The alimony payer will be able to deduct the life insurance premiums on his or her tax returns, provided that all proceeds of the policy are payable to the alimony recipient and the alimony recipient is the owner of the policy. Another tax benefit of life insurance is that the alimony recipient will receive the proceeds of the policy entirely tax-free.

THE TAX ASPECTS OF ALIMONY

The general rule is that alimony is tax deductible for the payer and taxable to the recipient. The alimony deduction is "above the line"—or deducted from gross income in computing adjusted gross income. Alimony payments are deductible even if the alimony payer does not itemize his or her deductions, and those provisions of the tax code that reduce itemized deductions do not affect the alimony deduction. Alimony does not have to be tax deductible to the payer and taxable to the payee. If the spouses agree, alimony can be non-deductible to the payer and non-taxable to the payee.

In order for alimony to be tax deductible to the payer, a relatively long list of requirements must be met:

- The alimony payments must be made in cash. No deduction is allowed for payments made in services or non-cash property (for example, stock).
- The alimony payments must be made pursuant to a divorce or separation instrument, such as a divorce decree or a settlement agreement.
- The alimony payments must be made to the supported spouse or to a third party on behalf of the supported spouse.
- The alimony payments must not terminate or decline because of a contingency relating to a child of the marriage—for example, alimony payments cannot terminate when the youngest child reaches the age of eighteen.

- The alimony payments cannot be designated as non-deductible.
- The alimony payments must terminate upon the death of the supported spouse.
- The spouses cannot be living together at the time that the alimony payments are made, unless the payments are made pursuant to a written separation agreement or temporary judicial support decree.
- The spouses cannot file a joint return for the year in which the deduction is claimed.
- The alimony recipient must supply his or her social security number to the alimony payer, and the alimony payer must disclose this information on his or her tax return.

If you provide your spouse with support payments while you are separated, but there is no separation agreement or decree that directs you to make such payments, you cannot deduct the alimony payments from your income. You also cannot "cure" the problem by entering into a retroactive agreement with your spouse. Rather, the divorce or separation agreement or decree must have already been in effect at the time that any payments are made in order for the payments to be tax deductible.

Payments to a third party on behalf of the supported spouse are tax deductible, provided that the divorce or separation agreement or decree requires alimony to be paid to a third party. For example, alimony paid in the form of mortgage payments on the supported spouse's home would be tax deductible. Paying alimony in the form of mortgage payments for a house owned by the supported spouse can be mutually tax advantageous: the alimony payer can deduct the alimony, and the alimony recipient (who must include the alimony as ordinary income on his or her tax return) may be able to take offsetting deductions for the mortgage interest and the property taxes. Tax-deductible alimony can also be paid in the form of tuition payments on behalf of the supported spouse or any other third-party payment that makes sense in any particular case. Even if your divorce or separation agreement provides that alimony payments will be made directly to the recipient, you and your spouse could modify your agreement at a later date to provide for alimony payments to be made directly to a third party.

Because of the favorable tax treatment accorded to alimony, people often attempt to disguise their child support payments as alimony. Unlike alimony, child support is neither deductible to the payer nor taxable to the recipient. The IRS has therefore placed several restrictions on alimony payments in order for them to qualify for tax deductibility. First, the alimony payments cannot terminate because of any child-related contingency. The IRS will presume that any payment that terminates within six months of when a child reaches eighteen years of age is non-deductible child support, rather than deductible alimony. The IRS will also presume that alimony payments are actually child support if there are two or more children and alimony payments decline at two or more fixed points. Second, alimony payments must end upon the death of the recipient. This is to ensure that the alimony payments are in fact provided for the support of one's former spouse, not the support of one's children. Once the former spouse is deceased, there should no longer be any need for spousal support payments.

The Recapture of Excessively Front-Loaded Alimony

To take advantage of the favorable tax treatment accorded to alimony payments, people will often attempt to restructure their marital property division as alimony. To prevent this from happening, the IRS will automatically recapture alimony payments—in other words, eliminate the tax deduction for alimony paid in the past—in either of the following circumstances:

- The alimony paid in the second post-separation year was more than $15,000 greater than the alimony paid in the third post-separation year, or
- The alimony paid in the first post-separation year exceeded the average of payments in the second and third post-separation years by more than $15,000.

In either case, the excess over $15,000 is considered ordinary income to the alimony payer in the third post-separation year. The alimony recipient is entitled to deduct an equivalent amount on his or her tax return that same year.

Let us consider two examples. Suppose first that Joe paid Mindy $30,000 a year in alimony for the first and second years following their divorce. In the third year following the divorce, he paid only $10,000. Joe's alimony payments to Mindy therefore declined by $20,000 from year two to year three. Because the alimony paid in year two was more than $15,000 greater than the alimony paid in year three, the IRS would deem Joe's alimony payments to be excessively front loaded. The IRS would therefore require him to include the excess over $15,000—or $5,000 ($20,000 - $15,000)—as ordinary income on his tax return in year three. The IRS would further allow Mindy to deduct $5,000 from her ordinary income for year three.

Now suppose that Joe paid Mindy $50,000 in alimony for the first year following their divorce. Suppose further that he paid only $25,000 total in alimony for the second and third years. The amount that Joe paid Mindy in alimony in year one exceeded by $25,000 the average of the amount that he paid in years two and three. The IRS would therefore consider Joe's alimony payments to be excessively front loaded. He would be required to include the excess over $15,000—or $10,000 ($25,000 - $10,000)—as ordinary income on his tax return in year three. Mindy would be allowed to deduct that same amount from her ordinary income in year three.

The alimony recapture rules do not apply to payments made pursuant to a temporary support decree. The recapture rules also are not triggered if the decrease in alimony payments is caused by the death of either spouse or the remarriage of the supported spouse. Finally, the recapture rules do not apply if the amount of alimony to be paid was a certain percentage of income from any particular source. For example, if Luis agreed to pay Nina 10 percent of the profits from his dry-cleaning business for five years as alimony, Luis's alimony payments would not be subject to recapture even if the amount paid in year three differed significantly from the amount paid in year one. Because Luis's dry-cleaning business profits are somewhat out of his control, the IRS would reason that Luis could not have been using the alimony rules as a way to achieve favorable tax treatment for his marital property division obligations.

To ensure that the alimony agreement in your case comports with all applicable IRS rules and does not run afoul of the recapture provisions, you should consult with your lawyer about the tax aspects of your alimony agreement. You may also want to ask your lawyer about alimony trusts and other tax-effective vehicles for alimony payment.

ALIMONY AND BANKRUPTCY

Even if the alimony payer files for bankruptcy, he or she must still meet his or her alimony obligations. In other words, alimony obligations are not dischargeable in bankruptcy. Property division obligations, however, are generally dischargeable in bankruptcy. For this reason, many settlement agreements include provisions recasting property division obligations as alimony in the event of bankruptcy.

QUESTIONS TO ASK YOUR LAWYER

- Is a judge likely to award either me or my spouse alimony? If so, approximately how much alimony would a judge likely award and for how long?
- What factors is a court likely to consider most relevant in awarding alimony in my case?
- When does alimony end?
- Is a judge likely to award temporary alimony in my case?
- Is a judge likely to award either me or my spouse attorney's fees?
- If I am likely to be paying alimony, can you recommend the most tax-advantageous method for meeting my alimony obligations?
- If I am the financially dependent spouse:
  - Do you recommend that I immediately seek temporary alimony?
  - Do you recommend that I seek temporary attorney's fees from my spouse?
  - What kinds of COBRA health insurance benefits do I qualify for?
  - Should I seek additional health insurance benefits as part of my alimony package?
  - Should I ask my spouse to purchase a life insurance policy as part of my alimony package?
- If I am the spouse of a military employee, do I qualify for military health insurance benefits?

Chapter Eight

Child Custody

Like Humpty Dumpty, a family, once broken by divorce, cannot be put back together in precisely the same way.
    —*Tropea v. Tropea* (New York Court of Appeals 1996)

One of the most emotionally difficult aspects of divorce is "dividing" your children between you and your spouse in a way that provides the best outcome for your children. This may mean that you will have sole custody of your children and your spouse will have the right to visit the children according to a particular schedule. Or it may mean that your spouse will live with your children and share in their lives on a daily basis, while you will be the visiting parent. It may even mean that you and your spouse will share custody of the children, with both of you having roughly equal time with the children and roughly equal input into the decisions that affect their lives. Irrespective of the custodial arrangement that you and your spouse ultimately agree on or a divorce court determines for you, one thing is virtually certain: you will no longer be able to spend every day, every holiday, every birthday, and every weekend with your children. Instead, you must share your children with your former spouse.

The prospect of "losing" one's child can be deeply frightening. Because children often mean more to people than anything else in their lives, child custody battles can be the most contentious and most protracted of all divorce-related disputes. Although parents may try to convince themselves that they are fighting for custody for the sake of their children, the sad reality is that custody disputes are usually devastating to the children involved. Too many parents do not keep their children's best interests in mind when engaging in legal warfare over child custody. Instead of trying to forge an out-of-court solution that makes the most sense for their children, parents frequently litigate custody for reasons that have nothing to do with their children's best interests: to punish their spouses, to extract economic concessions in other aspects of the divorce, or to obtain or avoid paying child support. As explained by the Alaska Supreme Court, "the custody of children is often merely another bargaining point between the divorcing parents, along with the questions of the property division, spousal support, child support, and visitation." *Veazey v. Veazey,* 560 P.2d 382, 389 (Alaska 1977).

Divorce courts recognize that children can become the accidental victims of the divorce process. The divorce laws are therefore designed to protect children and to promote the custodial arrangement that is in the best interests of the children. The divorce laws charge courts with the difficult task of determining which parent is best equipped to provide the child with a loving and nurturing environment, and what type of custodial arrangement would best promote the child's physical, emotional, intellectual, and moral growth. Unlike other aspects of divorce law, you cannot simply "opt out" of the child custody laws by entering into an out-of-court agreement on issues of custody. If a divorce court determines that the agreed-upon custodial arrangement is not in the best interests of the child, the court can invalidate your out-of-court agreement and impose a different custodial arrangement.

TYPES OF CUSTODIAL ARRANGEMENTS

When one parent is awarded custody of a child, that parent is generally granted *physical custody* as well as *legal custody.* Physical custody is the right to live with and provide a home for the child, and to make day-to-day decisions concerning the child. Legal custody is the right to make all major decisions involving the care, upbringing, health, religion, discipline, and education of the child. In some cases, a parent may be awarded sole physical custody but not sole legal custody, or vice versa.

Parents without legal custody still have access to the children's medical, dental, and educational records, but they have no legal right to participate in decision making with respect to the children. Often, however, the non-custodial parent will be allowed some informal input into the custodial parent's decision making. In addition, the non-custodial parent has the authority to make day-to-day decisions regarding the child during any time that the child is visiting with the non-custodial parent.

Parents may also be awarded *joint custody,* which generally means that they share legal and physical custody alike. *Joint legal custody* allows both parents to have significant rights and responsibilities with respect to all major decisions concerning the child. *Joint physical custody* means that the child lives with or spends time with both parents in a manner that provides the child with approximately equal contact with each parent. A court may award joint legal custody while providing one parent with sole physical custody, or vice versa.

Finally, *split custody* refers to an arrangement in which one parent has sole custody of one child while the other parent has sole custody of the other child. Split custody is very rarely awarded.

FACTORS CONSIDERED IN DETERMINING CUSTODY

The universal standard for deciding which parent should be awarded custody is the "best interests of the child" test. In order to determine the custodial arrangement that would be in the best interests of the child, divorce courts look to a series of different factors. The most commonly considered factors are:

- Which parent serves as the child's primary caretaker
- The time each parent has available to spend with the child
- The current custodial arrangement
- Each parent's ability to meet the child's educational and health needs
- Each parent's ability to foster a loving relationship and encourage frequent and continuing contact between the child and the other parent
- Whether either parent has abused or neglected the child
- Whether either parent has alcohol or drug problems
- Each parent's mental and physical health
- The child's preferences as to custody
- Each parent's extramarital relationships, to the extent they have an adverse impact on the child
- The nature of the home environment that each parent can offer

Factors that are comparatively much less important in custody determinations are:

- The parent's gender
- The parent's financial resources
- The parent's religious beliefs

Courts generally do not consider race when deciding custody. Courts also do not differentiate between an adoptive parent and a natural parent for custody purposes.

Divorce courts are obligated to take into account a number of different factors when determining custody, but they are free to weigh each factor in the manner they see fit. In other words, divorce courts have tremendous discretion in custody decisions. For example, one court may consider a child's preference to be paramount in awarding custody, while another court may be most interested in which parent has more time available to spend with the child. It is therefore difficult to predict with any certainty how a court will rule on a given custody dispute. As noted by one New York court, "[t]he only absolute in the law governing custody of children is that there are no absolutes." *Friederweitzer v. Friederweitzer,* 447 N.Y.S.2d 893, 895 (N.Y. 1982).

The major advantage of the "best interests of the child" custody standard is that it allows judges the freedom to consider each case on an individual basis and to tailor the custodial arrangement to the particular case. The major drawback of the "best interests of the child" standard is its lack of predictability. Some have argued that the uncertainty of the standard encourages parents to try their luck litigating instead of settling for a custodial arrangement that is less than their ideal.

The Role of Gender in Custody Determinations

Until as recently as the 1970s, divorce courts adhered rigorously to the "tender years doctrine," which provided that a mother should generally have custody of children of "tender years." The preference for awarding mothers custody of young children is a thing of the past. Divorce courts now recognize that fathers are equally suited to take care of young children, and that it is the quality of the parent rather than his or her gender that should dictate custody determinations. In all states, custody determinations must be made without reference to the gender of the parent, at least in theory.

Although the United States Supreme Court has yet to rule on the issue, divorce courts around the country agree that using gender as a basis for making custody determinations violates the United States Constitution. It is fundamental that people should not be treated differently based on their gender unless there is some very good reason for doing so. While divorce courts in the mid-1800s might have considered mothers to be better parents simply by virtue of their biology, there is absolutely no modern evidence that mothers are inherently better suited for parenting than fathers.

Having said all of this, some judges nevertheless prefer mothers in custody disputes. Judges are, after all, human beings with their own biases and perspectives. No matter what the statutes mandate, some judges continue to believe that women are simply more suited to parenting than men. These judges often use "backdoor" methods for considering gender. One method is to take into account the age and sex of the child. Some judges have held that very young children, or female children, need to be in their mother's custody. Another method is to use gender as "tiebreaker" when both the mother and the father appear equally fit as parents.

Just as there are judges who firmly believe that young girls belong with their mothers, other judges believe that active young boys belong with their fathers. In one Iowa case, the judge gave custody of two boys aged nine and eleven to their father on the grounds that the father would "be able to engage in various activities with the boys, such as athletic events, fishing, hunting, mechanical training and other activities that the boys are interested in." *In re Marriage of Treshak,* 297 N.W.2d 109, 112 (Iowa 1980), *quoting* trial court decision. Ironically, there was no evidence that the boys had any interest in such activities or that the father was better at such activities than the mother. Because the case had been decided purely on the basis of gender, the Iowa Supreme Court reversed the judge's decision and explained:

> Each case must be decided on its own facts. . . . [N]either parent has an edge on the other based merely on sex. The real issue is not the sex of the parent but which parent will do better in raising the children. (*Id.* at 112.)

The only situation in which gender can properly be considered without raising constitutional concerns is when the child is still nursing. Given the well-recognized benefits of breast feeding, it is entirely appropriate for divorce courts to award the mother custody of a nursing child until he or she is weaned. With the exception of this particular situation, gender should not be taken into account for custody determinations.

The Primary Caretaker

An extremely important factor in child custody determinations is whether either parent serves as the child's primary caretaker. The child's primary caretaker is the individual who meets the child's physical and emotional needs, and who supervises and cares for the child on a day-to-day basis.

Particularly when the child is relatively young, divorce courts place a great deal of weight on the primary caretaker factor for a number of reasons. First, the child is usually more dependent on and has a closer relationship with the primary caretaker parent. Second, the primary caretaker parent has more parenting experience with the child and understands how to meet the child's needs. Third, the primary caretaker has demonstrated that he or she is committed to taking care of the child. Finally and perhaps most important, it is extremely disruptive and perhaps even traumatic for a child to be taken away from the parent who has taken the most care of him or her. As explained by one Pennsylvania court:

> [W]here two natural parents are both fit, and the child is of tender years, the trial court must give positive consideration to the parent who has been the primary caretaker. Not to do so ignores the benefits likely to flow to the child from maintaining day to day contact with the parent on whom the child has depended for satisfying his basic physical and psychological needs.
> *Com. Ex. Rel. Jordan v. Jordan,* 448 A.2d 1113, 1115 (Pa. Super. Ct. 1982).

While the number of things that a primary caretaker does for a child can be virtually limitless, the West Virginia Supreme Court of Appeals has provided the following list of primary caretaker activities as guidance:

- Preparing and planning of meals
- Bathing, grooming, and dressing
- Purchasing, cleaning, and taking care of clothes
- Medical care, including nursing and trips to physicians
- Arranging for social interaction among peers after school—for example, transporting the child to friends' houses or to girl or boy scout meetings
- Arranging for alternative care, such as baby-sitting and day care
- Putting the child to bed at night, attending to the child in the middle of the night, waking the child in the morning
- Disciplining—for example, teaching general manners and toilet training
- Educating the child on religious, cultural, and social matters
- Teaching elementary skills—for example, helping the child with homework and teaching the child the basics of reading and arithmetic

This list may be helpful in determining which parent would be considered to be the child's primary caretaker by a divorce court.

If both parents work outside the home, a nanny or day care service may meet a child's day-to-day needs. This does not necessarily mean that neither parent is the child's primary caretaker. Rather, divorce courts recognize that one parent may nevertheless do the lion's share of parenting in the time he or she has available after work and on weekends. In one Minnesota case, the father attempted to argue that the mother was not the child's primary caretaker since she worked full-time outside the home. The court rejected the father's contention and gave custody to the mother, noting that she had stayed home with the children until the youngest was nine months old, took the children to the doctor when necessary, found day care and provided transportation to and from the day care center, cooked meals for the children, and changed their diapers.

Time Available to Spend with the Child

Another particularly important factor in the case of relatively young children is which parent has more time available to spend with the child. This factor favors parents who stay at home with their children or who have relatively flexible jobs. Correspondingly, this factor disfavors parents with extremely busy jobs or other commitments that limit the time they have available to spend with their children. Divorce courts will take into account not only the number of hours in the day that each parent has available, but also which hours. A parent who works the night shift or regularly works late in the evenings is at a disadvantage compared with a parent who works the same number of hours in the daytime.

In one well-known Washington, D.C., case, the mother worked extremely long hours, including many evenings and weekends, as chief counsel for the Republicans on the Senate Judiciary Committee. The father, on the other hand, had a comparatively relaxed schedule as assistant executive director of the American Federation of Television and Radio Artists and Screen Actors Guild. Notably, the father had switched jobs in order to be able to spend more time with his children. The trial court awarded custody to the father, finding that the mother was "simply more devoted to and absorbed by her work and her career than anything else in her life, including her health, her children and her family." *Prost v. Greene,* 652 A.2d 621, 624 (D.C. Ct. App. 1995), *quoting* trial court decision.

Many women have complained that divorce courts rely on the "time available" factor to penalize working women and to reward disproportionately those fathers who are even slightly more involved in their children's lives than the average father. These women charge that women with demanding jobs are judged far more harshly than their male peers by divorce courts.

The Current Custodial Arrangement

Because of the importance of stability to a child's well-being, divorce courts are generally reluctant to alter existing custodial arrangements. Courts tend to prefer awarding custody to the parent with whom the child is residing at the time of the custody dispute, in order to maintain continuity in the child's life. The longer the child has been living with a particular parent, the stronger this preference.

When one parent moves out of the family home, leaving his or her children behind, the other parent gains a tremendous advantage in any future custody dispute. For this reason, parents anticipating custody disputes should consult with their lawyers before moving out of the marital home. Parents should also discuss with their lawyers the option of filing for temporary custody while the divorce dispute is pending.

The Ability to Meet the Child's Educational and Health Needs

Divorce courts will generally favor the parent in whose care the child enjoys consistently good health and performs better in school. If a parent takes extra steps to address the child's educational or health needs—for example, by helping the child with his or her homework every evening, or by carefully monitoring the diet of a lactose-intolerant child—a court will take those efforts into account when considering which parent would be best suited to serve as the child's primary custodian. A parent with particular expertise in taking care of a child's special health or educational needs also stands a better chance of obtaining custody. In one West Virginia case, for example, the mother obtained custody when she knew how to take care of a hydrocephalic child but the father did not.

The Parent's Ability to Foster a Loving Relationship Between the Child and the Other Parent

Divorce courts firmly believe that children should have frequent and continuing contact and the opportunity to develop a loving relationship with both parents, even if one parent has been awarded sole custody. Accordingly, divorce courts will consider which parent is more likely to encourage the child to stay in touch with the other parent and to facilitate meetings between the child and the other parent when awarding custody. A parent who is inclined to interfere with the child's relationship with the other parent—for example, by refusing to allow the other parent to visit with the child regularly, saying negative things about the other parent to the child, and forcing the child to take sides in disputes between the parents—is unlikely to win custody. This is because divorce courts recognize that such actions can have a deeply damaging effect on the child's relationship with the other parent. The term "parental alienation syndrome" has been coined to describe a child's negative feelings for one parent that result from the other parent's efforts to sabotage the child's relationship with that parent.

As tempting as it may be to inform your child of every negative thing that your spouse has ever said and done, the most prudent and appropriate course of action is to avoid saying anything negative about your spouse to your child. You will be in a far better position to seek custody of your child if you can demonstrate that you have never stood in the way of your child's relationship with your spouse and, even better, you have actually encouraged your child to remain close with your spouse.

Abuse and Neglect

A parent who has physically or sexually abused a child is highly unlikely to receive custody. A parent who has neglected a child by ignoring the child's needs or by abandoning the child is also unlikely to receive custody. When a parent fails to supervise the child, keep the child clean and well fed, take care of the child's health needs, or ensure that a child's care providers are qualified, a parent may be deemed to have neglected the child. A parent's own abuse and neglect of the child is not the only relevant factor. If a parent lives or frequently visits with somebody who is abusive or neglectful of the child, a court will consider that fact when making a custody determination. For example, if Sheila is a good parent but her new boyfriend, Nick, has sexually abused his own daughter in the past, a divorce court might not award Sheila custody unless she ends her relationship with Nick.

When making custody determinations, divorce courts generally take domestic violence into account. Courts recognize that domestic violence has a tremendously negative impact on children. In fact, the United States Congress adopted a continuing resolution in 1990 declaring that courts should presume that it is detrimental to a child to be placed in the custody of a parent who has abused the other parent.

Because divorce courts will rarely award custody to an abusive parent, parents in heated custody disputes are occasionally tempted to make false abuse allegations against their spouses in order to obtain custody of their children. Divorce courts view such false accusations with extreme disapproval. If a court discovers that you have made false accusations of abuse against your spouse, it very likely could award your spouse custody of your children or even prevent you from visiting your child for a period of time. If your own ethics would not prevent you from launching false accusations of abuse against your spouse, a fear of the practical consequences most certainly should.

Alcohol and Drug Problems

If one parent suffers from alcohol or drug addiction, a divorce court is unlikely to award him or her custody of the child for the obvious reason that the addicted parent could place the child in danger as a result of his or her inebriation or altered mental state. For example, an alcoholic parent may drive a child to school while intoxicated and place the child and others at great risk.

Drug and alcohol problems are not always enough, in and of themselves, to justify a denial of custody. If the parent with the problem is making an earnest effort to overcome his or her addiction, and the parent has never placed the children in danger as a result of his or her alcohol or drug use, a court may award such a parent custody. A parent who has had alcohol or drug problems in the past but has successfully overcome those problems will not necessarily be denied custody merely on the basis that he or she could lapse back into old habits at some point in the future.

Mental Health

Divorce courts will generally only take severe mental health problems into account when making custody determinations. If a parent has attempted suicide in the past or has been hospitalized for mental health problems, a court is unlikely to award custody to such an individual. However, if a parent's mental health problem consists only of minor depression or can be addressed with weekly trips to a therapist, a divorce court probably will not deny custody to the parent.

The crux of the issue is whether a parent's mental health problems adversely affect the child in some way. In one New York case, for example, the divorce court awarded custody to the father with only supervised visitation to the mother, because she suffered from bipolar disorder, frequently failed to take the lithium prescribed for her condition, and exhibited bizarre behavior in the courtroom. The court explained that its duty was "to resolve custody disputes not out of sympathy for the circumstances of the parent, but out of concern for the best interest and welfare of the child." *James P.W. v. Eileen M.W.,* 136 A.D.2d 549, 550 (N.Y. App. Div. 1988).

Physical Health

As with mental health problems, a divorce court will only take into account physical health problems that adversely affect the child or interfere with the parent's ability to take care of the child in a way that cannot be corrected. A parent suffering from a disease or illness could certainly be awarded custody if he or she could demonstrate that the disease or illness does not affect his or her ability to care for the children and is not likely to shorten his or her life expectancy dramatically. Even if a parent is disabled, a divorce court will not automatically deny that parent custody without considering the parent's actual abilities and limitations more carefully.

The leading case on this issue is *Carney v. Carney,* decided by the California Supreme Court in 1979. In *Carney,* the father had been taking care of his two young sons for four years before a jeep accident left him quadriplegic. During those four years, the mother did not visit the children once. After the accident, the father's good friend assisted him with the care of his children. The father also had the financial ability and the intent to hire a caregiver if his friend left. Nevertheless, the mother fought the father for custody of the boys—then aged six and seven—and claimed that the father was too disabled to take care of them. The trial judge awarded custody to the mother on the grounds that the father "can't do anything for the boys except maybe talk to them, be a tutor, which is good but it's not enough." *Carney v. Carney,* 598 P.2d 36, 41 (Cal. 1979), *quoting* trial court decision. The judge was most concerned that the father would not be able to play baseball, go fishing, or engage in other such activities with the children.

The California Supreme Court reversed the trial judge's decision, explaining that the trial judge's ruling was based on "outdated stereotypes of both the parental role and the ability of the handicapped to fill that role." (*Id.* at 37.) The court stated that

> [T]he essence of parenting is not to be found in the harried rounds of daily carpooling endemic to modern suburban life, or even in the doggedly dutiful acts of "togetherness" committed every weekend by well-meaning fathers and mothers across America. Rather, its essence lies in the ethical, emotional and intellectual guidance the parent gives the child throughout his formative years, and often beyond. (*Id.* at 44.)

A divorce court will now generally make the following inquiries when considering whether a disabled individual should be granted custody:

- What are the person's actual and potential physical capabilities?
- How has the parent adapted to the disability and learned to manage its problems?
- How have the children adjusted to the parent's disability?
- What special contributions may the parent make to the family despite or even because of the disability?

A divorce court will evaluate all of these factors together when determining whether an individual's disability has an adverse impact on the child.

AIDS

Another recent issue is whether individuals infected with the HIV virus should be awarded custody despite their condition. The few divorce courts that have considered the issue to date have held that a parent's infection with the HIV virus should not in and of itself determine custody and visitation issues. Rather, courts have assessed whether the parent's condition would have an adverse impact on the child. These courts have recognized that the HIV virus is primarily transmitted through sexual contact, the sharing of needles by intravenous drug users, and blood transfusions. Because the HIV virus generally cannot be transmitted through everyday parent–child interactions, these courts have reached the conclusion that a parent infected with the HIV virus can be awarded custody and visitation in the same manner as a healthy parent.

The Child's Preferences

In general, divorce courts will take into account the preferences of a child who is old enough to make a reasoned assessment of his or her own circumstances. Although divorce courts would probably honor the wishes of a twelve-year-old provided his or her preference was reasonable, divorce courts would be unlikely to place much weight on the preferences of a five-year-old.

The child's age alone is not determinative. Courts also pay a great deal of attention to the reason for the child's preference in deciding whether to consider the child's wishes in a custody determination. If a child has been pressured by one parent to express a preference in that parent's favor, a divorce court will usually disregard the child's wishes entirely. The same holds true if a child prefers one parent simply because that parent provides more toys, less discipline, or the like. In one Louisiana case, a court awarded custody of a thirteen-year-old boy to the mother even though the child wished to live with his father because the father had showered the child with expensive gifts—including a horse, a motorcycle, two color televisions, and a shotgun—shortly before the custody hearing.

If a child expresses a preference for living with one parent and is able to articulate a valid reason for the preference, a court will generally award custody to the parent of the child's choosing. Examples of valid reasons for preferring one parent over another include a desire to escape an abusive parent, the child's sense that he or she has a much closer relationship with the preferred parent, and the child's desire to live with his or her half-siblings.

Before deciding to make your child's preferences a part of your custody dispute, be certain to take into account the effect that doing so may have on your child. Forcing your child to express a preference essentially requires your child to take sides between parents, something most children would rather not do. Moreover, your child may feel pressured to express a preference in favor of one parent when in fact he or she would rather remain with the other parent. Finally, your child may be required to testify as to his or her preferences in court and be examined by a social worker or a psychologist in order for the court to determine how much weight to assign to your child's preference. In the author's view, children should be kept out of nearly all custody disputes.

Extramarital Relationships

The majority view is that a parent's extramarital relationships should not be used as a factor in determining custody unless such relationships have a negative impact on the child. Divorce courts are in disagreement over when an extramarital relationship has a negative impact on a child. In some cases, divorce courts will simply presume that a parent's extramarital relationships have a negative impact on the child. In other cases, divorce courts have required specific proof of harm to the child before they will weigh in a parent's extramarital relationships for the purposes of custody. Still other courts have made it a condition of custody that parents have no overnight romantic visitors while the children are present.

The safest course of action is to steer clear of romantic relationships while your custody dispute is still brewing. If this is not an option for you, the next best strategy is to keep your extramarital relationships as discreet as possible. Do not bring lovers home overnight, and try to keep your romantic relationships separate from your relationship with your children. Make certain that your romantic relationships do not interfere with your ability to care for your children. If a court finds that you are too wrapped up in your new significant other to pay adequate attention to your child, it may be very reluctant to award you custody. Finally, try very hard to avoid entering into a succession of romantic relationships. Divorce courts tend to view multiple romantic relationships more harshly than a lengthy one. Many courts consider it disruptive and confusing for children to see their parents with a new lover every few weeks. Moreover, courts may view your numerous relationships as a sign of your general instability and promiscuity—very problematic characteristics if you are in the throes of a custody battle.

Homosexuality

Most courts do not consider a parent's homosexuality, in and of itself, to warrant a denial of custody. In many states, courts will use the same considerations they use to evaluate heterosexual relationships when assessing a parent's homosexual relationships. These states will not factor in a parent's homosexual relationships unless such relationships have an adverse impact on the child.

Courts in a minority of states, however, will not award custody to a homosexual parent. These courts rely on a number of different rationalizations for taking homosexuality into account for the purposes of custody determinations—ranging from morality to social stigmatization to the risk that the child will become homosexual. If homosexuality is an issue in your case, you should consult with your lawyer to see how courts in your state have recently decided cases involving homosexuality. Parents engaged in homosexual relationships should follow the same guidelines discussed in the last paragraph of the "Extramarital Relationships" section.

The Proposed Custodial Environment

In considering which parent should be awarded custody, courts consider the kind of home environment that each parent can provide. Factors include the cleanliness of the home; the habits and lifestyles of any other individuals who live in the home; the characteristics of the proposed child care providers; and the proximity of the home to the child's school, friends, and other family members. For example, a court may prefer to award custody to a parent who intends to remain in the child's hometown instead of to a parent whose job requires him or her to move to a different city every year.

Financial Resources

Divorce courts rarely take into account the financial resources of the parents when considering which parent would make a better custodian. If there is a tremendous disparity in incomes between the parents and one parent can offer the child substantial material advantages that the other cannot, the usual remedy is to direct the wealthier parent to pay more in child support to help bridge the gap. The only circumstances under which divorce courts do take financial resources into account are if one parent's lack of resources will prevent him or her from providing the child with a decent, stable home. Again, this problem can generally be corrected with child support if that parent is nevertheless better equipped to serve as the child's primary custodian.

Religion

Divorce courts are generally prohibited from considering religion in custody determinations because doing so raises constitutional concerns with respect to freedom of religion. If divorce courts were permitted to consider religion freely for custody purposes, there would be a significant risk that divorce courts would prefer one religion over another or prefer religious parents over nonreligious parents. In essence, judges would be able to impose their particular religious value systems on custody litigants.

Two exceptions exist to the general rule that a court may not consider a parent's religion or lack thereof when deciding custody. The first is when the child has been brought up with a certain amount of religious training or religious influence. In such cases, divorce courts can consider which parent is more likely to provide the child with continuity of religious training or religious influence for the sake of stability in the child's life. For example, if a child has attended Sunday school regularly for several years, a divorce court could properly take into account the fact that one parent is likely to continue sending that child to Sunday school whereas the other parent no longer believes that Sunday school is necessary or appropriate. Conversely, if a twelve-year-old child has been brought up in an entirely secular fashion, a court could take into account the fact that one parent has recently converted to a new religion and now wishes to have the child attend religious instead of public school.

The second circumstance in which divorce courts can consider religion for the purposes of custody determinations is if one parent's religious beliefs or activities are somehow harmful to the child. Because of judicial reluctance to make value judgments about religious beliefs, a parent's religious beliefs or activities must have a clear and significant negative impact on the child before courts will take such beliefs or activities into account when determining custody. For example, parental religious beliefs prohibiting the pledging of allegiance to the U.S. flag and requiring children to pass out religious literature from door to door have not been found to be sufficiently harmful to children to permit the courts to take religion into account for determining custody. Even parental religious beliefs prohibiting blood transfusions in emergencies have not been considered sufficiently harmful to children for custody purposes.

Race

The general view is that divorce courts are not constitutionally permitted to consider the race of either parent when making custody determinations, nor can they take into account the race of either parent's significant other or families. The most important case on this issue is *Palmore v. Sidoti,* decided by the U.S. Supreme Court in 1984. In *Palmore,* a white mother lost custody of her daughter when she married a black man. The trial court's decision was based on the fact that the little girl would face social stigmatization when she reached school age because her stepfather was black. The U.S. Supreme Court reversed the trial court's decision on the grounds that taking race into account for custody determinations violates the Constitution. The Supreme Court acknowledged that a child who has a stepparent of a different race may be subject to social stigmatization by her peers, but went on to explain as follows:

> The Constitution cannot control such prejudices but neither can it tolerate them. Private biases may be outside the reach of the law, but the law cannot, directly or indirectly, give them effect. *Palmore v. Sidoti,* 466 U.S. 429, 433 (1984).

JOINT CUSTODY

An alternative to an arrangement in which one parent "wins" sole custody of the child is joint custody, which allows both parents to share physical and legal custody of the child. In a joint custody arrangement, both parents have equal rights to make major decisions with respect to the child, such as medical and educational decisions, and each is entitled to spend roughly equal time with the child. Parents can be given joint legal custody without joint physical custody, and vice versa.

Courts are growing increasingly in favor of joint custody as a way to allow children to continue to enjoy the love and affection of both parents equally even after the parents have divorced. In a number of states, divorce courts have a general presumption in favor of joint custody. In other words, a court will order joint custody unless such a custodial arrangement would not be in the best interests of the child. In a number of other states, courts have a presumption in favor of joint custody if both parents agree to such an arrangement. To determine whether your state has any preference in favor of joint custody, please turn to appendix A.

The proponents of joint custody argue that such an arrangement provides children with the closest thing to a nuclear family. Unlike the case with sole custody arrangements, children in joint custody arrangements do not suffer the loss of one parent following the divorce. Another important advantage is that joint custody allows both parents continuing involvement in their children's lives, and neither parent feels cut off from the children after the divorce. The concept of joint custody also changes the landscape of custody battles. No longer are there "winners" and "losers," only parents who are both committed to the care and upbringing of their children.

The opponents of joint custody, on the other hand, contend that joint custody is extremely disruptive for children. Children are forced to shuttle back and forth between two parents, two homes, and two neighborhoods. Instead of ever feeling simply "at home," children always feel that they are either at "Mom's house" or "Dad's house." Opponents of joint custody contend that the entire concept of joint custody is based on a pie-in-the-sky notion that adults who could not cooperate to save their marriage can now interact regularly, without hostility, in a joint custodial arrangement. When cooperation between parents breaks down in joint custody settings, it is the children who are caught in the middle and suffer. Moreover, joint custody forces divorced spouses to interact far more regularly and intimately than they would in a sole custody arrangement.

Factors Considered in Awarding Joint Custody

Joint custody is practical and beneficial in some cases but not in others. In determining whether joint custody is in the best interests of the child in any given case, a court will consider first and foremost the parents' ability to cooperate and to place the needs of their child above their own. Joint custodial arrangements require tremendous cooperation between the parents, both on the day-to-day logistics of time sharing and on the larger issues of education, health, religion, and other decisions that may affect the child. If parents are unable to work together in this manner, courts recognize that a joint custodial arrangement is unlikely to remain feasible for very long. When one parent has been abusive to the other parent or to the child, courts recognize that joint custody is inappropriate.

Courts will also consider whether parents respect one another's parenting abilities and share basic values regarding child rearing. If two parents have dramatically different ideas of the role that religion should play in a child's life, or have other such deep differences, a joint custodial arrangement probably will not work. The same holds true if one parent believes that the other is incapable of properly caring for the children. Of course, if one parent is not fit to be a primary custodian for any reason, joint custody will not be awarded.

Courts will also take into account the preexisting relationship between the child and each parent. If a child has strong relationships with both parents, a court is more likely to award joint custody. If a child has a very poor or virtually nonexistent relationship with one parent, however, it would be a dramatic departure for both the child and the parent suddenly to spend substantial amounts of time together.

Finally, courts will consider the mechanics of a joint custodial arrangement. If parents live close to one another and the children could easily be shuttled back and forth, a court would be more willing to order joint custody. If, on the other hand, the parents live very far apart and a joint custodial arrangement would require a child to spend a great deal of time in transit, a court would be hesitant to order joint custody. A court will also take into account the age and nature of the child before ordering joint custody. In some cases, a joint custodial arrangement would simply be too disruptive for a child, and the child would fare much better by living in one home rather than two. A court will also consider whether the two home environments are roughly similar in terms of the resources available, the neighborhood, and so forth. Courts believe that children are better able to live in two homes if the homes are not drastically different from one another. Unfortunately, however, it may not always be possible to maintain two homes at roughly equal economic levels.

Parenting Plans

To evaluate the mechanics of a proposed joint custody arrangement, courts will often require parents to submit a parenting plan, providing the court with details of the proposed arrangement. Parents must inform the court of such things as when the child will be living with which parent; how the child will be transported back and forth; what kind of home each parent can provide; whether the two homes are comparable; what kinds of decisions have already been made as to the child's health, education, and religion; how the parents will be making decisions that affect the child in the future; and how the parents plan on resolving any disputes that may later arise between them. One of the key benefits of a parenting plan is that it forces parents to sit down and cooperate to arrive at an arrangement and a set of rules on which they agree. Preparing a parenting plan is also a good test for determining whether joint custody is an option in any given case, as parents may simply be unable to agree on the details of such a plan.

Even with a parenting plan in place, parents embarking on joint custody should understand that communication and cooperation are the ultimate keys to a successful joint custodial arrangement. As explained by the Louisiana Court of Appeals, "no plan, with or without ironclad guidelines, could possibly resolve the infinite number of conflicts which can and will arise between divorced parents in their quest to share their child's life." *Plemer v. Plemer,* 436 So.2d 1348, 1350 (La. Ct. App. 1983).

Joint Custody and Child Support

The wealthier parent generally pays substantially less in child support in a joint custodial arrangement than he or she would have had to pay in a sole custody arrangement. This is because the wealthier parent is already supporting the child during the time that the child spends with him or her. If parental incomes are roughly equivalent and the children spend approximately the same time living with each parent, it is possible that neither parent will be ordered to pay child support to the other.

Because of the relationship between joint custody and child support, some women have contended that men seek joint custody simply to reduce their child support obligations. Men, on the other hand, have argued that women are reluctant to enter into joint custodial arrangements because of a fear of lost income in the form of child support. Courts are aware of these issues and will take into account the fact that one parent is seeking or opposing joint custody for child support reasons when making a custody determination.

Though joint custody often reduces child support obligations, one parent may nevertheless be required to pay the other a significant amount in child support if the additional funds are necessary to enable that parent to provide the child with a proper living environment and the necessities of life. If one parent earns substantially more money than the other, or if the child spends much more time with one parent than with the other, sizeable child support payments may be required even in a joint custodial arrangement.

Joint custody can become very expensive. Instead of having one home for the child that contains all of the child's necessities, divorced parents must maintain two homes that are suitable for the child. Divorced parents must often buy duplicates of many items, such as shoes and clothing, to prevent the child from having to "pack up and move" with each trip back and forth from each house. Without child support payments, joint custody may become prohibitively expensive for the parent with less in the way of economic resources.

SPLIT CUSTODY

Courts are extremely reluctant to separate siblings between parents—a custodial arrangement known as *split custody*. This is because courts recognize that siblings depend on one another for friendship, companionship, and support. Unless there are exceptional and compelling reasons for separating the children, courts will not award custody of one sibling to one parent and custody of another to the other parent. In some cases, courts will apply this rule to half-siblings as well.

When one child expresses a strong and well-reasoned preference for staying with one parent while another child wishes to be with the other parent, courts may decide that split custody is appropriate. A court may also award split custody if one parent is better suited to raise one child and another parent is better suited to raise the other. For example, in one New York case, the court awarded custody of the sons to the father and custody of the daughter to the mother. In that case, the oldest son was learning disabled and the father had been actively involved in the child's education. The daughter, on the other hand, had trouble with her toilet training when she was separated from her mother.

MODIFICATION OF CUSTODY

Child custody decisions are not set in stone for the remainder of the child's youth. These arrangements may be modified where the circumstances warrant a change. Custody determinations can be modified in a number of ways: sole custody may be switched from one parent to the other; sole custody may be modified to joint custody; or physical custody may be changed without affecting legal custody, and vice versa. Divorce

courts are authorized to modify custodial arrangements when appropriate, but they are very reluctant to do so. Courts recognize that stability
and continuity are critical to a child's sense of well-being. Modifying
custodial arrangements uproots children and forces them to adjust to
major changes in their lives.

Courts also understand that petitions to modify custody are frequently
abused by the parent who did not receive the desired custodial arrangement in the first instance. Parents often feel that they have nothing to lose
by simply relitigating custody, even if the only purpose of doing so is to
seek revenge on the "winning" parent. In order to provide some sort of
closure to custody decisions, courts will consider petitions to modify
custody only if there is some legitimate reason for a change. Moreover,
courts usually require that parents seeking modification wait a reasonable amount of time after the initial custody determination, to allow
enough time for the child to settle into the arrangement and to give the
arrangement a chance to work. Finally, courts will only consider new
facts—facts arising after the initial custody determination—in evaluating petitions to modify custody. Otherwise, parents could simply reliti-
gate their entire custody disputes again and again.

In most states, courts will not modify custody arrangements unless a
significant change in circumstances has occurred since the time of the
original custody determination. The majority rule is that an improvement
in the circumstances of the non-custodial parent is not sufficient, in and
of itself, to justify a change of custody. For example, if the non-custodial
parent has obtained a better job, recovered from alcohol or drug problems, or has remarried and can now provide a more stable home environment, these changes alone will not be enough for a court to modify a
custodial arrangement. Courts usually require that there have been some
substantial or material change with respect to the custodial parent. For
example, if the custodial parent has become romantically involved with
an individual who has abused children in the past, a court may consider
that to be a substantial change in circumstances warranting a change in
custody.

In a handful of states, courts will modify custody arrangements based
simply upon a showing that modification is in the best interests of the
child. Although courts in these states will only consider facts arising
since the initial custody determination, these courts will reevaluate the
fitness of each parent. If the non-custodial parent's circumstances have
improved substantially while the custodial parent's circumstances have
remained the same, courts in these states would consider awarding the
non-custodial parent with custody.

Finally, a small number of states allow a modification of custody only if the child is endangered by the current custodial arrangement or if the custodial parent has consented to a modification of custody. These states make it very difficult to obtain a modification of custody. Even a significant change in the circumstances of the custodial parent is not enough to justify a modification of custody if the change does not threaten the child's physical, mental, moral, or emotional well-being.

Despite the different standards used in different states for modifying custody, courts in virtually every state would consider modifying custody if the custodial parent denied adequate visitation to the non-custodial parent or attempted to destroy the child's relationship with that parent. In one California case, the court switched custody from the mother to the father on the grounds that the father was more likely to encourage frequent and continuing contact and a loving relationship between the child and his mother. The court explained that the mother had "engaged in an ongoing course of conduct designed to frustrate visitation rights and interfere with the normal development of a healthy father-son relationship." *Catherine D. v. Dennis B.,* 220 Cal. App. 3d 922, 932 (Cal. Ct. App. 1990). For example, the mother had told the son that the father had not provided them with adequate financial support and had tried to discourage Christmas visitation with the father by promising extra gifts if the child remained with her over the holidays. Remember, if you are awarded custody in your case you have an obligation to foster a warm and loving relationship between your child and his or her other parent. A failure to do so could result in a modification of custody.

Courts will also consider modifying custody if the custodial parent remarries and the child has a rocky relationship with his new stepparent and stepsiblings. In one Louisiana case, for example, the court switched custody from the mother to the father because the mother and her new husband suffered from significant personal problems and had, in the court's words, "an emotionally draining relationship." *Moffatt v. Moffatt,* 508 So.2d 851, 853 (La. Ct. App. 1987). The father's new wife, on the other hand, had a very good relationship with the children. Because children often take time to adjust to a new stepfamily, courts will usually require that the non-custodial parent allow a reasonable amount of time to pass—perhaps as long as a year—before considering a modification petition on these grounds.

If a modification petition is based primarily on the child's preference to live with the non-custodial parent, courts will look closely at the reason for the child's preference. Has the child been pressured by the non-custodial parent to express such a preference? Is the child simply rebelling against the custodial parent's rules and discipline? Unless there is a legitimate reason for the child's preference, such as abuse by the custodial parent, courts will not modify custody based solely on the wishes of the child. In considering modification petitions based on the child's preference, courts will consider whether the child has been thriving under the care of the custodial parent. If the child has been doing well in school, and is well adjusted socially and in good health, a court would be very reluctant to modify custody even if the child desires a change.

MODIFICATION OF JOINT CUSTODY

Courts are much more flexible with requests to modify joint custody than with requests to modify a sole custody arrangement. Instead of requiring a substantial change in circumstances, courts will generally modify a joint custodial arrangement simply upon a showing that there has been a breakdown in parental cooperation and communication. Courts recognize that parental tensions can destroy a joint custodial arrangement, and children suffer as a result.

However, parents cannot come running to the courthouse at the first sign of disagreement in a joint custodial arrangement. Rather, parents have an obligation to make a good-faith effort at joint custody. Courts will not look favorably upon a parent who sabotages a joint custodial arrangement in an effort to obtain sole custody. If a parent violates the terms of a joint custody plan—for example, by refusing to allow the child to spend the weekend with the other parent as provided for in the joint custody schedule—a court is likely to switch the child from joint custody to the custody of the other parent.

Despite parental disagreements over aspects of the joint custodial arrangement, sometimes the child is nevertheless happy and well settled. In such cases, a court will not modify joint custody because it is in the best interests of the child for the parents to continue sharing custody. Parents must remember that even in happy marriages, parental disagreements over child-rearing issues arise. The fact that divorced parents face more disagreements over child-rearing issues should come as no surprise.

At times, joint custody will need to be modified to sole custody because of purely practical considerations. For example, if one parent is forced to move out of state, joint physical custody may be very difficult to maintain because of the long-distance travel involved. Or one parent's job responsibilities or work schedule may have changed to such an extent that it is impossible for that parent to take care of the child on a roughly equal basis. In such cases, joint custody may be modified to sole custody with liberal visitation for the other parent.

RELOCATION BY THE CUSTODIAL PARENT

The general rule in most states is that if the custodial parent has a legitimate reason for relocating out of state, that parent will be allowed to move away with the child. This is because courts believe that the custodial parent should have as much freedom to seek a better life for him- or herself by finding a new job or starting a new life in another state as the non-custodial parent. In a minority of states, courts will require the custodial parent to demonstrate not only a good reason for moving but also that the relocation is in the child's best interests.

In evaluating a custodial parent's request for relocation, courts in all states will consider:

- The prospective advantages of the move for the child and the custodial parent.
- The motives of the parent seeking the move.
- The motives of the parent opposing the move.
- The relationship between the child and the non-custodial parent.
- Whether visitation can be restructured to allow the non-custodial parent to continue to have a meaningful relationship with the child, and whether the custodial parent will encourage such visitation.

If the custodial parent wishes to move to obtain a better job, to accompany his or her spouse to another state because of a change in that spouse's employment, or to be closer to relatives, courts will usually consider the custodial parent to have a valid reason for moving. If, on the other hand, it appears that the custodial parent would like to relocate primarily in order to limit contact between the child and the non-custodial parent, a court will deny the request.

With respect to the non-custodial parent's reasons for opposing the move, courts are more likely to respect the non-custodial parent's position if he or she has regularly exercised visitation in the past and has developed a close relationship with the child. Courts are sympathetic to the concerns of non-custodial parents who fear that the custodial parent's relocation will adversely impact their well-established relationships with their children. On the other hand, courts tend to be suspicious of parents who have not exercised visitation in the past and who have limited relationships with their children. These parents may be opposing relocation simply to punish the custodial parents or to obtain leverage to reduce their child support obligations.

In most cases, visitation schedules can be adjusted to provide the non-custodial parent with adequate visitation after the custodial parent has relocated, provided that at least one of the parents is well-off and can afford the costs of transportation, and there are no other practical obstacles to having the non-custodial parent visit with the child.

Where it appears that the custodial parent's proposed relocation would interfere dramatically with the non-custodial parent's ability to visit with the child, however, courts will be very reluctant to allow the move. In one New Jersey case, for example, the court rejected the custodial father's proposed move from New Jersey to Florida where both parents had limited resources and the mother could not afford frequent trips to Florida to visit her eight-year-old daughter. Moreover, the mother had remarried and had a new young child, so trips to Florida would have been logistically very difficult.

STEPPARENT RIGHTS

Courts around the country generally award custody to natural parents only. However, courts have occasionally awarded custody to stepparents in cases where the stepparents have been very active in raising their stepchildren and have treated their stepchildren as their own. Stepparents have been awarded custody when:

- They have custody of the child's half-siblings, and the court believes it would be in the child's best interests to live in the same household as his or her half-siblings.
- They have a significantly closer relationship with the child than the natural parents.
- The natural parents are unfit.

As the list above illustrates, stepparents will only be awarded custody in rare circumstances. If this is an issue in your case, you should consult with your lawyer about how courts in your state have recently considered custody petitions from stepparents.

THE TAX ASPECTS OF CUSTODY

The custodial parent is automatically entitled to claim the dependency exemption and the child tax credit for any child who resides with him or her. This exemption is phased out for parents earning above a certain amount. The parent entitled to claim the dependency exemption is also eligible to claim two education-related tax credits: the Hope Scholarship Credit and the Lifetime Learning Credit. Both the Hope Scholarship Credit and the Lifetime Learning Credit are phased out for parents earning above a certain amount. In addition, the parent entitled to claim the dependency exemption may be eligible to deduct some amount of the interest on loans used to pay the child's educational expenses.

Although the non-custodial parent cannot claim the dependency exemption, that parent can deduct a child's medical expenses to the extent they exceed 7.5 percent of adjusted gross income, provided the non-custodial parent actually paid those expenses.

In cases of joint custody, parents may choose to alternate the dependency exemption year by year. To do so, the parent waiving the right to a dependency exemption must execute IRS Form 8332.

QUESTIONS TO ASK YOUR LAWYER

- Given the particular facts of my case, what type of custodial arrangement do you recommend? Would joint custody make sense in my case?
- What type of custodial arrangement is a judge likely to order in my case?
- What factors is a judge likely to consider most relevant in determining custody in my case?
- If I anticipate a custody dispute, what steps can I take to increase my chances of being awarded custody?
- Should I seek temporary custody?
- Under what circumstances can custody be modified in my state?
- How does my state view relocation by the custodial parent?
- Should my settlement agreement include limitations on the custodial parent's ability to relocate?
- How do courts in my state view petitions for custody from stepparents?
- Given the facts of my case, is a judge likely to award custody to someone other than the natural parent(s)?

Chapter Nine

Visitation

Divorce courts around the country firmly believe that it is important for a child to have continued access to the love and care of both parents, even if the parents are divorced and one parent has been awarded sole physical and legal custody. Courts therefore automatically grant reasonable and regular visitation to the non-custodial parent except in the extremely rare cases in which it would not be in a child's best interests to see that parent.

The term *visitation* refers to the scheduled time that a non-custodial parent spends with the child on weekends, holidays, and so forth. Visitation is viewed as the natural right of both the non-custodial parent and the child. Divorce courts consider visitation so important that they sometimes even grant visitation when one parent is incarcerated.

VISITATION SCHEDULES

Courts will often grant "liberal" or "reasonable" visitation and leave it up to the parents to come up with a workable schedule. If parents are unable to negotiate a visitation schedule on their own, a court may specify one or refer the parents to a mediation service, mental health professional, or social service agency to help them arrive at a reasonable schedule.

There is no single visitation schedule that will work well in every case. The general rule, however, is that the non-custodial parent is entitled to a reasonable amount of weekend and overnight visitation, even if the children are very young. The non-custodial parent is usually not entitled to visit with the children every weekend, as the custodial parent is also entitled to spend weekend time with the children. In addition to weekend time, courts may provide for weeknight visitation one day a week. Courts normally also grant extended visitation during summer and winter vacations. If the non-custodial parent lives far away, a visitation schedule involving weekends and weeknight visitation will probably be impractical. The more appropriate schedule in such cases is blocks of visitation time during summer and winter vacations.

With respect to holidays, courts generally require parents to divide the holidays between them, with one parent having the children at Thanksgiving and the other parent having the children at Christmas, for example. Mother's Day and Father's Day are usually spent with the mother and father, respectively, along with the mother's birthday and the father's birthday. For the child's birthday, courts may encourage parents to share the day, perhaps by dividing the day in half, or to spend alternating birthdays with the child.

Irrespective of your visitation schedule, you should remember that none—however detailed—will cover every possible visitation-related issue. You and your spouse should prepare to be flexible and to cooperate with one another to make adjustments to the schedule when necessary. A visitation schedule may have to be completely reworked from time to time to accommodate extracurricular activities, changes in job responsibilities, and the changing needs and interests of the child. A schedule that works well when your children are very young may not work at all when they are older.

RESTRICTIONS DURING VISITATION

Custodial parents often wish to place limits on what non-custodial parents can and cannot do with the children during visitation. The general rule is that courts will not impose restrictions on visitation unless a child would be physically, mentally, or emotionally harmed without such restrictions. Although the parent with legal custody has the right to make major decisions affecting the child, courts usually allow the non-custodial parent to make all day-to-day decisions with respect to the child during visitation.

One issue that often comes up is recreational activities that the custodial parent considers harmful to the child, such as flying in private planes and motorcycle riding. Courts usually will not limit the non-custodial parent's recreational activities with the child unless it is clear that such activities pose a serious risk to the child. For example, a court would probably not interfere with a non-custodial parent's efforts to teach a child horseback riding provided the non-custodial parent did so in a safe manner. A court would, however, be more likely to prevent a non-custodial parent from taking a child flying before that parent had completed flying lessons.

Another common concern among custodial parents is having the non-custodial parent's girlfriend or boyfriend spend the night while the child is visiting. Many courts are uncomfortable with placing restrictions on what non-custodial parents can and cannot do in the privacy of their own homes. Unless it is clear that having lovers remain overnight would somehow be harmful to the child in question, most courts will not impose such restrictions.

A potential problem arises when the custodial parent wishes to restrict the non-custodial parent's religious activities during visitation. Even though the custodial parent has the right to make all decisions regarding the child's religious upbringing, courts are reluctant to interfere with the non-custodial parent's efforts to introduce the child to his or her religious beliefs during visitation. However, courts may step in to restrict religious activities during visitation if it is clear that the non-custodial parent is interfering with the custodial parent's right to choose the child's religion or if the non-custodial parent's religious activities are confusing or harmful to the child.

In one Massachusetts case, for example, the court placed restrictions on the non-custodial father's religious activities during visitation after he took his Jewish children to a Christian church where the children were taught that those who did not accept the church's particular brand of Christianity would be damned to hell. The father also cut off the boys' sideburns—symbols of their faith—and threatened to cut off their religiously significant clothing tassels. The court allowed the father to continue including the children in Easter and Christmas celebrations, but it prohibited him from taking the children to any church where they would be taught that nonbelievers would go to hell. The father was further restricted from interfering with outward symbols of the children's faith.

FAILURE TO EXERCISE VISITATION RIGHTS

Though courts can order the custodial parent to allow the non-custodial parent to visit with the child, they cannot require the non-custodial parent to exercise his or her visitation rights. As explained by one Illinois court, "[a] court simply cannot order a parent to love his or her children or to maintain a meaningful relationship with them. We are not convinced that forcing the children to spend time with a parent who views the visit as a punishment or obligation would truly be in the child's best interests." *In re Marriage of Mitchell,* 319 Ill.App.3d 17, 23 (Ill. App. Ct. 2001).

WHEN VISITATION IS DENIED

Visitation will be denied only in those extraordinary cases where the child's physical, mental, or emotional health would be endangered by contact with the non-custodial parent. If the non-custodial parent is less than perfect at parenting, or has a strained relationship with the child, that is usually not enough to justify a denial of visitation. Rather, the non-custodial parent must usually have exhibited extreme and clearly damaging behavior for a court to deny visitation. In one Pennsylvania case, for example, visitation was denied to a father who had shot the mother while she was holding their three-year-old child and had also held the mother and child hostage for eight hours. Visitation was similarly denied in a Washington, D.C., case where a schizophrenic father had, on at least a dozen occasions, locked the mother and the child in a room and sprayed them with mace. If the facts in your case are not anywhere near as exceptional as these cases, chances are that a court will grant visitation to the non-custodial parent.

A court will usually award visitation even if a child does not wish to see the non-custodial parent. Courts understand that children often express such preferences because of pressure from their custodial parents. Because courts consider visitation to be good for children in the long run, courts will often override a child's short-term preference not to see one parent. Courts are more likely to honor an older child's desire not to see one parent if the child can articulate a valid reason. Even in the case of an older child, however, courts may provide for visitation against the child's wishes. In one New York case, for example, the court ordered girls aged fifteen and seventeen to visit with their mother even though neither girl wished to see her.

SUPERVISED VISITATION

Before a court will take the extreme step of denying visitation altogether, a court will often order supervised visitation. In a supervised visitation arrangement, the non-custodial parent may spend time with the child only if a relative, social worker, or other trusted supervisor is present. A court will order supervised visitation only if there is a substantial risk that the parent could seriously endanger the child if visitation were unsupervised.

It is up to the custodial parent to demonstrate that supervised visitation is necessary. Because courts understand that a parent–child relationship cannot develop in the same way if a parent and child spend time together only in the presence of a third person, courts are very reluctant to order supervised visitation without a very good reason for doing so.

Supervised visitation may be appropriate if:

• A parent or a member of the parent's household has sexually, physically, or emotionally abused the child.
• A parent has been abusive to his or her spouse in the presence of the child.
• A parent has drug or alcohol problems that could impair his or her ability to care for the child.
• A parent is likely to kidnap his or her child.

With the exception of the cases just listed, a court will generally grant unsupervised visitation to the non-custodial parent.

STEPPARENT VISITATION

When stepparents have established unusually close bonds with their stepchildren, courts have granted visitation to them. Courts recognize that it is not in a child's best interests to be separated from someone he or she has grown to love, even if that individual is not technically related to the child.

In considering a petition for visitation from a stepparent, courts will take into account the amount of time that the stepparent lived with the child, whether the stepparent acted as a substitute parent to the child, and the nature of the stepparent's relationship with the child. If stepparent visitation is an issue in your case, you should consult with your lawyer about how courts in your state have recently considered visitation requests from stepparents.

THE RELATIONSHIP BETWEEN VISITATION AND CHILD SUPPORT

Courts consider visitation and child support to be two totally separate rights and obligations. The non-custodial parent cannot stop paying child support simply because the custodial parent has been interfering with visitation. Similarly, the custodial parent cannot interfere with visitation just because the non-custodial parent has failed to pay child support. The proper remedy in both cases is to turn to the court for help.

QUESTIONS TO ASK YOUR LAWYER

- What type of visitation schedule do you recommend, based on the particular facts of my case?
- What type of visitation schedule is a judge likely to order in my case?
- Is a judge likely to deny visitation to the non-custodial parent in my case?
- Is a judge likely to order supervised visitation for the non-custodial parent in my case?
- Is a judge likely to uphold any relevant restrictions on visitation in my case—such as a provision that the non-custodial parent cannot have overnight romantic visitors during visitation?

Chapter Ten

Child Support

Parents—whether married or divorced—have an obligation to provide for the financial needs of their natural and adopted children until the children reach an age where they are reasonably capable of supporting themselves. Mothers and fathers are equally responsible for supporting their children.

In intact families, parents usually work together to provide for their children's financial needs. Once parents divorce, however, the economic burden of raising children generally falls on the custodial parent's shoulders. To ensure that the custodial parent does not bear more than his or her fair share of child-rearing costs, all states require the non-custodial parent to pay child support according to his or her means. Each state has established child support guidelines that dictate the amount of child support that must be paid on a regular basis by the non-custodial parent to the custodial parent. In addition to basic child support, many states also require the non-custodial parent to contribute toward the child's health, educational, and child care expenses.

Parents cannot simply "opt out" of the child support laws. Because all children have the right to be supported by their parents, parents are not entitled to waive child support or to provide for dramatically less child support than the guidelines require. Parents can, however, agree to more than the guideline amount because it is almost always in a child's best interests to receive more in the way of child support.

Child support must be paid in cash to the custodial parent, or to a third party—such as the child's private school—in accordance with the parents' agreement or the court's order. The non-custodial parent must pay the full amount of child support owed even if he or she showers the child with clothes and presents during every visit. This is because child support is designed to help offset the custodial parent's costs of providing the child with a proper home, a proper automobile to travel in, and the like. If non-custodial parents were permitted to substitute toys and other gifts for child support, custodial parents would be left shouldering a disproportionate share of the children's basic expenses.

THE CHILD SUPPORT GUIDELINES

Every state has established child support guidelines specifying the amount of child support that the non-custodial parent must pay. Unless your income exceeds the maximum income to which the guidelines are applicable, or the court determines that the guidelines provide for an inappropriate amount of child support given the particular facts of your case, the court will order child support in the amount provided for under the child support guidelines.

The details of each state's child support guidelines vary tremendously. However, there are three basic models used for calculating child support: the income-shares model, the variable percentage model, and the Melson formula. These three models are discussed below. Because the child support formulas can be somewhat complex, and because the formulas are regularly updated to reflect inflation and other relevant changes, appendix A will only tell you which model applies to your state. You should consult with your lawyer or your local child support office about the specifics of your state's child support guidelines. Your lawyer or your local child support office will help you calculate the child support that will be due under the guidelines in your case as well as determine whether a court is likely to deviate from the guidelines in your case.

The Income-Shares Model

Most states use the income-shares model for calculating child support. Under this model, courts take into account the income of both parents when determining a basic child support obligation. Some states will multiply the parents' combined income by a certain percentage—based on the number of children—to arrive at a basic child support obligation. In New York, for example, the basic child support obligation is determined by multiplying the parents' combined income by 17 percent for one child, 25 percent for two children, 29 percent for three children, 31 percent for four children, and no less than 35 percent for five or more children.

Other states use child support tables instead of fixed percentages. These child support tables allow courts simply to look up the parents' combined income and the number of children to determine the basic child support obligation. A child support table generally looks like the following, and will specify child support obligations for a wide range of incomes.

Combined Monthly Adjusted Parental Gross Income	One Child	Two Children	Three Children	Four Children	Five Children	Six or More Children
$900	$180	$261	$266	$271	$276	$281
$1,000	$195	$303	$325	$330	$335	$340
$1,100	$212	$324	$384	$389	$394	$399
$1,200	$229	$346	$433	$446	$451	$456
$1,300	$246	$367	$460	$504	$510	$515
$1,400	$262	$392	$491	$554	$576	$582
$1,500	$277	$417	$522	$588	$642	$650
$1,600	$293	$437	$548	$618	$674	$717
$1,700	$308	$458	$574	$647	$706	$755

Once the basic child support obligation is determined, the child support amount is then divided between the parents according to their incomes. The court will order the non-custodial parent to pay his or her proportionate share of the basic child support obligation to the custodial parent. The custodial parent will not have to make any payments to the non-custodial parent, because the court will assume that the custodial parent will spend at least his or her share of the basic child support obligation for the care of the children during the time that they spend living with him or her.

Let us consider an example of a basic child support calculation under the income-shares model. For the sake of simplicity, we will assume that the guidelines use gross income rather than net income. Yvonne earns $50,000 per year and Blake earns $80,000. They have two children, and Yvonne will have custody of both. Under their state's child support guidelines, the relevant percentage for two children is 15 percent. A court would arrive at the basic child support obligation by adding Yvonne's and Blake's incomes ($50,000 + $80,000 = $130,000) and then multiplying that amount by the relevant percentage ($130,000 x 0.15 =

$19,500) to arrive at a basic child support amount of $19,500. A court would then divide this amount between Yvonne and Blake according to their incomes: Yvonne would be responsible for $^{5}/_{13}$ ($50,000 ÷ $130,000), and Blake would be responsible for $^{8}/_{13}$ ($80,000 ÷ $130,000). Yvonne's share of the child support would be $7,500 ($^{5}/_{13}$ x $19,500), while Blake's share of the child support would be $12,000 ($^{8}/_{13}$ x $19,500). Blake would therefore have to pay $12,000 a year—or $1,000 a month—in child support.

The Variable Percentage Model

The second model for calculating child support—the variable percentage model—bases the child support obligation solely on the non-custodial parent's income. This model tends to involve a great deal less math. As is the case with the states that use the income-shares model, some states calculate the basic child support obligation using a simple percentage of income while others rely on child support tables.

Let us consider an example. Suppose that Yvonne and Blake, described above, live in a state that applies the variable percentage model rather than the income-shares model. For the sake of simplicity, suppose the guidelines use gross income rather than net income. Under their state's child support guidelines, the relevant percentage for two children is 12 percent. In this case, a court would take only Blake's income into account when calculating Blake's child support obligation. Blake's child support obligation would be calculated by multiplying his income ($80,000) by 12 percent to arrive at a basic child support obligation of $9,600. Blake would therefore owe approximately $800 per month.

The Melson Formula

The third model for calculating child support—the Melson formula—is used in only three states: Delaware, Hawaii, and Montana. Like the income-shares model, the Melson formula takes into account the income of both parents for the purposes of determining a basic child support obligation. Of the three models, the Melson formula involves by far the most math and the most steps:

1. Determine the monthly net income that each parent has available for child support.
2. Subtract a "self-support reserve," which is the absolute minimum amount of money that a parent needs to cover his or her basic needs, such as food and shelter.

3. Determine a primary child support obligation. This primary child support obligation is determined according to a table of child support guidelines.
4. Divide the primary child support obligation proportionately between the parents, according to their incomes.
5. Subtract the non-custodial parent's share of the primary child support obligation from his or her net income.
6. Multiply the foregoing amount by the standard of living allowance (SOLA). The SOLA is a percentage set forth in the child support guidelines.
7. Add the non-custodial parent's share of the primary child support obligation to the SOLA amount (calculated in step six).

Let us consider again the case of Yvonne and Blake. Suppose now that Yvonne and Blake live in a state that uses the Melson formula. Yvonne's net income is $30,000 per year (her gross income was $50,000) and Blake's net income is $48,000 per year (his gross income was $80,000). The first step is to determine each parent's monthly net income. Yvonne's monthly net income is $2,500 ($30,000 ÷ 12), and Blake's monthly net income is $4,000 ($48,000 ÷ 12).

The second step is to subtract a self-support reserve from each parent's net income. Suppose that the self-support reserve is $750 per month. Yvonne's monthly net income minus the self-support reserve would be $1,750 per month ($2,500 − $750 = $1,750). Blake's monthly net income minus the self-support reserve would be $3,250 ($4,000 − $750 = $3,250). The total monthly net income available for support is $5,000 (Yvonne's available income of $1,750 + Blake's available income of $3,250). Blake earns 65 percent of the income available for child support ($3,250 ÷ 5,000 = 0.65), while Yvonne earns 35 percent ($1,750 ÷ $5,000 = 0.35).

The third step is to determine a primary support obligation. Suppose that the primary support obligation for two children is $575. The fourth step is to divide this between the parents according to their net income minus their self-support reserve. Blake would owe 65 percent of $575, or approximately $375 ($575 x 0.65 = $374). Yvonne would owe 35 percent, or approximately $200 ($575 x 0.35 = $201).

The fifth step is to subtract this primary support obligation from each parent's available net income. Yvonne has $1,750 in available net income. After subtracting her share of the primary support obligation ($200), Yvonne only has approximately $1,500 in available net income ($1,750 − $200 = $1,550). Blake has $3,250 in available net income. After subtracting his share of the primary support obligation ($375),

Blake has approximately $2,900 in available net income ($3,250 − $375 = $2,875).

The sixth step is to determine the SOLA. Suppose that the SOLA percentage for two children is 26 percent. Yvonne's SOLA child support amount would be her available net income ($1,550) multiplied by 26 percent—or approximately $400 ($1,550 x 0.26 = $403). Blake's SOLA support amount would be his available net income ($2,900) multiplied by 26 percent—or approximately $750 ($2,900 x 0.26 = $754).

The final step would be to add the primary child support obligation to the SOLA support amount, to arrive at a basic child support obligation. Yvonne's basic child support obligation would be her share of the primary child support obligation ($200) plus her SOLA amount ($400)—amounting to a total monthly child support obligation of $600 per month. Blake's child support obligation would be his share of the primary support obligation ($375) plus his SOLA support amount ($750)—amounting to a total monthly child support obligation of $1,125.

If you find the Melson formula confusing, do not worry. Your lawyer or child support office will help you to apply the formula in your case, and will handle all of the child support calculations for you.

DETERMINING A PARENT'S INCOME

Courts will take into account a parent's income from all sources when calculating child support. For example, courts will include income from overtime and second jobs if the income is regular and likely to continue. Courts will also factor in bonuses, tips, and job-related perks—such as a company car or company housing—when determining a parent's income. If a parent has little actual income but substantial asset holdings, courts will consider that parent's investments, real estate, and other assets when determining how much child support he or she can pay.

If a parent is voluntarily unemployed or underemployed, a court may impute income to that parent for the purposes of calculating child support. For example, suppose a Harvard-educated lawyer quit his $200,000 a year job in order to avoid his child support obligations. In that case, the court may use the lawyer's original income of $200,000 as the basis for calculating child support. Courts will not impute income to parents whose income declines for reasons outside of their control. If a consultant lost her $150,000 a year job due to a bad economy, a court would not use her prior income of $150,000 for purposes of determining child support.

Courts will also not impute income to parents who do not work outside the home because they are caring for young children. However, where parents do not work simply because their needs are provided for by their new spouses, courts may take their spouses' incomes into account when determining their child support obligations. Courts reason that since the new spouse has assumed responsibility for the support of the parent, the new spouse has also assumed responsibility for that parent's obligations.

Gross Income Versus Net Income

Some states use gross income for calculating child support, others use net income. Gross income consists of a parent's total income before any taxes or other deductions. Net income is calculated by taking a parent's gross income and then subtracting taxes, mandatory union dues, mandatory retirement contributions, preexisting spousal and child support obligations, and certain other specified expenses. To determine whether your state uses gross income or net income in calculating child support, check with your lawyer or your local child support office.

DEVIATING FROM THE CHILD SUPPORT GUIDELINES

If the guideline amount of child support is inappropriate given the particular facts of a case, courts will deviate from the guidelines—in other words, they will provide for a different amount of child support than the guidelines require. For example, a court may award more child support than the guideline amount if a child has extraordinary educational or health care needs. Similarly, a court may grant less child support when the child spends an unusual amount of time living with the non-custodial parent.

In determining whether the guideline amount is appropriate in any given case, courts will consider:

- The income and other resources of the parents
- The needs of the parents and the child, including the child's health, educational, and child care expenses
- The custodial arrangement
- The standard of living the child enjoyed while the parents were married
- The child's own financial resources

The Parents' Economic Circumstances

Perhaps the most important consideration in determining child support is the economic circumstances of each parent. If the custodial parent has a very high income or substantial assets, a court may provide for less child support than the guideline amount. Courts will also consider the extent to which the custodial parent's share of marital property will help offset his or her need for child support. For example, if a court awards the custodial parent with exclusive use and occupancy of the marital home until the child reaches the age of majority, a court may determine that the full guideline amount of child support is not necessary.

The economic circumstances of the non-custodial parent are equally important in determining child support. For example, a very wealthy non-custodial parent may be required to pay more than the guideline amount of child support. In some states, the child support guidelines apply only up to a certain income level. If a parent's income exceeds the uppermost limit of the child support guidelines, courts in these states sometimes deviate from the guidelines to arrive at an appropriate child support amount. Other states' child support formulas apply irrespective of the non-custodial parent's income. Applying the guidelines even when parents have extraordinarily high incomes can result in excessively high child support amounts that bear no relationship to a child's actual needs. Courts in those states often provide for less child support than the guideline amount in such cases.

A non-custodial parent with very limited resources may be exempted from paying the full amount of child support due under the guidelines. Still, courts will generally require a non-custodial parent to make some kind of child support payments, believing that parents have an absolute obligation to support their children, irrespective of their financial conditions.

The Needs of the Parents and the Children

Courts will take into account a parent's own needs and preexisting obligations when determining how much child support he or she can afford to pay. For example, a parent with a debilitating disease and substantial unreimbursed medical costs will be required to pay much less in child support than a healthy parent with the same income. Most courts would recognize that ill parents need more resources to meet their own needs. A parent with preexisting spousal and child support obligations may also be required to pay less than the guideline amount if such obligations limit the parent's available resources.

Conversely, a parent whose own needs are unusually low may be required to pay more in child support than the guideline amount. For example, a parent with a very wealthy new spouse may have to pay more in child support because most of his or her living expenses are taken care of by the new spouse.

Courts will also consider the child's needs when determining whether the guideline amount of child support is sufficient. If a child has special health or educational needs that warrant significant additional expenses, such as the services of a speech therapist or a team of after-school tutors, the guideline amount may be insufficient. The same holds true if both parents work long hours and the cost of child care is substantial. In a number of states, courts will require the non-custodial parent to pay a proportional share of the child's health, educational, and child care expenses—such as day care or orthodonture costs—in addition to the guideline amount of child support.

The Custodial Arrangement

The child support guidelines in most states are based on a custodial arrangement in which one parent has primary physical custody and the other parent has reasonable visitation. Where parents share physical custody, or the child spends a substantial amount of time living with the non-custodial parent, applying the guidelines may result in an excessively high child support amount. This is because the non-custodial parent has much more in the way of child-related expenses in a joint custodial arrangement as compared with a sole custody arrangement. Some states have modified child support guidelines that apply in cases of joint custody. Courts in other states will deviate from the child support guidelines when the parents will be sharing custody.

In most joint custody cases, the wealthier parent will still have to pay some amount of child support. This is because the less well-off parent often lacks the resources to support the child at an appropriate level on his or her income alone. Moreover, while joint custodial arrangements increase the child care costs borne by the "non-custodial" parent, joint custody does not substantially reduce the "custodial" parent's child care costs. The "custodial" parent still has to provide an adequate home and an adequate means of transportation for the children, even if the children spend only half their time living with him or her.

Let us consider an example. Suppose that Laura earns $70,000 a year while her ex-husband, Seth, earns $180,000 a year. Laura and Seth have joint custody of their three children. In this case, a court would likely order Seth to pay a reasonable amount of child support to Laura to enable her to offer the children a similar lifestyle to the one they enjoy when they are spending time with their father.

Courts may deviate from the guidelines even in sole custody arrangements if there are extraordinary expenses associated with visitation. A custodial parent who relocates with the child to France, for example, may have to accept substantially less in child support to account for the expenses associated with the non-custodial parent's trips to France and the child's trips to the United States.

The Child's Standard of Living While the Parents Were Married

Courts around the country prefer to see children of divorced parents enjoy the same standard of living that they would have enjoyed had their parents not divorced. Courts recognize that the divorce process is difficult enough for children without the added burdens of having to give up hobbies, lessons, and other childhood enjoyments.

When adequate resources are available, courts will try to ensure that children maintain their standard of living after a divorce. If a seventh-grader has always attended private school, for example, a court would factor in the costs of private school tuition when determining whether the guideline amount of child support is appropriate. Courts will also take into account the costs of housing in a neighborhood and style that the child was accustomed to, as well as the costs of hobbies, lessons, summer camps, and travel abroad that the child enjoyed prior to the divorce, when calculating child support.

In many cases, however, it is impossible for children to maintain the same standard of living following their parents' divorce. Because many American families tend to live above their means, dividing one household into two can result in a dramatic drop in every family member's standard of living.

The Child's Own Financial Resources

Courts will factor in a child's own resources in determining whether the guideline amount of child support is appropriate. Some children are the beneficiaries of healthy trust funds or may have inherited a substantial amount of money from a grandparent or other relative. In such cases, the child's own resources may have been used during the marriage to pay for the child's private school tuition, summer camps, private tutors, and other luxuries. A court may determine that no increase in the guideline amount is necessary to enable that child to continue living at a high standard even after the divorce. If a child's own resources are sizeable, a court may even conclude that less child support than the guideline amount is warranted. Courts will not completely eliminate a parent's child support obligation even when a child has extraordinary independent wealth, believing that parents have a financial obligation irrespective of their children's own resources.

THE RELATIONSHIP BETWEEN CHILD SUPPORT AND VISITATION

Non-custodial parents often claim that their child support obligations should be decreased—or even eliminated—during periods of extended visitation, such as summer holidays. Courts generally require non-custodial parents to pay the full amount of child support owed even during an extended visitation, however, because courts take visitation into account when awarding child support.

Some non-custodial parents have argued that they should not be required to pay child support if they do not exercise their right to visitation. Courts have uniformly rejected such arguments on the grounds that visitation and child support are completely independent rights and obligations. Parents must provide for their children's needs regardless of whether they visit them once a week or once a year. Arguably, a parent who does not exercise visitation rights should be liable for more child support because the custodial parent must bear additional child care costs—such as expenses for food and recreation—during the time that the child would otherwise have spent with the non-custodial parent.

HEALTH INSURANCE

Courts can order non-custodial parents to maintain health insurance or to contribute toward health insurance costs as part of their child support obligations. In many cases, the cost of doing so will be minimal because children continue to be designated as "beneficiaries" on parents' health insurance plans even after a divorce.

Ensuring continuity of health insurance coverage for children is critical in every case. If both parents have access to employer-subsidized health insurance at minimal expense, they should consider maintaining dual insurance for their children. Doing so will minimize the risk that parents might be faced with substantial unreimbursed health care expenses for their children at some later time.

LIFE AND DISABILITY INSURANCE

In order to ensure that children will be adequately provided for even after the death or disability of their non-custodial parents, courts may require that non-custodial parents purchase life and/or disability insurance policies that name the children as beneficiaries. Generally, parents are allowed to discontinue such policies once their children reach the age of majority.

WHEN CHILD SUPPORT ENDS

Child support ends when the child reaches the age of majority (eighteen to twenty-one, depending on the state) or when the child is otherwise deemed emancipated. A child can become emancipated by getting married (an act most courts consider to be a sign of adulthood), becoming self-supporting (as in the case of teenage Internet millionaires), or abandoning the parental home. Courts are generally reluctant to consider a child of divorced parents emancipated, because of the impact that emancipation has on child support.

Some states provide that child support continues until the age of eighteen or when the child graduates from high school, whichever is later. Others end child support when the child reaches eighteen irrespective of school completion. Non-custodial parents in those states may be able to stop paying child support before their children have graduated from high school. If this could be an issue in your case, consult with your lawyer about including a provision in your settlement agreement extending child support until your child graduates from high school.

Children who are mentally impaired or physically disabled may require support even after they reach the age of majority. Therefore, courts may extend child support obligations in such cases.

COLLEGE EXPENSES

College tuition costs are generally not covered by standard child support, primarily because college is a post-majority expense. Courts in some states will, however, require non-custodial parents to contribute toward college tuition under certain circumstances. In determining whether to require a parent to pay for college-related expenses, courts will consider the following questions:

1. Would the parent have paid for a child's college-related expenses if the parent were still living in the same household as the child?
2. Is it reasonable for the child to expect that his or her parent would contribute to college expenses in light of the family's educational background, values, and goals?
3. What is the likelihood that the child would benefit from a college education, given the child's motivation to attend college and his or her past academic performance?
4. What is the cost of the particular school that the child wishes to attend and the amount of parental contribution sought by the child?
5. What is the relationship between the parent and the child?

A court that orders a parent to contribute to college expenses will usually not require that parent to pay the full cost of college expenses. Courts expect students to pay at least part of their college expenses through student loans, work-study programs, and part-time jobs.

Courts are less likely to order non-custodial parents to contribute to educational expenses as children progress up the educational ladder. Courts generally consider graduate school students to be of an age and responsibility level where they should be able to meet their own educational expenses, either through student loans or their own resources.

To ensure that the non-custodial parent in your case will be required to contribute to college or graduate school tuition, you must include a provision in your settlement agreement to that effect. While many courts are reluctant to order non-custodial parents to pay for post-majority educational expenses, courts around the country will enforce written agreements providing that the non-custodial parent will pay all or part of a child's college or graduate school expenses.

MODIFICATION OF CHILD SUPPORT

Like custody orders, child support orders are not set in stone for the remainder of the child's youth. Courts will modify child support if circumstances have changed substantially since the time of the original order. For example, if the income of the non-custodial parent has risen substantially, a court may increase child support. Similarly, if the non-custodial parent has suffered a decline in income through no fault of his or her own—such as the loss of a job or a downturn in business—a court might decrease child support.

Changes in the custodial parent's financial circumstances are also relevant. For example, if the custodial parent wins the lottery, a court may determine that he or she needs less child support to provide the child with the necessities of life. If, on the other hand, the custodial parent experiences financial difficulties, a court may require the non-custodial parent to pay more child support.

Courts will also consider increasing child support in cases of significant inflation or if the costs associated with child care have gone up. For example, if tuition at a child's private school has doubled since the time of the court's original order, a court may decide that additional child support is necessary. Some courts use automatic adjustment clauses to account for the effects of inflation. With these clauses, child support automatically increases by a fixed percentage after a certain number of years.

If one of multiple children reaches the age of majority, courts may reduce child support. Courts usually do not reduce child support proportionally, because the costs of raising children increase only marginally with each additional child. For example, suppose that Adam was originally paying $1,200 per month in child support for his three children. After the eldest child turned eighteen, Adam petitioned the court for a one-third reduction in his child support obligation because one out of three of his children had reached the age of majority. The court might decrease Adam's child support obligation, but probably not by one-third. The court would recognize that it does not cost three times as much to raise three children than it does to raise one child. Moreover, if Adam's income had increased since the time of the original order, the court might decide that Adam should pay the same amount—or more—in child support.

If a court determines that a reduction in child support is appropriate in any given case, a court will generally apply that reduction only to future child support payments. The usual rule is that reductions in child support cannot be applied retroactively. For example, suppose that Maggie owed her ex-husband, Brian, $4,000 in child support. She successfully petitioned the court for a 50 percent reduction in her child support payments, from $500 per month to $250 per month, based on her changed financial circumstances. In this case, Maggie would still owe Brian the full $4,000 in child support arrears. She could not reduce her outstanding child support arrears by half ($4,000 x ½ = $2,000), the amount of the court's reduction in her future child support obligations.

TEMPORARY CHILD SUPPORT

Courts routinely award temporary child support at the outset of a case to ensure that children do not suffer a decline in their standard of living pending the outcome of the divorce dispute. In determining an appropriate amount of temporary child support, courts will generally rely on the child support guidelines because there are insufficient facts to determine whether or not a deviation is warranted.

Oftentimes, the amount of permanent child support awarded is the same as the amount of temporary child support. Courts may conclude that the temporary child support amount is appropriate if the children enjoyed their usual standard of living while the divorce dispute was pending. Because of the risk that the amount of support initially awarded could become the final amount of child support, it is important for the custodial parent to seek an appropriate amount of temporary child support.

STEPPARENTS AND CHILD SUPPORT

Stepparents are usually not obligated to support their stepchildren. Only in rare cases have courts ordered stepparents to pay child support. Courts have required stepparents to support their stepchildren if:

- The stepparent has interfered with the stepchild's ability to obtain support from his or her natural parent.
- The stepparent has sought visitation.
- The stepparent has agreed to pay child support in a divorce settlement agreement.

As the list illustrates, stepparents may have to pay child support only in unusual circumstances. If this is a concern for you, consult with your lawyer about how courts in your state have recently addressed the issue of a stepparent's obligation to support his or her stepchild.

THE TAX ASPECTS OF CHILD SUPPORT

Unlike spousal support, child support is not tax deductible by either the non-custodial or the custodial parent.

CHILD SUPPORT AND BANKRUPTCY

Non-custodial parents must meet their child support obligations even if they file for bankruptcy. In other words, child support is not discharge-able in bankruptcy. A court will not eliminate or modify any past-due child support amounts because the non-custodial parent filed for bank-ruptcy, but it may determine that the non-custodial parent's financial sit-uation requires a reduction of his or her future child support obligations.

WHEN A PARENT FAILS TO PAY CHILD SUPPORT

The penalties for failing to pay child support have been substantially en-hanced in recent years. Every state now imposes a criminal penalty on parents who fail to pay child support. Some states even condition the granting or renewal of professional and driver's licenses upon the pay-ment of child support.

The federal government also imposes criminal penalties on parents who have fled a state in order to avoid paying child support. These penal-ties apply to any parent who owes more than $5,000, or who has not paid child support arrears for more than one year. The first offense is a misde-meanor punishable by fine or imprisonment for up to six months, or both. Repeat offenders could face up to two years in prison in addition to a fine. Felony charges apply to state-hopping parents who have willfully failed to pay more than $10,000 in child support for more than two years. In addition to these criminal penalties, the federal government may deny issuance of or revoke passports of parents who owe more than $5,000 in child support arrears.

If you think the non-custodial parent is likely to evade his or her child support obligations in your case, talk to your lawyer about using your state's IV-D ("four-D") services to collect child support. Instead of hav-ing child support paid directly to you, child support may be paid to a IV-D agency, which will then forward the money to you. The advantage of using these services is that IV-D agencies monitor and provide a record of child support payments and can make it much easier for you to seek remedies—such as the interception of your former spouse's tax re-fund—in the event that your spouse does not meet his or her child sup-port obligations.

Another option in many states is to provide for automatic deduction of child support from the non-custodial parent's wages. Automatic de-duction is extremely convenient for the non-custodial parent and provides the custodial parent with a sense of security that child support will be paid in full and on time.

QUESTIONS TO ASK YOUR LAWYER

- How much child support will be owed in my case under my state's child support guidelines?
- Is the court likely to deviate from the child support guidelines in my case?
- What factors is a judge likely to consider most relevant in determining whether to deviate from the guidelines in my case?
- Under what circumstances will a court in my state modify the child support amount? Does my state provide for a periodic review of the child support amount?
- If I am likely to be the custodial parent:
    - Should I seek additional child support to cover "extras" such as private school tuition, extracurricular activities, summer camp, and orthodonture?
    - Should I seek additional child support to cover the costs of health insurance, or will those costs be adequately provided for by the basic child support amount?
    - Should my child support package mandate my spouse to purchase life and disability insurance naming my child as the beneficiary?
    - Should I negotiate with my spouse to have child support continue for some period of time after the age of majority—for example, until the child is twenty-two years old?
    - Should I negotiate with my spouse to determine in advance the conditions under which child support can be increased or decreased?
    - Should I obtain some security for the child support payments?
- How do courts in my state approach the question of college tuition?
- Would a court be likely to award college tuition in my case?
- What are the various options available for paying child support? Which option do you recommend?
- What penalties are available in my state if child support is not paid?

PART TWO

The Out-of-Court Agreement: Minimizing the Costs and Uncertainty of Divorce

Chapter Eleven

Why Choose an Out-of-Court Agreement?

The two ways to resolve a divorce dispute are: First, proceed to trial, and leave it up to a judge to decide the terms of your divorce. Second, negotiate an out-of-court agreement with your spouse. This chapter explains in detail why settling your divorce dispute out of court is the least expensive, most efficient, and least traumatic way to divorce your spouse.

Although it may be tempting to insist on having your day in court, proceeding to trial on a divorce case can be a very risky proposition, because judges have a tremendous amount of discretion in any divorce dispute. A good lawyer will be able to tell you how a judge is likely to decide your case, but no lawyer—no matter how talented or experienced—can predict the outcome of your divorce trial with absolute certainty.

When you proceed to trial on your divorce case, you not only run the risk of having a judge rule completely in your ex-spouse's favor, but you also have very few avenues of recourse in the event that the judge does so. It is extremely difficult to appeal a judge's decision in a divorce case, and appellate courts will overturn trial judges' decisions only in those very rare cases when the judge committed an *abuse of discretion*—in other words, when the judge's decision or handling of the trial was far outside the bounds of the law.

Since trial is such a high-stakes bet, very few divorcing couples—less than 10 percent—ultimately battle it out before a judge. The majority of divorcing couples settle their differences out of court, but not always before spending thousands of dollars engaging in legal warfare. What these couples should have known is that the most successful divorces are those that are settled out of court as *quickly as possible.*

Even though the benefits of settling your divorce dispute out of court are almost too numerous to list, here are some of the most important advantages:

• *Settling out of court can save you thousands of dollars—if not more—in divorce-related legal fees.* The sooner you and your spouse can reach agreement on the issues, the less you will ultimately end up paying your lawyers, and the more that you will have to divide between yourselves.

• *Settling out of court is the most efficient way to end your marriage and move on with your separate lives.* The litigation process can take months, if not years. Depending on your judge's trial docket, your trial date may be an eternity away. Settlement, on the other hand, can happen within a matter of weeks, or even less if you and your spouse reach agreement on the issues before filing for divorce.

• *Settling out of court lets you and your spouse decide the rules of your divorce.* While you will likely negotiate your settlement agreement with the divorce laws in mind, settling out of court allows you to tailor the divorce laws to your specific case. If you and your spouse agree, you can even opt out of the divorce laws entirely.

• *Settling out of court puts you and your spouse in control of your post-divorce destiny.* Rather than leaving such important life decisions as property division and custody to a complete stranger (albeit a very well-educated one), settling out of court allows you and your spouse to make the decisions that will affect your lives for years to come.

• *Settling out of court is more likely to resolve—permanently—all the issues of your divorce.* Because divorce often entails obligations that continue well after the date the divorce decree is issued—such as child support, alimony, and visitation—the potential for divorce-related disputes with your spouse continues as well. As you have already learned, your spouse can drag you back into litigation well after your divorce is finalized to change custody and visitation arrangements, and to challenge child support and alimony amounts. If the judge rules in your favor on custody, child support, or alimony, your spouse will have nothing to lose but legal fees by recommencing litigation against you. Where divorcing spouses settle their differences out of court, however, studies have shown that they are more willing to abide by the terms of their divorce decrees. This stands to reason: adhering to the terms of an agreement that you yourself negotiated is an easier pill to swallow than complying with the orders of a powerful stranger.

• *Settling out of court is the least antagonistic way to end your marriage.* Though you and your spouse may not emerge from the divorce process as friends, settling out of court makes it far more likely that you will part on civil terms, ending a once-significant relationship with courtesy and respect. This can be particularly important if you have children in common and a continued relationship with your spouse is inevitable.

• *Settling out of court is the least traumatic way to end your marriage.* Aggressive litigation pits you and your spouse against one another in a legal boxing ring, with each of you struggling to inflict as much personal and financial pain on the other as possible. This may seem like an excellent way to punish your spouse, but remember that your spouse is likely to use the legal process to punish you right back. For example, if you instruct your lawyer to present the court with the sordid details of your spouse's behavior, your spouse is likely to ask his or her lawyer to do the same, painting you in the worst light possible. Make sure you will be able to handle such blows before deciding against settlement.

• *Settling out of court is generally much better for your children.* Having parents divorce and adjusting to the many life changes that accompany divorce is difficult enough for children. Seeing parents at each other's throats in a legal battle can be terribly psychologically damaging to children.

• *Settling out of court is the most private and discreet way to end your marriage.* Although the details of your divorce might not merit the front page of the *National Enquirer,* your divorce will probably make for quite interesting gossip among neighbors, friends, and even family. The more quietly that you and your spouse can reach agreement on the issues before going your separate ways, the easier it will be for you both to continue on with your lives once the divorce is behind you.

To put it simply, the advantages of settling your divorce dispute out of court far outweigh the potential benefits of proceeding to trial. Even if you and your spouse ultimately cannot agree on all of the issues in dispute, it is in your best interests to reach at least a partial out-of-court settlement with your spouse. Always bear in mind that the more issues you and your spouse can resolve without going to court, the more efficient and economical your divorce will be.

Chapter Twelve

Taking Stock

Regardless of whether you expect a full-scale divorce trial or a quiet and discreet out-of-court settlement, taking stock of your assets and liabilities—as well as the needs and wants of everyone involved—is an integral part of the divorce process. It is impossible to begin negotiation or litigation without all of the facts at hand and a realistic set of goals.

ASSETS AND LIABILITIES

The first step is to obtain a complete inventory of all property—including both marital property and separate property—owned by you and your spouse. It would be ideal if you and your spouse could work together to arrive at a list of assets and liabilities, and collect the necessary documentation. If you and your spouse are unwilling to cooperate with each other in this regard, your lawyers will have to serve discovery requests in order to obtain the same information that you could simply provide to each other. The end result will be the same, because divorcing spouses are generally required by law to furnish thorough details of their financial situations to one another.

Failing to provide your spouse with complete financial disclosure can have very serious consequences. Settlement agreements reached without adequate financial disclosure may be invalidated, and inadequate disclosure may be grounds to nullify a divorce court's decision. Refusing to comply informally with the financial disclosure requirements will simply increase legal costs for both you and your spouse and prolong your divorce process.

When compiling a list of the assets your spouse and you own, be certain to include all assets of any kind. Do not limit your list to stocks, bonds, real estate, automobiles, and savings accounts. Instead, take an expansive view of the term "property" when listing your assets. Remember to include pensions, stock options, professional practices, closely held corporations, small businesses, disability benefits, inheritances, professional licenses and degrees, gifts (including those you received from your spouse), accrued vacation time with a cash value, intellectual property (books, songs, and screenplays authored by you or your spouse; inventions by you or your spouse), and even frequent flier benefits. Also include personal property such as jewelry, furs, art, antiques, furniture, and collectibles. To prevent your list from becoming unwieldy, group certain items together. For example, your list may simply have a category for "dining room furniture."

Your list should furnish as much information about each category of property as possible. Be certain to include identification information, such as bank account and license numbers, registration, make, model, and year for automobiles. Also list when each category of property was acquired, for how much, and where the funds were obtained to acquire the property. Do not forget to include "negative" property on your list—that is, debts and liabilities. For each liability, list who incurred the liability, when it was incurred, for what purpose, the original amount of the liability, the current balance, and any relevant account information.

To help you understand the kinds of information that you want to include in this list, look at the sample list for "Joseph and Maria Meyers," a hypothetical couple from Minnesota (see below). You can either follow the format of the sample list or check with your lawyer to see whether there is a format that he or she prefers. Depending on the facts of your case, your list may be much simpler than the sample list, or vastly more complicated. It may even be necessary to consult a financial professional to assist you in the preparation of this list if your finances are sufficiently complex.

LIST OF ASSETS AND LIABILITIES OF
JOSEPH AND MARIA MEYERS

Date of Marriage: July 6, 1997

1. House located at 125 Walnut Street, Maple Grove, Minnesota

Date of purchase:	May 5, 1998
Purchase price:	$350,000
Title:	Joseph and Maria Meyers
Down payment amount:	$50,000
Source of down payment:	$25,000 from Maria's inheritance; $25,000 from Joseph and Maria's joint checking/savings account (Chemical Bank account 3142325)
Source of closing costs:	Joseph & Maria's joint checking/ savings account (Chemical Bank account 3142325)
Original mortgage amount:	$300,000 (North Fork Bank, loan 214288)
Current mortgage balance:	$250,000 (North Fork Bank, loan 214288)
Source of mortgage payments:	Joseph and Maria's joint checking/ savings account (Chemical Bank account 314325)

2. Joseph and Maria Meyers's joint checking/savings account: Chemical Bank account 314325

Current balance:	$13,500
Source of funds:	Joseph and Maria's biweekly paychecks
Date account opened:	July 1997

3. Maria Meyers's savings account: Chase Bank account 412332

Current balance:	$20,000
Source of funds:	Inheritance from Maria's grandmother
Date account opened:	December 1997

4. Joseph Meyers's 401(k) plan: Fidelity Investments account 378-67-9030

Current balance:	$29,350

Source of funds: Contributions from Joseph, matched by contributions from his employer, from January 1994 to the present

Date account opened: · January 1994

5. Maria Meyers's 401(k) plan: Vanguard Investments account 329-32-5455

Current balance: $7,200
Source of funds: Contributions from Maria from September of 1997 to the present
Date account opened: September 1997

6. Maria Meyers's student loan: Sallie Mae Corporation account 1239876

Current balance: $12,500
Original balance: $18,500
Date loan accrued: Between September 1995 and June 1997, when Maria was pursuing a master's degree at the University of Minnesota
Source of loan payments: Joseph and Maria's joint checking/savings account (Chemical Bank account 314325); began making payments in September 1997

7. Joseph and Maria's joint credit card account: MBNA MasterCard account 4432903393

Current balance: $5,500
Original balance: $0
Date debt accrued: July 1997
Date account opened: July 1997
Reason for debt: Honeymoon in Jamaica ($2,000); wedding rings ($2,000)
Source of payments: Joseph and Maria's joint checking/savings account (Chemical Bank account 314325); began making payments in September 1997

8. Joseph Meyers's automobile: 1996 Toyota Camry, license plate BZM-23J

Original cost: $22,680 (fully paid up; no car loan)

Source of funds: Joseph's parents (very belated
                                graduation gift)
Date acquired: December 1996

9. Joseph and Maria Meyers's wedding rings

Original cost: $2,000
Source of funds: Joseph and Maria's joint credit
                                card account (MBNA MasterCard
                                account 4432903393)

10. Maria Meyers's engagement ring

Original cost: $3,000
Source of funds: Joseph's savings
Date purchased: July 1996

11. Joseph and Maria Meyers's household furnishings

Consists of: Furniture from Ethan Allen,
                                Pottery Barn, and flea markets;
                                inexpensive artwork; rugs; etc.
Original cost: Approximately $10,000 in total
Source of funds: Joseph and Maria's joint checking/
                                savings account (Chemical Bank
                                account 314325)

If the thought of preparing such a comprehensive list of assets and liabilities strikes you as tedious and overwhelming, rest assured that you are not alone. The divorce process requires you to assemble a mountain of financial information that will rival any mortgage application or tax audit you may have had the burden of handling. Be sure to allow yourself sufficient time to complete this daunting task. If you are one of those rare individuals whose finances are completely organized and alphabetized, you may be able to complete this task in an afternoon. For most individuals, however, compiling this list is likely to take several afternoons and much haggling about who paid for what. Do not worry if some of the information is disputed. For example, you may believe that you paid for your car with your inheritance funds but your spouse may insist that you paid for it using money you earned during your marriage. You should simply make a note of any disputed information and begin gathering documentation that will help prove your position or at least help to shed some light on the issue.

That brings us to the next tedious task: documentation. You will need to gather as much financial documentation as you possibly can. At a minimum, you will need to collect your tax returns for the last several years (including your W-2s), your bank statements, your 401(k) statements, your credit card statements, your mortgage statements, your student loan statements, and the deed to your home. While you will not need to collect every bank statement going back for ten years, having a year or two worth of bank statements would probably be very helpful. If a business is involved, you will need to gather tax returns for the business, profit and loss statements, and so forth. You should check with your lawyer to see whether he or she can provide you with a list of necessary documents.

Be certain to gather documentation with an eye to your legal case. If you are going to be tracing your separate property interest in marital property, or demonstrating that a particular asset was obtained in exchange for separate property (see chapter four), you will need to collect documentation—such as bank statements and canceled checks—that will help you (or your lawyer) convince your spouse of your position. If you are going to be claiming that separate property was used for marital purposes—for example, that your spouse paid your mortgage using rents he or she received from his or her separate property townhouse—collect documentation that will help prove this.

When you are compiling your financial information and documentation, remember that you and your spouse will be taking the material to your respective lawyers. You will save on legal fees if you and your spouse take the time to organize the information as well as you possibly can. You need not do anything fancy; a simple system of folders and labels should work nicely. Tempting as it may be, resist the urge to pile all of your documents into shoeboxes and ask your lawyer to sort through the mess. Not only will your lawyer be unhappy, but you will be, too, when you receive a bill for hours of paralegal time spent sorting through your financial paperwork.

INCOME AND EXPENSES

Once you and your spouse have tackled your assets and liabilities, you will have to turn to your income and your expenses—essentially, the "ins" and the "outs" of your finances. You will be pleased to learn that this part is usually much easier than the list of assets and liabilities. Because the list of income and expenses is directly relevant for the purposes of both alimony and child support, it is worth taking the time to complete the list as carefully as you can. Even if alimony and child support are unlikely to be issues in your case, this list is nevertheless useful in obtaining an understanding of your spending patterns during your marriage. Determining how you lived during your marriage might help tell you whether or not you can maintain a comparable standard of living after your divorce.

To help you get a sense of the kind of information that you should include in this list, review the sample list for our hypothetical family from Minnesota, Joseph and Maria Meyers and their infant daughter, Suzie. You can either follow the format of the sample list, or check with your lawyer to see whether there is a format that he or she prefers.

LIST OF INCOME AND EXPENSES FOR
JOSEPH AND MARIA MEYERS

1. Joseph Meyers's income

   - Salary of $75,000 per year
   - Bonus of $5,000 to $10,000 per year
   - Approximately $45,000 per year after taxes—or $3,750 per month

2. Maria Meyers's income

   - Salary of $50,000 per year (works part-time)
   - Approximately $28,000 per year after taxes—or $2,333 per month

3. Mortgage payments (including real estate taxes)

   - $2,250 per month

4. Homeowners' insurance

   - $70 per month

5. Utilities

   - $60 per month

6. Cable

   - $55 per month

7. Telephone

   - $75 per month

8. Car insurance (for Joseph Meyers's car)

   - $150 per month

9. Gas and tolls (for Joseph Meyers's car)

   - $55 per month

10. Train fare (for Maria Meyers)

    - $50 per month

11. Groceries

    - $300 per month

12. Eating out
    • $150 per month

13. Movies and other entertainment
    • $50 per month

14. Health and dental insurance
    • $200 per month (paid by Joseph Meyers; employer-subsidized)

15. Clothing/shoes/etc. for Maria Meyers
    • $75 per month

16. Clothing/shoes/etc. for Joseph Meyers
    • $50 per month

17. Clothing/shoes/etc. for Suzie Meyers:
    • $50 per month

18. Diapers for Suzie Meyers
    • $30 per month

19. Formula/baby food for Suzie Meyers
    • $45 per month

20. Day care costs for Suzie Meyers
    • $600 per month (part-time)

21. Toys/books for Suzie Meyers
    • $30 per month

22. MBNA credit card payments
    • $60 minimum due per month

23. Maria Meyers's student loan payments
    • $200 minimum due per month

Total after-tax income per month $6,083
Total expenses per month $4,605

YOUR CHILDREN

When it comes to your children, you will need to take stock not only of their financial needs but also of their emotional needs. You will need to consider their needs and wants with respect to spending time with each of their parents, remaining in touch with friends and relatives, participating in after-school activities, and so forth. Let us start out with the nonfinancial matters this time.

To assess your children's emotional needs, you must evaluate what your children—rather than you and your spouse—truly need and want in terms of a post-divorce custodial arrangement. If at all possible, you and your spouse should sit down together to discuss the children and the types of living and visitation arrangements in which your children will best thrive after you are divorced. Consider the following questions:

- Do you each view the other as a good and caring parent, whatever your marital differences?
- Who currently takes care of the majority of the children's needs? (Is one parent the children's primary caretaker?)
- Are the children used to spending time with both parents on the weekends and after work?
- Do one or both parents have a job with long or unpredictable hours?
- Do one or both parents plan to move far away from the children's current hometown?

If one parent has abused the children or suffers from drug or alcohol addiction, it is virtually certain that the other parent will receive custody. In most cases, however, things are much less black and white and both parents deserve to maintain close bonds with their children after the divorce. Always remember that as a parent, it is your job to ensure that your child has the opportunity to share the love and affection of both parents on a regular basis.

If you and your spouse feel that you can still communicate and cooperate well despite the breakdown of your marriage, consider the possibility of joint custody to allow you both to continue to play an active role in your children's lives. Joint custody need not mean that you each have custody of the children for exactly equal amounts of time. Rather, you can have a joint custodial arrangement wherein the children live primarily with one parent but visit very frequently with the other. Though joint custody may seem like too much of a compromise at the outset, consider whether you are willing to shoulder the burden of child rearing largely on your own. Sharing custody of your children with your spouse may provide you with the extra time you need to pursue your career more aggressively, have a more fulfilling social life, or (one day) pursue a romantic relationship.

In addition to considering where your child should live and how often your child should visit with the other parent, you should think about how child-rearing decisions will be made after your divorce. Should only one of you make all of the decisions with respect to the children? Or should you have equal say over such issues as religion and discipline? You and your spouse may want to consider making some of these decisions in advance. For example, you could agree that your child will be raised in a certain religion, held to certain academic standards, required to be home by a certain hour, and so forth. No matter how much you agree to in advance, however, issues will always arise in the future and decisions will need to be revisited. You and your spouse should think about how future decisions will be made and what actions either of you can and cannot take without the other's consent. For example, you might agree that neither of you can allow the children to take a trip out of the country without first checking with the other.

Now let's turn to financial matters. The first thing that you and your spouse should do is to determine the amount of child support due under your state's child support guidelines. After reviewing the information contained in chapter ten, you should consult with your lawyer or local child support office to learn the specifics of the child support guidelines in your state. Your lawyer or local child support office will also be able to help you calculate the child support amount that would be due under the guidelines.

Once you have determined the basic child support amount, you and your spouse will need to assess whether that amount of child support would be insufficient or excessive in your case. Consider whether your children have any special educational, health, or recreational needs that will require either more child support or child support supplements on an as-needed basis. Now is the time to think about such matters as private school, swimming lessons, orthodonture, and speech therapy. You should also take into account the children's need for health insurance and who should be responsible for those premiums. Finally, you should consider the issue of college tuition, even if your children are only infants. Because college tuition is generally not a required component of child support, you and your spouse will need to reach an out-of-court agreement in order for either spouse to be obligated to contribute to college tuition expenses.

If you and your spouse will be sharing custody, or if one of you will have far more visitation than the average non-custodial parent, consider whether a reduction in child support is warranted in your case. Determining an appropriate reduction in child support should be relatively simple if your state provides for modified child support guidelines for use in joint custody situations. If your state has no such modified guidelines, consult with your lawyers about the appropriate amount of such a reduction.

YOUR PRIORITIES

Too many divorcing spouses begin the divorce process with the simple "priority" of getting as much as they possibly can in the way of property division, alimony, child support, and even custody. This approach is based on the flawed notion that there are "winners" and "losers" in divorce. The reality in the overwhelming majority of cases is that each spouse walks away from the marriage with a fair deal given the facts and circumstances of the case. It is very rare when the "winner" takes all, or even most.

As you are inventorying what you own, what you owe, and what you and your children need and want, it is going to become clear to you that there are some things that mean a great deal to you and other things that matter much less. You should take the time to think about your real priorities. For example, you may be very emotionally attached to your marital home and cannot bear the thought of losing it after your divorce, while you may have very little interest in obtaining a share of your spouse's accounting practice even though you know it constitutes marital property. Coming up with a list of your real priorities will help you and your lawyer to achieve a negotiated settlement that you find acceptable.

In the case of our hypothetical couple from Minnesota, Joseph and Maria Meyers, their lists of priorities looked like this:

Maria Meyers's Priorities

1. Be able to afford to work only part-time.
2. Have custody of Suzie.
3. Keep inheritance from grandmother free and clear.
4. Get back inheritance funds contributed to house.
5. Keep 401(k) free and clear.
6. Be debt-free.

Joseph Meyers's Priorities

1. Pay no alimony.
2. Sell the house and keep a substantial amount of the proceeds.
3. Be able to spend lots of time with Suzie.
4. Keep 401(k) free and clear.
5. Keep car.

Unlike the other lists that we have suggested you make, this is one list you should not share with your spouse. One of the main purposes of creating a list of your priorities is to understand what you would be willing to bargain away. If your spouse is aware of your priorities to begin with, you will not have the ability to make "concessions" to your spouse in the form of items or issues that you do not care as much about.

THE LAW

We have saved the most important aspect of taking stock for last: understanding the law in your state on the issues that are most important in your case. Although this book provides you a good general introduction to divorce law, you will still need to consult with a lawyer or at least a legal clinic to determine the law in your state as it relates to the facts of your case. There are three reasons for this. First, the law is constantly changing, at a rate much faster than this book can be updated. You need to check with a lawyer to ensure that there have been no significant new changes in your state's laws that will affect your case. Second, there may be unique issues in your case that are not addressed in this book, or unique facts that would significantly impact how a judge would determine your case. Third, a lawyer can provide you with a realistic assessment of your case given the facts of your case and the law in your state. Consulting with a lawyer will help you evaluate whether your list of priorities is reasonable or whether you are asking for too little or too much.

After reviewing this book and consulting with your lawyer, you should be able to determine which assets count as marital property and which count as separate property; how a judge in your state would divide your marital property; whether you are likely to receive or owe alimony; how a judge in your state would rule on custody and visitation; the amount of child support that would be due under the guidelines; and whether a deviation from the child support guidelines is warranted in your case. You should use this information to define the parameters of an acceptable out-of-court settlement and to assess whether your goals for the outcome of your divorce dispute are reasonable.

A SAMPLE CASE: JOSEPH AND MARIA MEYERS

To help you understand how the law is applied to the facts in a "real life" divorce case, let us once again consider the case of Joseph and Maria Meyers. You have already seen their lists of assets and liabilities, income and expenses, and priorities. Although you probably already know some of this from reading the Meyers's lists, the facts of the Meyers's case are as follows:

• *Income and Assets.* Joseph earns $75,000 per year plus a bonus of $5,000 to $10,000. Maria earns $50,000 per year working part-time. Joseph and Maria contribute their paychecks to a joint checking account, which has a current balance of $13,500. The Meyers purchased a house during their marriage for $350,000. Maria contributed $25,000 of her inheritance funds toward the down payment. The current outstanding balance on their home mortgage is $250,000. Joseph and Maria each have 401(k) plans. Joseph's is worth $29,350 while Maria's is worth $7,200. Joseph earned part of his 401(k) before his marriage to Maria, but Maria earned her entire 401(k) during her marriage to Joseph. Joseph drives a car originally purchased for $22,680 before his marriage to Maria. Maria maintains a separate savings account with a balance of $20,000 that contains the rest of her inheritance. In terms of jewelry, Maria's engagement ring was purchased for $3,000, and the Meyers's wedding rings were purchased for $2,000. The Meyers estimate that their household furnishings are worth approximately $10,000.

• *Liabilities.* Maria came into the marriage with $18,500 worth of student loan debt. She paid off $6,000 worth of this debt during her marriage. In addition, Joseph and Maria have $5,500 in joint credit card debt, which they incurred for wedding-related expenses.

• *Children.* The Meyers have a small infant named Suzie. Maria works three days a week and takes care of Suzie full-time two days a week. Joseph is unable to help out much with Suzie during the week because he often works late and travels for business. On the weekends, Joseph and Maria share child care responsibilities and they both enjoy spending time with Suzie.

Now that we have a handle on the facts, it is time to consider the law. Imagine that Joseph and Maria each read a copy of this book and consulted with their respective lawyers. They know that all assets acquired during the marriage—including pensions and other retirement benefits—count as marital property. They also know that inheritance funds and property acquired before the marriage count as separate property. Finally, they know that marital property is divided equitably in Minnesota.

Joseph and Maria determine that Maria's inheritance account and her engagement ring count as her separate property, and her student loan debt counts as her separate debt. The Meyers also determine that Joseph's automobile and the part of his pension that he earned before his marriage to Maria count as his separate property. Joseph and Maria agree that their marital property therefore consists of their house, the funds in their joint checking account, the funds in Maria's 401(k) plan, the funds in Joseph's 401(k) plan to the extent that they were earned during the marriage, the Meyers's wedding rings, and their household furniture. Their marital debt consists of their mortgage and credit card debt. To allocate their marital property and debt, the Meyers realize that they will need some help determining the marital portion of Joseph's 401(k) plan and the current market value of their house.

Joseph and Maria have two initial points of disagreement. The first issue is whether Maria is entitled to a refund of the $25,000 that she contributed toward the down payment for the house. Joseph believes that Maria's inheritance funds have become marital property because the funds were mixed with marital property, while Maria believes that she deserves reimbursement for her contribution to the house. The second issue is whether Joseph is entitled to a refund of any part of the $6,000 in marital funds that Maria spent reducing her student loan debt during their marriage. Maria believes that because she earned money during their marriage, she was entitled to use some of that money to pay down her separate debt. Joseph takes the position that because marital funds were used to benefit separate property, the marital estate should be reimbursed.

Fortunately, Joseph and Maria have no dispute over alimony. Because Maria earns a good living on her own and has a $20,000 nest egg from her inheritance, both Joseph and Maria agree that a court would be unlikely to award her alimony. Joseph and Maria also agree that Joseph should not be entitled to alimony because he earns more than Maria.

The Meyers have serious differences when it comes to custody of little Suzie. They recognize that the state of Minnesota makes custody determinations according to the best interests of the child, without regard to the gender of the parent. They also understand that Minnesota does tend to favor the parent who is the primary caretaker and has more time available to spend with the child. Based on these criteria, it appears that Maria would receive custody of Suzie. However, Joseph is very concerned about being relegated to the status of second-class parent. He does not want to lose touch with his baby daughter after the divorce. Joseph also recognizes that Maria will only be able to afford to work part-time if he pays child support. He is uncomfortable with subsidizing Maria's ability to spend time with Suzie at the expense of his own ability to spend time with his daughter.

Now that Joseph and Maria have completed the process of taking stock of the facts of their case, their priorities, and the law, they are ready to turn to the negotiations. We will come back and see how Joseph and Maria settle their differences at the end of chapter thirteen.

Chapter Thirteen

Reaching an Out-of-Court Agreement

Once you and your spouse have completed the process of taking stock, you will be ready to begin negotiations. The three main ways in which you and your spouse can negotiate an out-of-court agreement are: (1) direct negotiations with each other; (2) negotiations through your respective lawyers; or (3) mediation. You can even use a combination of these methods to resolve your divorce dispute out of court. Before discussing negotiation in more detail, let us review the ground rules for a valid out-of-court agreement.

THE GROUND RULES

You and your spouse have complete freedom to reach any out-of-court agreement that you find acceptable, subject to certain limitations. First, while you can be a tough negotiator, you cannot force your spouse to enter an out-of-court agreement or accept any of its provisions against his or her will. Forcing your spouse to an agreement—known in legal-speak as *duress* or *overreaching*—renders the agreement invalid. In one New York case, for example, the court nullified an out-of-court agreement that the wife signed only because her husband threatened to refuse her a Jewish divorce if she did not consent to the agreement. Notably, not all pressure to settle out of court is unacceptable. If you simply threaten to litigate the case to its fullest if your spouse does not consent to an out-of-court agreement, a court will not consider that to constitute duress or overreaching.

Second, you cannot reach an out-of-court agreement that is so unfair to your spouse that it shocks the conscience. In one Florida case, for example, the court invalidated an out-of-court agreement that a deeply depressed wife signed only after her husband told her that she would lose her home and all of her belongings if she did not consent to the agreement. The agreement provided that she would waive alimony and any interest in her husband's shopping centers and other real estate—valued at over $10 million—in exchange for the marital residence, worth only $100,000. To ensure that your out-of-court agreement will withstand any challenges later on, be certain that the agreement is fundamentally fair and reasonable. You should also double-check the agreement itself to make sure it contains language stating that each spouse considers the agreement to be fair and reasonable.

Third, you cannot reach an out-of-court agreement based on fraud or misrepresentation. If you do not disclose to your spouse the existence of an offshore bank account containing substantial funds, for example, your spouse could later move to invalidate the agreement on the grounds that he or she would never have entered into the agreement had he or she been aware of the additional funds. Even nonfinancial fraud and misrepresentation is relevant. If you do not disclose your plans to marry your lover in the very near future and you manage to convince your spouse to agree to continue paying alimony even in the event you remarry, your spouse could move to invalidate the agreement on the grounds that he or she never would have agreed to continue paying alimony in the event of your remarriage if he or she knew that you already had plans to remarry. The most prudent course of action is to disclose all relevant assets, liabilities, and other facts before or during your negotiations.

Fourth, any agreement you make with respect to custody and child support is subject to the approval of the court. A court will only approve a custody and visitation agreement that is in the best interests of the child. For example, a court is unlikely to approve an agreement in which one spouse has absolutely no visitation with his child. A court may also be reluctant to approve an arrangement in which the child stays with a different parent every night. In addition, a court will not permit you to agree to deviate from the child support guidelines unless you have good reasons for doing so.

Finally, you can reach any agreement with respect to alimony except one that would leave either spouse dependent on public assistance. This is because former spouses have a continuing obligation to support each other and to ensure that the burden of support does not rest on the state.

Having each spouse represented by his or her own lawyer is not a prerequisite for a valid out-of-court agreement; however, a court is much more likely to find an out-of-court agreement to be valid if each spouse was represented by an independent lawyer of his or her choosing. If you and your spouse decide to negotiate an out-of-court agreement on your own and then hire one attorney to draft the agreement, be aware that agreements involving only one lawyer are more susceptible to invalidation at a later date. For example, the spouse who ended up with less than she desired may argue that the lawyer who drafted the agreement was biased toward her ex-husband.

PRELIMINARY MATTERS

Before diving headfirst into negotiations, it would be helpful if you and your spouse could agree—either on your own or with the assistance of counsel—on a few preliminary matters. The first is the cutoff date for the acquisition of marital property. It would not bode too well for the rest of your negotiations if you began the process embroiled in a huge debate over whether or not post-separation earnings count as marital property. Consider using the date of the commencement of the divorce or the date that one of you finally and officially moved out of the marital home as the cutoff date for the acquisition of marital property. Regardless of which particular date you choose, the important thing is that you and your spouse both agree that any property either of you acquire after that date is your own separate property.

The second is a commitment that with the exception of reasonable and necessary living expenses, neither of you will dispose of any property—marital or not—or incur any new liabilities without the other spouse's consent until your divorce is settled. Agreeing to this will do much to help reduce conflict and avoid unpleasant surprises during the negotiation process. For example, you would probably be very unhappy if your spouse took out a huge pension loan just as you were in the process of negotiating for a share of his or her pension. As part and parcel of this agreement, you and your spouse may want to consider closing any joint credit card accounts after ensuring that you both have established credit histories and will have no trouble obtaining credit in the future. This will keep you from incurring any new liabilities for your spouse's spending in the time between your separation and your divorce.

The third is an agreement that you and your spouse will jointly appoint any experts or other financial professionals required to value property. If you and your spouse were each to hire your own experts to evaluate a professional practice, for example, the experts would be likely to arrive at wildly different figures. This is because the expert retained by the non-professional spouse would be aiming for the highest valuation possible, while the expert retained by the professional spouse would be aiming for the lowest. Because financial experts and lawyers tend to bill at hefty hourly rates, you and your spouse would each spend a sizeable sum obtaining competing valuations of the same asset.

It is always more efficient and far less costly for divorcing spouses to hire one expert or financial professional to evaluate the asset at issue. An expert hired by both spouses has no incentive to reach a very high or low valuation—rather, his or her goal is to reach a fair and reasonable valuation. If you and your spouse decide to take this approach to valuation, be certain to involve your respective lawyers in the selection process for an expert or other financial professional. Your lawyer will help to ensure that the financial professional you select is not biased toward your spouse or his or her position.

DIRECT NEGOTIATIONS WITH YOUR SPOUSE

Once you and your spouse have a thorough understanding of the facts of your case and the law in your state, there is no reason why you and your spouse cannot negotiate some or all of the terms of your out-of-court agreement entirely on your own. Before beginning any direct negotiations, have a thorough discussion with your lawyer and make sure that your lawyer is in agreement with any proposals you plan to put on the table. The worst thing that you can do is to reach an agreement with your spouse, only to talk it over with your lawyer to learn that you settled for much less than you could have. Another important benefit of consulting with your lawyer in advance of negotiations with your spouse is that he or she may be able to come up with creative or tax-advantageous options that you would not have thought of yourself. Finally, checking with your lawyer will ensure that you have considered all the issues and will not leave out something important—such as health or life insurance—from your final settlement.

Even if you don't want to negotiate the key issues directly with your spouse, many lawyers will ask you to divide your household furnishings and other personal items between yourselves on your own. Don't underestimate the importance of the "little things"—many divorce settlements have broken down over who gets to keep the family albums or the wedding china. Here are a few approaches you could take to dividing your personal items: One, agree on a valuation for each item, then take turns picking what you want, with the understanding that you will each "pay" for what you pick by taking less in the way of other items. For example, our hypothetical couple, Joseph and Maria Meyers, might agree that the dining room furniture is worth $2,000, the living room furniture is worth $1,500, and their china and other collectibles are worth $500. If Maria were to pick the dining room furniture, Joseph would be able to pick both the living room furniture and the china and other collectibles. Second, have one spouse make two equal lists of all personal items, then have the other person select the list of items he or she would prefer. Finally, if all else fails, you may want to consider selling everything and simply dividing the proceeds.

In some cases, it would not be appropriate or advisable to resolve a divorce dispute through direct negotiations with one's spouse. Where one spouse has been abusive to the other, or if one spouse is intimidated or overpowered by his or her spouse, direct negotiations are likely to lead to a very unfair result. In such cases, negotiations through counsel are the only option.

NEGOTIATIONS THROUGH COUNSEL

Another option for negotiating some or all of your divorce settlement is for your lawyer to negotiate with your spouse's lawyer. If there is a power imbalance between you and your spouse, or if the two of you cannot be in the same room together without a screaming match ensuing, negotiating through counsel is a wise option. It also makes sense to negotiate through counsel when some aspects of your divorce settlement—such as dividing shares of a closely held corporation—are too complex for you to hammer out on your own.

Rest assured that your lawyer can only make firm proposals to your spouse's lawyer that you have discussed and approved in advance. For example, if you have agreed to pay no more than $1,000 per month in alimony, your lawyer cannot offer $1,500 just to close the deal more quickly. Your lawyer may only communicate with your spouse's lawyer, unless your spouse has not retained a lawyer. This is because ethical rules prohibit a lawyer from directly contacting an individual who is represented by counsel. While it may be tempting to have your lawyer reason directly with your spouse when you've reached an impasse, it is not permitted under the law.

If you decide to negotiate through counsel, remember that you do not have to negotiate every aspect of your divorce settlement through your lawyers. For example, you and your spouse may be able to decide the custody and visitation issues on your own, but you need a little help coming to agreement on child support. Different issues sometimes require different types of negotiation.

MEDIATION

A third option for negotiating the terms of your divorce settlement is mediation. Mediation is widely respected as a good way to resolve divorce disputes. Courts in a number of states have the authority to require couples to attempt mediation before proceeding with a trial. In mediation, you and your spouse negotiate directly with one another in the presence of a neutral third party. Mediators may be lawyers, psychologists, or social workers. They are usually well trained in the process of conflict resolution. In general, the spouses' separate lawyers are not present during mediation sessions, but you and your spouse could choose to include your lawyers in the process.

Although mediators moderate negotiations and help each spouse to see the other spouse's perspective, they have no authority to compel either spouse to reach an agreement. A mediator is therefore very different from a judge. Both spouses can walk away from the mediation table at any time, even after a complete agreement in principle has been reached.

Like direct negotiations, mediation is not for everyone. Mediation is not appropriate if one spouse has been abusive to the other, or if one spouse is intimidated or overpowered by the other. This is because mediation requires divorcing spouses to deal with each other as equals, in a fairly civilized negotiation process.

If you like the idea of negotiating with a neutral third party present but are uncomfortable with the nonbinding nature of mediation, you may want to consider arbitration. Unlike a mediator, an arbitrator has the power to issue a binding decision on your divorce dispute. Arbitrations are run quite a bit differently from mediations. In practice, arbitrations are often more like informal minitrials, and the arbitrator assumes the role of a judge. As a result, arbitrations are considerably more adversarial than mediations, which are designed to help the spouses themselves—rather than some third party—make a decision about their future.

A SAMPLE CASE: JOSEPH AND MARIA MEYERS

In the case of our hypothetical couple, Joseph and Maria Meyers, the Meyers ultimately used all three negotiation options to settle their divorce dispute.

Part One: Direct Negotiations

Joseph and Maria first sat down and discussed the issues on their own, after consulting with their separate lawyers. The Meyers were able to find common ground almost immediately. Both Joseph and Maria agreed that the house—their most valuable asset—should be sold and the proceeds divided equally between them. Neither felt that he or she could manage the mortgage payments alone. Moreover, both knew that unless one person was able to take over the entire mortgage—an unlikely situation since neither could realistically afford the mortgage alone—both Joseph and Maria would continue to be liable for the entire mortgage in the event of default. They agreed that selling the house was really the only option.

Joseph and Maria consulted a real estate agent and were pleased to discover that their house, which was originally purchased for $350,000, had appreciated to $450,000. Thus, the Meyers would earn approximately $100,000 tax-free upon the sale of their house before expenses such as the real estate agency commission. Both Joseph and Maria agreed that the proceeds from the sale of the house should be divided equally between them. However, Maria insisted that she first receive a reimbursement of the $25,000 that she contributed to the down payment from her inheritance. Joseph argued that her inheritance money had become marital property through commingling. The Meyers decided to let their lawyers take over the negotiations for this last issue.

The Meyers then turned to the issue of their 401(k) plans. After checking with their lawyers, the Meyers learned that they could determine the marital property portion of Joseph's 401(k) using the time rule fraction. The numerator would be the number of years that the Meyers were married and Joseph was contributing to his 401(k), and the denominator would be the total number of years that Joseph was contributing to his 401(k). Because the Meyers were married for five of the eight years that Joseph was contributing to his 401(k), they determined that $\frac{5}{8}$ of Joseph's 401(k) plan—or $18,344 out of $29,350—constituted marital property. They also determined that Maria's entire 401(k) worth $7,200 constituted marital property.

The Meyers agreed that all of their marital property should be divided in half. They agreed that Maria's 401(k) funds could be offset by $7,200 of Joseph's 401(k) funds. This left approximately $11,000 of Joseph's 401(k) funds to be divided. According to their 50-50 plan of division, Joseph therefore owed Maria $5,500. In exchange for keeping all of the funds in his 401(k) plan free and clear, Joseph offered to take on complete responsibility for the $5,500 in credit card debt. Maria considered this to be a tremendously fair solution and agreed immediately.

The Meyers then turned to the $13,500 in their joint checking account. Maria argued that she was entitled to half—or $6,750. Joseph contended that Maria had no right to that $6,750 in checking account funds because she paid down over $6,000 of her student loan debt during their marriage using marital funds. Maria checked with her lawyer on this point and learned that a judge would probably order her to reimburse Joseph for his share of those funds. Assuming Maria contributed an even $6,000 of marital funds toward her student loan debt, she would owe Joseph one-half—or $3,000. Maria knew that she probably paid a bit more than $6,000, so she probably owed Joseph around $3,500. Maria then offered to give Joseph the first $3,500 in their joint checking account. She then proposed that they split the remaining $10,000—entitling her to $5,000. Joseph checked with his lawyer and determined that this was a fair solution.

The only other marital property that Joseph and Maria owned was their wedding rings and their home furnishings. They agreed that they would keep their wedding rings. They also agreed that Maria would keep the bedroom and den furniture, while Joseph would keep the living room and dining room furniture. Maria would keep the computer, while Joseph would keep the television.

After Joseph and Maria made substantial progress with respect to property division, they turned to the issues of custody, visitation, and child support. It is here that the Meyers ran into extreme difficulty. Maria insisted that she was entitled to sole custody and child support. Joseph, however, believed that they should have joint custody and neither should pay the other child support. He argued that if Maria went back to work full-time, their incomes would be approximately equal and no child support would be warranted. The Meyers found themselves in the middle of a heated argument over custody and child support and realized that they could not handle this issue on their own. After consulting with their lawyers, the Meyers decided to try mediation to resolve this aspect of their dispute.

Part Two: Negotiations Through Counsel

Joseph and Maria relied on their lawyers to negotiate the issue of whether Maria was entitled to a reimbursement of the $25,000 she contributed toward the down payment on their marital home. Joseph's lawyer argued that because Maria's inheritance money had been commingled with marital property, Maria's inheritance had become marital property. Joseph's lawyer pointed out that Maria did not place any conditions on her inheritance money when she contributed it toward the house. For example, she did not inform Joseph that she expected to receive her $25,000 back if they ever sold the house. Joseph's lawyer also noted that Maria kept the rest of her inheritance money segregated in an account in her name only. Thus, Maria knew that she had to keep her separate property separate if she did not want it to become part of the marital estate.

Maria's lawyer argued that Maria's inheritance funds had not become so commingled with marital property that it was impossible to trace her separate property. Because there was no dispute that Maria had contributed $25,000 to the house, Maria was entitled to a reimbursement of those funds.

After much discussion, the lawyers were unable to reach a settlement. This is because Maria was insistent on receiving her $25,000 back, while Joseph was insistent that she should not. Maria's lawyer came back and explained to her that Joseph had the better legal argument here. If Maria were to go to court, a judge would likely order her to share that $25,000 with Joseph on a 50-50 basis. Maria's lawyer pointed out that Maria was likely to spend a great deal on legal bills and end up losing half the inheritance money anyway. Maria's lawyer proposed that Maria agree to give up $10,000 of her inheritance funds to Joseph and keep $15,000. This way, Maria would make $2,500 because a judge would likely order her to give $12,500 of the money to Joseph. Joseph's lawyer conducted a similar negotiation with Joseph. He explained that Joseph would make at most $12,500 from a successful resolution of the case. He proposed that Joseph agree to take something less—perhaps $9,000 or $10,000—just to settle the matter.

After much convincing by their lawyers, Joseph and Maria agreed that Maria would receive a reimbursement of $15,000 and Joseph would receive a reimbursement of $10,000. The remaining proceeds from the sale of the house would be divided between them on a 50-50 basis. Fortunately for the Meyers, the house ended up selling for $485,000. After payment of the remaining mortgage balance and other expenses associated with the sale of the house, the Meyers earned a total of $225,000. The

Meyers first took their respective reimbursements—totaling $25,000—and then divided the remaining $200,000 between them. Maria came out with $115,000 in tax-free funds, and Joseph with $110,000 in tax-free funds. When all was said and done, even Maria agreed that the settlement was fair. She knew that she never would have been able to afford to purchase the property without Joseph's income, and she would therefore not have profited from the substantial increase in home values.

Part Three: Mediation

When Joseph told his lawyer that he and Maria were having difficulty coming up with an acceptable arrangement for custody and child support, Joseph's lawyer suggested that they consider mediation, explaining that mediation would help Maria and Joseph see each other's perspective on this very emotional issue. When Joseph suggested the idea to Maria, she was willing to give it a try.

With the help of their lawyers, the Meyers selected a mediator who had special expertise in the area of custody disputes. Joseph and Maria decided that it would be better to have mediation sessions outside of the presence of counsel. This way, they both would feel more comfortable airing their concerns openly.

The mediation sessions began with a focus on what Joseph and Maria each wanted to see happen with respect to custody, and why each had issues with the other's plan. Maria began by explaining that she cherished the current arrangement she had in taking care of Suzie. Maria worked three days a week but devoted another two full days to taking care of Suzie. Maria believed that she and Suzie had formed a very close bond, and Suzie would suffer if she did not get to spend that time with Maria. Maria explained that she would need financial assistance from Joseph in order to continue the arrangement, which she felt was in Suzie's best interests.

Joseph expressed a concern that he would be cut out of Suzie's life after the divorce. If Maria had sole custody, he worried that he would not be able to continue playing a major role in Suzie's life. He also said that it was unfair for him to pay Maria in order to allow her to spend more time with Suzie.

After much negotiation, the mediator managed to get Joseph and Maria to agree that Suzie would benefit from spending as much time as possible with both of her parents. The mediator suggested something that neither Joseph nor Maria had considered: making adjustments to their work situations in order to allow them both to spend more time with

Suzie. Joseph went home and mulled over the possibility of changing his work–life balance a little. After talking it over with his boss, Joseph decided to scale back his workweek to only four days. Joseph reasoned that if money became a problem, he would take weekend shifts to earn overtime funds.

Maria, for her part, talked to her boss about overtime options for the weekends. Maria's boss informed her that the company had no such options, but put her in touch with an agency that offered frequent freelance work opportunities. Maria calculated that she would be able to make 15 percent more money doing freelance work on the weekends, and this would help offset some of her day care and other costs.

At the next mediation session, Joseph proposed that he take care of Suzie one weekday per week while Maria was at work. Joseph explained that this would reduce Maria's day care costs and give him a chance to spend time with Suzie. Maria proposed that Joseph take Suzie every other weekend, from Friday night until Sunday night. This would give Maria a chance to work on her freelance projects and provide Joseph with some time with Suzie. Before making this proposal, Maria had checked with her lawyer and learned that a judge would probably award Joseph with one or two complete weekends of visitation per month. According to the schedule, Maria would have Suzie for two full days a week, plus most evenings, and two full weekends a month. Joseph would have Suzie for one full day and night a week, plus two full weekends a month. This schedule made both Maria and Joseph relatively happy. Maria did not feel she was giving up too much time with Suzie, while Joseph felt that he would likely end up spending more hours with Suzie after the divorce than he had while he was married.

The next issue was child support. With a 20 percent decrease in income, Joseph would now be making approximately $64,000 per year— or approximately $2,917 per month after taxes. Maria, with a 15 percent increase in income, would be making approximately $57,500. The real difference in their incomes was now only $6,500 before taxes. The Meyers determined that under the Minnesota Child Support Guidelines, Joseph would owe $729 per month in child support. Both Joseph and Maria agreed that this amount seemed a bit excessive. Instead, Joseph offered to pay for Suzie's health care and contribute $300 per month toward her day care costs, if Maria would agree that no further child support would be due. Joseph explained that he would also regularly purchase clothes for Suzie, as well as toys, to offset some of those costs. This proposal would leave Maria responsible for only $100 per month in child care costs, as Joseph's new work arrangement cut her costs by one-third. After talking the proposal over with her lawyer, Maria agreed to the arrangement.

Once Maria and Joseph agreed on the big custody and child support issues, they had no trouble agreeing to joint legal custody and dividing up major holidays between them. They also agreed that they would each save $125 per month to fund Suzie's eventual educational expenses. Overall, the Meyers were quite happy with the results of their mediation. Although it took quite a few mediation sessions to hammer out an agreement, Joseph and Maria emerged from the sessions feeling like they could deal with each other in a civil and cooperative way as they shared parenting responsibilities for Suzie over the years to come.

Chapter Fourteen

The Final Agreement

Once you and your spouse have reached agreement on all of the issues in your divorce dispute, the final settlement agreement can be prepared. Usually one spouse's lawyer drafts the agreement and the other spouse's lawyer "marks up" the draft agreement with comments and suggestions. Only after both lawyers and both spouses have signed off on the terms of the agreement is the agreement finalized and signed.

In rare cases, divorcing spouses who have reached agreement on their own will hire one lawyer to draft the final agreement. This may seem like a very economical idea, but having one lawyer represent both spouses often raises conflicts of interest. Moreover, courts are much more suspicious of agreements wherein both spouses were represented by one lawyer. Judges recognize that there is a risk that the lawyer will end up—consciously or unconsciously—favoring one spouse. The spouse who emerges from the divorce with less than he or she had hoped may later challenge the agreement on the grounds that he or she did not have independent legal counsel. Because of all of these problems, most lawyers will not represent both divorcing spouses in drafting a final agreement.

Some divorcing spouses decide to leave lawyers out of the process entirely and draft their own settlement agreements. It is generally not advisable to attempt to draft a settlement agreement on your own. There are several reasons for this. First, you may accidentally omit important clauses that you must include in order for your agreement to survive a subsequent challenge. Second, you may draft an agreement that is less comprehensive than it should be. Lawyers tend to draft agreements that cover every possible contingency to avoid conflicts and confusion in the future. Third, having a lawyer draft your agreement ensures that a lawyer has checked over the agreement and confirmed that it is a fair and legally proper settlement.

THE CONTENTS OF A FINAL SETTLEMENT AGREEMENT

Irrespective of who drafts your settlement agreement, you and your spouse should insist that the agreement be written in simple English. If you or your spouse cannot understand any part of the agreement, have your lawyer explain it to you. Consider asking your lawyer to redraft any paragraphs that confuse you, because you may have to consult your settlement agreement if disputes arise in the future. You will save yourselves a great deal of trouble if you and your spouse can work out minor disputes on your own simply by reference to the agreement.

One way of simplifying a settlement agreement is to make sure that the document is not unnecessarily wordy. If you think that the agreement is using ten words to say something that could be said in five, consider pointing this out to your lawyer. It may be that the extra five words have some importance, or it may be that they are extraneous and should be omitted. Make sure that you and your spouse are referred to using simple shorthand—using your first names or something easy like "Husband" and "Wife." It will make the agreement much easier to read.

Also, be certain that your settlement agreement covers every contingency. For example, if your settlement agreement provides that your spouse will visit with the children every Wednesday, make sure your agreement specifies what happens if your spouse is sick and cannot make his or her Wednesday visitation. Providing for contingencies will help you and your spouse avoid arguments in the future. Of course, there is a reasonable limit to the number of contingencies that you can provide for in your agreement. If you include a provision for every possibility that life may throw your way, your settlement agreement will be longer than the Yellow Pages.

In terms of what actually goes into a final agreement, settlement agreements usually begin with what are known as "recitals." The recitals set forth basic information such as the names of the spouses, where they live, the date and place of their marriage, and the names and ages of the children. The recitals note that the spouses have separated and intend to file for divorce, and explain that both spouses desire to settle all the issues of their divorce through the agreement. By way of a disclaimer, the recitals also usually state that each spouse was represented by independent counsel of his or her own choosing; each spouse is fully aware of all of his or her rights; each spouse has provided the other with full financial disclosure; and each spouse agrees that the terms of the agreement are fair and reasonable.

After the recitals, there is a transition clause that usually reads something like this: "Now therefore, in consideration of the premises and the mutual promises and covenants contained herein, and for other good and valuable consideration, the parties agree as follows." The agreement will then set forth a "no molestation" provision. This provision states that each spouse is free to live his or her life as he or she chooses following the divorce, and the other spouse may not interfere in any way with his or her decisions.

The agreement will then address the nitty-gritty aspects of the divorce settlement. With respect to property division, the agreement will generally annex a complete list of each spouse's assets and liabilities. The agreement will list which property is marital, which property is separate, and how it will be divided. The agreement will also specify which spouse is responsible for each debt or liability.

If one spouse is assigned jointly held debt, the agreement will generally contain a "hold harmless" provision to protect the other spouse in the event of a default. This provision requires the responsible spouse to reimburse the other spouse in full in the event the responsible spouse defaults on the jointly held debt and the creditor goes after the other spouse for payment.

In addition, the agreement will generally include a protection provision in the event of bankruptcy. Because property division obligations are dischargeable in bankruptcy while spousal support obligations are not, such a provision may recast some or all of the property division obligations as spousal support in the event of bankruptcy.

To ensure that one spouse cannot later bring an additional claim with respect to property addressed in the agreement, the agreement will contain a general release providing that each spouse releases the other from any further claim that he or she may have.

If one spouse will be paying alimony, the agreement will specify the amount and duration of the alimony. The agreement will also specify whether or not alimony is tax deductible to the payer and what events trigger termination of alimony. The agreement will usually also provide for some security—such as life insurance—to protect the alimony recipient in the event that the payer dies before completing his or her spousal support obligations.

If there are children involved, the agreement will state the terms of the custody and visitation arrangement in some detail. The agreement may also specify how decisions affecting the child will be made. The agreement will state the amount of child support due, when it will terminate, and any other arrangements that the spouses have made with respect to providing for their children. If the child support amount is different from the guideline amount, the agreement will have to specify the reasons for the deviation. The agreement will generally provide for some security—such as life insurance—to protect the child in the event that the parent dies while his or her child is still a minor. The agreement may also require each spouse to make certain testamentary dispositions—in other words, provisions in his or her will—for the benefit of the children.

The agreement will generally specify whether each spouse will pay his or her own attorneys' fees, or whether one spouse will pay part or all of the other's fees. If a religious divorce is involved, the agreement will require each spouse to take all steps necessary to obtain a religious divorce. If one spouse has the unilateral power to refuse a religious divorce, the agreement may provide that certain marital property will not be transferred until the religious divorce is granted.

The agreement will also usually provide that each spouse waives any rights he or she may have with respect to the other's estate. In general, individuals are entitled to a specified percentage of their spouse's estates, even if their spouses left nothing to them in their wills. This is known as an "elective share." A provision of this nature protects each spouse's estate in the event that the spouse dies between the signing of the agreement and the granting of the official divorce decree.

The agreement will specify what actions constitute a breach of the agreement and may provide for automatic penalties in the event of a breach. For example, an agreement may provide that paying alimony more than fifteen days late will constitute a breach of the agreement. The agreement may further provide that there will be a penalty of $100 per day thereafter that alimony is delinquent. To keep spouses from running to the courthouse upon every breach and disagreement, many agreements require spouses to engage in mediation or even arbitration before recommencing litigation.

Finally, the agreement will contain a number of provisions designed to limit each spouse's ability to challenge the agreement in court at a later time. The first is a "no oral modification" clause, which provides that the agreement can be amended only in writing, with all modifications signed and agreed to by both parties.

The second is a "no waiver" clause, which protects the ability of each spouse to take action for a breach of the agreement at any time, even if it has been months since the breach occurred. For example, if your spouse paid $200 less in child support each month and you did not sue for breach until the sixth month, a "no waiver" clause would limit your spouse's ability to claim that you waived your right to obtain the full amount of child support.

The third is a provision stating that the agreement constitutes the entire agreement between you and your spouse; this will prevent your spouse from later claiming that there were additional settlement terms that you agreed to orally.

The fourth is a "severability" clause. In the event that a court later invalidates any one paragraph or portion of your settlement agreement, the "severability" clause will ensure that the rest of the agreement still stands.

To give you a sense of what a final agreement looks like, we have prepared a settlement agreement for Joseph and Maria Meyers, our hypothetical couple from Minnesota.

SAMPLE SETTLEMENT AGREEMENT

AGREEMENT made this 20th day of November 2002 between JOSEPH FRANCIS MEYERS, residing at 22 Palm Court, Cider Hill, Minnesota 55425 (hereinafter referred to as "Joseph") and MARIA MAY MEYERS, residing at 62 Bailey Road, Maple Grove, Minnesota 55426 (hereinafter referred to as "Maria").

RECITALS:

A. WHEREAS Joseph and Maria were married on July 6, 1997, in Minneapolis, Minnesota, in an Episcopal ceremony;
B. WHEREAS there is one child of the marriage, Suzanne Marie, born on October 2, 2001 (hereinafter referred to as "Suzie");
C. WHEREAS the marriage between Joseph and Maria has broken down irretrievably;
D. WHEREAS Joseph and Maria are now living separate and apart from each other;
E. WHEREAS Joseph and Maria desire by this Agreement to settle their property rights with respect to any and all property owned by Joseph and/or Maria, as well as all matters relating to the custody and visitation of Suzie, and the support and maintenance of Suzie, Joseph, and Maria;
F. WHEREAS Joseph and Maria have each been advised, separately and independently by counsel of his or her choice, of his or her legal rights, remedies, and obligations arising out of the marriage, and Joseph and Maria have been fully apprised of the nature and extent of all property and liabilities owned or owed by the other, and the income and prospects of the other;
G. WHEREAS Joseph and Maria warrant and represent to the other that each fully understands his or her rights and obligations under the Agreement, and believes the Agreement to be fair, just and reasonable; and

NOW, THEREFORE, in consideration of the premises and the mutual promises and undertakings herein contained, and for other good and valuable consideration, Joseph and Maria agree as follows:

Article I: Separation And Non-Molestation

1. It is and shall be lawful for Joseph and Maria to live separate and apart from one another at all times, to reside wherever each sees fit, to asso-

ciate with whomever each sees fit, and to engage in any employment, business or profession he or she so wishes, without control, restraint, or interference from the other, as if he or she were single and unmarried.

2. Neither Joseph nor Maria shall compel the other to associate or cohabit with him or her by any action for the restoration of conjugal rights or by any means whatsoever. Neither Joseph nor Maria shall molest, harass, injure, or annoy the other, or interfere with the other's freedom, peace, or comfort in any way.

Article II: Division Of Marital Property

1. Joseph and Maria have together evaluated and divided their separate property, their marital property, and their debts in accordance with the guidelines set forth in Minnesota's equitable distribution statute, Minn. Stat. Ann. Ch. 518.58. Both Joseph and Maria agree that the terms of the property division are fair and reasonable, and in the best interests of both. The terms of their agreement are set forth in the following paragraphs.

2. Joseph and Maria, together or separately as specified, own the following assets. Joseph and Maria each represents and warrants to the other that this list comprises any and all property, wherever situated and in whatever form, owned by him or her:

   a. A house located at 125 Walnut Street, Maple Grove, Minnesota, originally purchased for $350,000 by Joseph and Maria in 1998;
   b. A joint checking account (Chemical Bank account 314325) with a balance of $13,500;
   c. A savings account in Maria's name (Chase Bank account 412332) with a balance of $20,000;
   d. Joseph's 401(k) plan (Fidelity Investments account 378-67-9030) with a balance of $29,350;
   e. Maria's 401(k) plan (Vanguard Investments account 329-32-5455) with a balance of $7,200;
   f. Joseph's automobile (1996 Toyota Camry, license plate BZM-23J), originally purchased for $22,680;
   g. Joseph's and Maria's wedding rings, originally purchased together for $2,000;
   h. Maria's engagement ring, originally purchased for $3,000; and
   i. Assorted household furnishings, with a collective value of approximately $10,000.

3. Joseph and Maria agree to divide their property as follows:

a. The house at 125 Walnut Street, Maple Grove, Minnesota, will be sold as quickly as possible following the execution of this agreement. Joseph and Maria agree to cooperate with one another and to facilitate the expeditious sale of the house. After payment of all taxes and expenses associated with the sale of the house, the proceeds will be divided as follows:

   i. The outstanding mortgage balance of $250,000 will be paid off in full;

   ii. Maria will receive $15,000 and Joseph will receive $10,000; and

   iii. The remaining proceeds will be divided in half between Joseph and Maria.

b. The $13,500 in funds in the joint checking account (Chemical Bank account 314325) will be divided as follows: Joseph will receive $8,500 and Maria will receive $5,000;

c. The $20,000 in funds in Maria's savings account in Maria's name (Chase Bank account 412332) will be assigned entirely to Maria, and Joseph waives and relinquishes any claim he has to those funds. The funds were inherited from Maria's grandmother and constitute Maria's separate property;

d. Joseph's 401(k) plan will be assigned entirely to Joseph, and Maria waives and relinquishes any claim she has to those funds. A substantial portion of the funds in Joseph's 401(k) were earned prior to his marriage to Maria and therefore constitute his separate property. Maria agrees that she will execute any spousal waivers as may be necessary, although this document may substitute for any other statement, prepared form, or document that may be required by Fidelity Investments;

e. Maria's 401(k) plan will be assigned entirely to Maria, and Joseph waives and relinquishes any claim he has to those funds. Joseph agrees that he will execute any spousal waivers as may be necessary, although this document may substitute for any other statement, prepared form, or document that may be required by Vanguard Investments;

f. Joseph's automobile will be assigned entirely to Joseph, and Maria waives and relinquishes any claim she has to the vehicle. Joseph acquired the vehicle prior to his marriage to Maria, and the vehicle therefore constitutes his separate property;

g. Joseph's wedding ring will be assigned to him, and Maria's wedding ring will be assigned to her;

h. Maria's engagement ring will be assigned entirely to Maria, and

Joseph waives and relinquishes any claim he has to the ring. Joseph gave Maria the ring before their marriage as a conditional gift, contingent on their marriage. The ring therefore constitutes Maria's separate property; and

i. The household furnishings will be divided as follows:

    i. Maria will receive the bedroom and den furniture, as well as the computer; and

    ii. Joseph will receive the living room and dining room furniture, as well as the television.

4. Joseph and Maria, together or separately as specified, owe the following debts. Joseph and Maria each represents and warrants to the other that this list comprises any and all debts and liabilities, wherever situated and in whatever form, owed by him/her:

    a. A joint mortgage debt for the property located at 125 Walnut Street, Maple Grove, Minnesota, with a balance of $250,000;

    b. A joint credit card debt (MBNA MasterCard account 4432903393) with a balance of $5,500; and

    c. Maria's student loan debt (Sallie Mae Corporation account 1239876), with a balance of $12,500.

5. Joseph and Maria agree to divide their debt as follows:

    a. The mortgage debt will be paid off in full using the proceeds from the sale of the property located at 125 Walnut Street, Maple Grove, Minnesota.

    b. Joseph will assume, pay and hold Maria harmless with respect to the joint credit card debt of $5,500. Simultaneously with the execution of this agreement, Maria shall give Joseph all credit cards in her possession with respect to this account. Maria shall incur no additional debt in this account;

    c. Maria will assume her student loan debt in full. Maria acquired the debt prior to her marriage to Joseph, and the debt therefore constitutes her separate debt. Maria waives and relinquishes any claim for reimbursement or contribution against Joseph with respect to this debt.

6. Except as otherwise set forth in the foregoing paragraphs of this Agreement, Joseph and Maria hereby mutually waive their rights and release each other from any claims for spousal support, the distribution of marital property, distributive awards, or any special relief or claims regarding separate property or the increase in value thereof. Joseph and Maria agree that they are accepting the provisions of this Agreement in

full satisfaction of any claim each may have to the property of the other, whether owned individually or jointly or by any third party or parties, and whether separate or marital.

7. Except as otherwise set forth in the foregoing paragraphs, Joseph and Maria represent and agree that neither has to date or will in the future incur any debt, obligation, or liability for which the other may be liable. Both Joseph and Maria agree to hold the other harmless from all loss, expenses, reasonable attorney's fees, and damages in connection with a breach of this representation and agreement.

Article III: Spousal Support

1. Because Joseph and Maria are each fully capable of supporting themselves, and have reasonable assets sufficient to provide for their needs, neither Joseph nor Maria seeks spousal support from the other. Accordingly, no provision for the support of either Joseph or Maria is made in this Agreement.
2. Joseph and Maria waive any and all rights each may have to receive support from the other. Both Joseph and Maria acknowledge that the Agreement, and the release and waiver of spousal support, is fair and reasonable.

Article IV: Custody And Visitation

1. Joseph and Maria will have joint legal and physical custody of Suzie because this custodial arrangement is in Suzie's best interests. Physical custody of Suzie will be shared according to the following schedule:

   a. Suzie shall spend every Wednesday day and night with Joseph. Joseph will pick up Suzie at 8:00 A.M. on Wednesday morning and shall return Suzie to Maria at 8:00 A.M. on Thursday morning.
   b. Suzie shall spend Monday, Tuesday, Thursday, and Friday days and Monday, Tuesday, and Thursday nights with Maria. Suzie will be left in the care of a baby-sitter or qualified day care institution on Thursdays and Fridays, from 8:00 A.M. until 6:00 P.M.
   c. Suzie shall spend every other weekend with Joseph and every other weekend with Maria. The weekend will begin at 6:00 P.M. on Friday evening and will continue until 6:00 P.M. on Sunday evening.
   d. Once Suzie is old enough to attend school, Suzie will spend the summer holidays with Joseph and Maria in alternating two-week blocks. Suzie will also spend half of her winter holidays with Maria and half with Joseph.
   e. Notwithstanding the foregoing provisions, Suzie shall spend the day

with Maria on Mother's Day and Maria's birthday. Suzie shall also spend the day with Joseph on Father's Day and Joseph's birthday. Joseph and Maria shall spend the day with Suzie on alternate birthdays, Christmases, and Easters, with the understanding that if Suzie spends Christmas with one parent on a given year, she will spend Easter with the other, and so on.

2. Joseph and Maria recognize that life is subject to change, and hereby agree to cooperate and to be reasonable with one another in making accommodations to the foregoing schedule as necessary. If either Joseph's or Maria's circumstances have changed to the point where a completely new schedule must be devised, Joseph and Maria agree to work with one another to come up with an acceptable schedule. In the event that Joseph and Maria are unable to reach agreement on their own, they hereby covenant to reach agreement through mediation. Litigation may only be commenced if Joseph and Maria are unable to reach agreement after six months of good-faith mediation.

3. Joseph and Maria further agree that it is important that Suzie have complete and continuing access to the love, affection, and support of both of her parents. In recognition of this fact, both Joseph and Maria agree to include the other in special events in Suzie's life—such as soccer games, school plays, and the like—that occur while Suzie is in his or her custody. Joseph and Maria further agree that each will encourage Suzie to call and keep in touch with the other while Suzie is in his or her custody.

4. Joseph and Maria may each vacation with Suzie. Prior to scheduling any such vacation, Joseph and Maria agree to confer with one another and reach agreement on the location, duration, and other aspects of such a vacation.

5. Joseph and Maria hereby agree that each will continue residing within a fifteen-mile radius of Maple Grove, Minnesota. In the event that either moves outside of this radius, Joseph and Maria agree that this custodial arrangement will be renegotiated to accommodate the changed circumstances. If Joseph and Maria cannot reach agreement regarding a revised custodial arrangement on their own, they hereby covenant that they will seek mediation. Litigation may only be commenced if Joseph and Maria are unable to reach agreement after six months of good-faith mediation.

6. Joseph and Maria agree to confer with one another and reach decisions together on all significant matters relating to Suzie's health, education, religion, discipline, and general upbringing. Both Joseph and Maria are entitled to obtain copies of Suzie's complete educational and health

records, and both Joseph and Maria are entitled to attend school con-
ferences, doctor's appointments, and any other events affecting Suzie's
education, health, or welfare. Notwithstanding the foregoing provisions, both Joseph and Maria are entitled to make day-to-day decisions
with respect to Suzie at any time during which Suzie is in his or her
custody.

7. Joseph and Maria agree that each shall undertake his or her best efforts
to foster a loving and open relationship between Suzie and the other
parent. Neither shall interfere with Suzie's relationship with the other
parent in any way.

8. Joseph and Maria agree that they will not allow Suzie to be called by
any surname other than "Meyers," and that they will not initiate or permit the designations of "Mommy" and/or "Daddy" or their equivalents
to be used by Suzie with reference to any person other than Joseph and
Maria.

9. In the event of the death of either Joseph or Maria, the surviving parent
shall have sole physical and legal custody of Suzie. The surviving parent shall make every effort to ensure continuing and frequent contact
between Suzie and her grandparents and relatives from her deceased
parent's side of the family, and to foster any relationships that Suzie
may have had with extended family members before the death of one
of her parents.

Article V: Child Support

1. As and for child support, Joseph shall pay to Maria $300 per month, on
the first of every month, commencing on the first month after the date
hereof and continuing until Suzie reaches the age of eighteen. In addition, Joseph shall provide for Suzie's medical and dental insurance
needs, including any unreimbursed health care costs. Unreimbursed
health care costs shall mean necessary medical, dental, and psychiatric
expenses, as well as prescription drug expenses. The monthly amount
of child support was determined after a consideration of the amount of
time that Suzie will be spending in each parent's home, and modifications to Joseph's work schedule and a corresponding decrease in income undertaken in order to spend more time with Suzie.

2. Joseph and Maria further agree that each will contribute $125 per
month to a savings account in Suzie's name. The funds in this savings
account will be used to fund Suzie's college tuition or, if Joseph and
Maria agree, to fund private school tuition or other educational needs
for Suzie.

3. Joseph and Maria hereby agree that a deviation from the amount that

Joseph would otherwise owe under the Minnesota Child Support Guidelines is warranted in this case and is in Suzie's best interests. Joseph's net income of $2,917 per month, multiplied by the required percentage of 25 percent, yields a child support obligation of $729 per month. Joseph and Maria agree that this amount is excessive in light of the fact that Joseph and Maria will be sharing physical custody of Suzie, and will be sharing the costs associated with raising and nurturing Suzie.

4. Joseph and Maria acknowledge that they are fully familiar with the Minnesota Child Support Guidelines, which they understand would govern child support issues in the absence of this Agreement. Joseph and Maria have been fully informed of the manner in which the Child Support Guidelines would affect their rights and obligations with respect to child support. Notwithstanding this knowledge, Joseph and Maria agree that all child support obligations between them shall be governed by this Agreement and they waive application of the Child Support Guidelines.

5. Joseph and Maria hereby agree that each will name Suzie as a beneficiary under their respective employer-subsidized health insurance plans, and that each will maintain health insurance for Suzie until Suzie reaches age eighteen.

6. To ensure that Suzie will be adequately provided for in the event of the death of either or both Joseph and Maria, both Joseph and Maria hereby covenant to obtain life insurance in the amount of $500,000, with Suzie to be named as the beneficiary. Both Joseph and Maria further covenant that each will leave at least one-fourth of their estates to Suzie in their wills. Joseph and Maria further covenant that neither will make a transfer of property to a third party in their lifetimes that will substantially diminish the amount that Suzie would receive in the event of the death of either of them.

7. With respect to any costs associated with Suzie that may arise in the future and that may be in excess of $150, Joseph and Maria will confer with one another in order to determine whether the expense is necessary and warranted. If Joseph and Maria agree that a particular expense—such as horseback riding lessons—would provide Suzie with material benefits and is within the budgets of both Joseph and Maria, Joseph and Maria shall share such expenses in proportion to their incomes.

8. Joseph and Maria will confer with one another in December of each year to determine whether a modification to the child support amount is necessary in light of inflation, an increase or decrease in either spouse's income, or other changed circumstances. In the event that

Joseph and Maria cannot agree to an appropriate revised child support amount, Joseph and Maria agree to pursue mediation. Litigation may only be commenced after six months of good-faith mediation.

Article VI: Tax Issues

1. Joseph and Maria filed joint returns during the marriage. Joseph and Maria represent and warrant to the other that each reported his or her income in full on those joint returns and that all deductions taken were appropriate. Joseph and Maria agree that they will cooperate with one another in the event of a tax audit or if it becomes necessary to amend tax returns for prior years. In the event of any liability for additional taxes, or any penalties or interest, Joseph and Maria will each pay one-half of the amount due and one-half of any expenses incurred in connection with the tax proceedings.
2. Joseph and Maria agree that they will file taxes separately for 2002.
3. Maria shall have the right to claim Suzie as a dependent for the year 2002 and for all future years. Maria's social security number is 329-32-5455. Joseph's social security number is 378-67-9030. Joseph agrees to execute IRS Form 8332 and to complete any other paperwork necessary to enable Maria to claim Suzie as a dependent.

Article VII: Mutual Waivers and Releases

1. Except for the express provisions of this Agreement, Joseph and Maria release and forever discharge one another from all causes of action, rights, and demands whatsoever, in law or equity, known or unknown, past, present, or future, which either may have had or may in the future have against the other. Both Joseph and Maria shall have the unrestricted right to dispose of their property free of any claims or demands from the other, as if Joseph and Maria had never been married to one another.
2. Without limiting the foregoing release, Joseph and Maria each expressly relinquish any and all rights of election, statutory allowance, dower, curtesy, homestead, distribution in intestacy, or right of election against the will of the other. Both Joseph and Maria renounce any right of administration with respect to the estate of the other, and both agree to make no objections to any provisions in the will or other testamentary dispositions of the other. Both Joseph and Maria hereby agree to execute any documentation necessary to extinguish their rights with respect to the other's estate.
3. Nothing in this Agreement shall be interpreted to prevent either Joseph

or Maria from suing for divorce in any jurisdiction based on the past or future conduct of the other, or to bar the other from defending any action for divorce.

4. This Agreement shall be incorporated in any decree for divorce that may be granted but will survive such incorporation and shall not be merged into such decree.

Article VIII: Default Under the Agreement

1. Except as otherwise provided herein, Joseph and Maria agree that each is entitled to bring a suit to enforce the terms of this Agreement in the event that either fails to comply with any payment or other obligation under this Agreement. The defaulting spouse shall indemnify the other for any costs and expenses, including reasonable attorney's fees, incurred to enforce the terms of this Agreement.

Article IX: Representation by Counsel and Counsel Fees

1. Both Joseph and Maria acknowledge that each was represented by independent counsel of his or her own choosing. Both Joseph and Maria further acknowledge that his or her counsel fully informed him or her of his or her rights and obligations under Minnesota law, and that each considers the Agreement to be fair and reasonable.
2. Joseph and Maria shall each be responsible for their own attorney's fees in connection with the negotiation and drafting of this Agreement, and with any and all other aspects of their divorce.

Article X: General Provisions

1. This Agreement and the rights and obligations hereunder shall be construed and interpreted in accordance with Minnesota law.
2. Joseph and Maria reached this Agreement voluntarily, without fraud, duress, coercion, or undue pressure. Both Joseph and Maria acknowledge that they fully understand all terms and provisions of the Agreement.
3. Both Joseph and Maria acknowledge that this Agreement contains the entire understanding between them with respect to the terms of their divorce, and that there are no agreements or understandings between them that are not specifically mentioned in the Agreement. Both Joseph and Maria further agree that this Agreement supersedes any prior agreements, whether oral or in writing.

4. This Agreement may be modified only in writing, signed and acknowl-edged by both Joseph and Maria. No oral modifications of the Agree-ment may be made.

5. If either Joseph or Maria fails to insist upon strict performance of any right or obligation under the Agreement, such failure shall not be con-strued as a waiver of his or her right to insist upon strict performance in the future and to seek remedies for any prior breach.

6. Each right and obligation under the Agreement is independent of any other paragraph or provision of the Agreement. If any paragraph or provision of this Agreement is deemed invalid for any reason, that shall not invalidate or in any way affect the remaining paragraphs and provi-sions of the Agreement.

7. Joseph and Maria agree to execute and deliver any additional docu-mentation required in order to give full force and effect to the provi-sions of this Agreement.

8. All notices or communications to be made by Joseph to Maria shall be in writing and mailed to 62 Bailey Road, Maple Grove, Minnesota 55426. All notices or communications to be made by Maria to Joseph shall be in writing and mailed to 22 Palm Court, Cider Hill, Minnesota 55425. Both Joseph and Maria shall immediately inform one another of any change in address.

9. The headings of the Articles and Recitals of this Agreement are for convenience only and are not intended to impart any substantive mean-ing to the text.

IN WITNESS WHEREOF, Joseph and Maria have set their hands and seals to six counterparts of this Agreement, each of which shall constitute an orig-inal, this 20th day of November 2002, in the city of Minneapolis, state of Minnesota.

Joseph F. Meyers
JOSEPH FRANCIS MEYERS

Maria May Meyers
MARIA MAY MEYERS

Acknowledgment

STATE OF MINNESOTA   )

                                             ss:

COUNTY OF MINNEAPOLIS   )

On this 20th day of November 2002, before me personally appeared JOSEPH FRANCIS MEYERS, to me known and known to me to be the individual described in and who executed the within instrument, and he acknowledged to me that he executed the same.

John D. Public
NOTARY PUBLIC

Acknowledgment

STATE OF MINNESOTA)

ss:

COUNTY OF MINNEAPOLIS)

On this 20th day of November 2002, before me personally appeared MARIE MAY MEYERS, to me known and known to me to be the individual described in and who executed the within instrument, and she acknowledged to me that she executed the same.

John D. Public
NOTARY PUBLIC

Appendix A

State-by-State Summary of the Divorce Laws

Alabama

residency requirement: If the respondent does not live in Alabama, the petitioner must have lived in Alabama for at least six months immediately prior to the application for divorce. The six-month residency requirement does not apply if the respondent is a resident of Alabama.

grounds for divorce: (1) Irretrievable breakdown of the marriage; (2) complete incompatibility of temperament such that the couple can no longer live together; (3) adultery; (4) abandonment for one year; (5) imprisonment for two years pursuant to a sentence of at least seven years; (6) commission of a crime against nature; (7) drug or alcohol abuse; (8) living separate and apart for over two years during which time the husband has not supported the wife and the wife has lived in Alabama (available to the wife only); (9) confinement for incurable insanity for over five years; (10) wife pregnant by another at the time of the marriage without the husband's knowledge; and (11) physical abuse or reasonable fear of physical abuse.

marital property: Marital property consists of all property acquired during the marriage. Marital property does not include gifts, inheritances, or property acquired prior to marriage unless such property or the income from such property was used regularly for the spouses' common benefit during the marriage. Pensions may only count as marital property to the extent that (a) they were earned during the marriage, and (b) the spouses were married for at least ten pension-qualifying years.

property division: Marital property is divided equitably. The court may consider marital fault if the grounds for divorce are fault-based. The court may not distribute more than half of a pension to the non-pension-holder spouse.

alimony: The court has the discretion to award alimony in an amount and duration it deems proper. The court may consider marital fault if the grounds for divorce are fault-based. Alimony terminates when the recipient remarries or begins cohabiting with someone of the opposite sex.

custody: Child custody decisions are made in accordance with the best interests of the child. Alabama favors joint custodial arrangements if such an arrangement is in the best interests of the child and the parents agree. The court will consider joint custody in every case. The court will presume that it is not in a child's best interests to award custody to a parent who has committed domestic violence. Where a wife abandons a husband, her husband is granted custody of children over the age of seven if he is a suitable person to have custody.

child support: Child support is determined according to the income shares model. The age of majority is nineteen.

Alaska

residency requirement: One spouse must live in Alaska.

grounds for divorce: (1) Incompatibility of temperament; (2) personal indignities rendering life burdensome; (3) cruel and inhuman treatment calculated to impair health or endanger life; (4) adultery; (5) abandonment for one year; (6) conviction of a felony; (7) alcohol abuse arising after the marriage and continuing for one year prior to the application for divorce; (8) confinement for incurable insanity for at least eighteen months immediately prior to the application for divorce; (9) drug abuse arising after the marriage; and (10) failure to consummate the marriage.

marital property: Marital property consists of all property acquired during the marriage. Marital property does not include property acquired prior to the marriage. Where justice requires it, the court may include property acquired prior to the marriage as marital property.

property division: Marital property is divided equitably, without regard to marital fault. The court will presume that an equal division of marital property is equitable.

alimony: The court has the discretion to award alimony in an amount and duration it deems proper, without regard to marital fault.

custody: Child custody decisions are made in accordance with the best interests of the child. The court must take domestic violence into account. There is no preference in favor of joint custody.

child support: Child support is determined according to the variable percentage method. The age of majority is eighteen. The court may extend child support beyond age eighteen if the child is still in high school at age eighteen.

Arizona

residency requirement: One spouse must have lived in Arizona for at least ninety days immediately prior to the application for divorce.

grounds for divorce: Irretrievable breakdown of the marriage.

marital property: Marital property consists of all property acquired during the marriage. Marital property does not include gifts, inheritances, or property acquired prior to marriage. Marital property also does not include the appreciation of separate property or income from separate property. The cutoff date for the acquisition of marital property is the date of service of a petition for divorce, legal separation, or annulment.

property division: Marital property is divided equitably, without regard to marital fault.

alimony: The court has the discretion to award alimony in an amount and duration it deems proper, without regard to marital fault. Alimony terminates upon the death of either spouse or the remarriage of the recipient.

child custody: Child custody decisions are made in accordance with the best interests of the child. There is no preference in favor of joint custody. The court may award joint custody over the objection of one parent if the court determines that joint custody is in the child's best interests.

child support: Child support is determined according to the income-shares model. The age of majority is eighteen, but if the child is still in high school at age eighteen, child support continues until the child graduates from high school.

Arkansas

residency requirement: One spouse must have lived in Arkansas for at least sixty days immediately prior to the application for divorce. In addition, that spouse must have lived in Arkansas for at least ninety days before the final judgment granting the decree of divorce.

grounds for divorce: (1) Living separate and apart for eighteen continuous months without cohabitation for any reason other than incurable insanity; (2) cruel and barbarous treatment so as to endanger the life of the other; (3) indignities to the other spouse rendering his or her condition intolerable; (4) impotency at the time of the marriage and continuing until the time of divorce; (5) conviction for a felony or other infamous crime; (6) alcohol abuse for one year; (7) adultery; and (8) living separate and apart for three years without cohabitation where one spouse was committed to an institution for insanity for three or more years prior to the application for divorce.

marital property: Marital property consists of all property acquired during the marriage. Marital property does not include gifts, inheritances, property acquired prior to marriage, compensation for a personal injury, or workers' compensation benefits. Marital property also does not include property acquired in exchange for separate property, the appreciation of separate property, or income from separate property. Where justice requires it, the court may include property acquired prior to marriage as marital property. The cutoff date for the acquisition of marital property is the date of the divorce decree.

property division: Marital property is divided equally, unless it would be inequitable to do so. Marital fault is not listed as a factor for consideration.

alimony: The court has the discretion to award alimony in an amount and duration it deems proper. Marital fault is generally not a factor for consideration. Alimony terminates upon the death of either spouse or the remarriage of the recipient. Alimony also terminates when the recipient produces a child with someone else and a court either orders the recipient to pay support for that child, or orders the other parent to pay support to the recipient for that child.

child custody: Child custody decisions are made in accordance with the best interests of the child. The court must take domestic violence into account. The court will presume that it is not in a child's best interests to be placed in the custody of a parent who has committed domestic violence. There is no preference in favor of joint custody.

child support: Child support is determined according to the variable percentage method. The age of majority is eighteen. The court may extend child support beyond age eighteen if the child is still in high school at age eighteen.

California

residency requirement: One spouse must have lived in California for six months immediately prior to the application for divorce.

grounds for divorce: (1) Irreconcilable differences which have caused the irremediable breakdown of the marriage; and (2) incurable insanity.

marital property: Marital property consists of all property acquired during the marriage. Marital property does not include gifts, inheritances, or property acquired prior to marriage. Marital property also does not include income from separate property. However, marital property includes the appreciation of separate property and income from separate property to the extent that it resulted from either spouse's efforts during the marriage. Separate property will only be deemed transmuted into marital property if there is a written agreement to that effect. However, if separate property has been so commingled with marital property that it is impossible to trace the separate property, the commingled property will be deemed marital property. The cutoff date for the acquisition of marital property is the date of the spouses' final physical separation or the date of the spouses' legal separation, whichever is earlier.

property division: Marital property is divided equally. Each spouse shall be reimbursed for separate property contributions to marital property. The term "contributions" includes down payments, payments for improvements, and payments that decrease the principal of a loan used to finance the improvement or purchase of property. The term "contributions" does not include interest payments on a loan or payments made for maintenance, insurance, or taxation. Each spouse shall also be reimbursed for contributions to the education or training of the other, unless such a reimbursement would be inequitable under the circumstances of the case. If one spouse misappropriates marital property, the court may reimburse the other spouse for his or her share of the misappropriated property. Property received as compensation for personal injury is generally awarded to the spouse who suffered the injury, provided that the marital estate has been compensated for any expenses associated with the personal injury. Where justice requires, up to one-half of property received as compensation for personal injury may be awarded to the spouse who did not suffer the injury.

alimony: The court has the discretion to award alimony in an amount and duration it deems proper. The court may not consider any marital fault except domestic violence. Alimony terminates upon the death of either party or the remarriage of the recipient.

custody: Child custody decisions are made in accordance with the best interests of the child. The court must take domestic violence into account. The court may order joint custody over the objection of one parent. If both parents agree to joint custody, the court will presume that joint custody is in the child's best interests.

child support: Child support is determined according to a variation of the income shares model. The age of majority is eighteen, unless the child is still in high school at the age of eighteen, in which case child support continues until the child graduates from high school or reaches age nineteen, whichever occurs first.

Colorado

residency requirement: One spouse must have lived in Colorado for ninety days immediately prior to the application for divorce.

grounds for divorce: Irretrievable breakdown of the marriage.

marital property: Marital property consists of all property acquired during the marriage. Marital property does not include gifts, inheritances, or property acquired prior to marriage. Marital property also does not include property acquired in exchange for separate property. The cutoff date for the acquisition of marital property is the date of the decree of legal separation.

property division: Marital property is divided equitably, without regard to marital fault.

alimony: The court has the discretion to award alimony in an amount and duration it deems proper, without regard to marital fault.

custody: Child custody decisions are made in accordance with the best interests of the child. The court must take domestic violence into account. There is no preference in favor of joint custody.

child support: Child support is determined according to the income-shares model. The age of majority is nineteen unless the child is still in high school at age nineteen, in which case child support continues until the end of the month following graduation from high school, but in no event shall child support continue past the age of twenty-one.

Connecticut

residency requirement: One spouse must live in Connecticut. However, a divorce decree will only be issued if: (1) one spouse was living in Connecticut for twelve months immediately prior to the date of the application for divorce or the date of the divorce decree; (2) the spouses lived in Connecticut during the marriage and one of the spouses returned to Connecticut with the intention of residing there permanently; or (3) the grounds for divorce occurred in Connecticut.

grounds for divorce: (1) Irretrievable breakdown of the marriage; (2) living separate and apart by reason of incompatibility for eighteen months and without any reasonable prospect of reconciliation; (3) adultery; (4) fraudulent contract; (5) abandonment for one year with total neglect of spousal duties; (6) seven years' absence, during which time the absent spouse has not been heard from; (7) alcohol abuse; (8) intolerable cruelty; (9) sentence to imprisonment for life or the commission of any infamous crime involving a violation of conjugal duty and punishable by imprisonment for a period in excess of one year; and (10) confinement for mental illness for at least five out of the six years immediately prior to the application for divorce.

marital property: Marital property consists of all property owned by both spouses.

property division: Marital property is divided equitably. The court may consider marital fault.

alimony: The court has the discretion to award alimony in an amount and duration it deems proper. The court may consider marital fault.

custody: Child custody decisions are made in accordance with the best interests of the child. The court will presume that joint custody is in the best interests of the child if both parents have agreed to joint custody.

child support: Child support is determined according to the income-shares model. The age of majority is eighteen unless the child is still in high school at age eighteen, in which case child support continues until the child graduates from high school or reaches age nineteen, whichever occurs first.

Delaware

residency requirement: One spouse must have lived in Delaware for six months immediately prior to the application for divorce.

grounds for divorce: Irretrievable breakdown of the marriage where reconciliation is improbable.

marital property: Marital property consists of all property acquired during the marriage. Marital property does not include gifts, inheritances, or property acquired prior to marriage. Gifts are considered separate property only if the property is titled and maintained in the sole name of the spouse who received the property, a gift tax return is filed reporting the transfer of the gifted property in the sole name of the spouse who received the property, or a notarized document is executed before or at the same time as the gift naming the spouse who received the property the sole owner of such property. Marital property also does not include property acquired in exchange for property acquired prior to the marriage, or the appreciation of property acquired prior to the marriage.

property division: Marital property is divided equitably, without regard to marital fault.

alimony: The court has the discretion to award alimony in an amount and duration it deems proper, without regard to marital fault. Except in marriages of twenty years or longer, the duration of alimony shall not exceed half the length of the marriage. Alimony terminates upon the death of either spouse. Alimony also terminates if the recipient remarries or begins cohabiting with someone else.

custody: Child custody decisions are made in accordance with the best interests of the child. The court must take domestic violence into account. There is no preference in favor of joint custody.

child support: Child support is determined according to the Melson formula. The age of majority is eighteen unless the child is still in high school at age eighteen, in which case child support continues until the child graduates from high school or reaches age nineteen, whichever occurs first.

District of Columbia (Washington, D.C.)

residency requirement: One spouse must have lived in the District of Columbia for six months immediately prior to the application for divorce.

grounds for divorce: (1) Voluntarily living separate and apart without cohabitation for at least six months immediately prior to the application for divorce; and (2) living separate and apart for one year immediately prior to the application for divorce. Spouses may be deemed to be living separate and apart even if they reside under the same roof, provided they do not engage in sexual relations during their period of separation.

marital property: Marital property consists of all property acquired during the marriage. Marital property does not include gifts, inheritances, or property acquired prior to marriage. Marital property also does not include property acquired in exchange for separate property or the increase in value of separate property.

property division: Marital property is divided equitably. The court may consider marital fault.

alimony: The court has the discretion to award alimony in an amount and duration it deems proper. The court may consider marital fault.

custody: Child custody decisions are made in accordance with the best interests of the child. The court must take domestic violence into account. The court will presume that joint custody is in the best interests of the child, except in cases where intrafamily violence, child abuse, child neglect, or parental kidnaping has occurred.

child support: Child support is determined according to the variable percentage method. The age of majority is twenty-one.

Florida

residency requirement: One spouse must have lived in Florida for at least six months immediately prior to the application for divorce.

grounds for divorce: (1) Irretrievable breakdown of the marriage; and (2) mental incapacity of one of the spouses, provided that the spouse was adjudged incapacitated for at least three years prior to the commencement of divorce proceedings.

marital property: Marital property consists of all property acquired during the marriage, including all vested and unvested retirement benefits, and all real estate held by the spouses jointly with rights of survivorship. Marital property does not include gifts, inheritances, or property acquired prior to marriage. Marital property also does not include property acquired in exchange for separate property. Marital property also does not include the income from separate property unless the income was treated as a marital asset during the marriage. Where separate property appreciated during the marriage as a result of the efforts of either spouse or the contribution of marital assets, that appreciation constitutes marital property. The cutoff date for the acquisition of marital property is the earliest of: (1) the date the spouses enter into a valid separation agreement; (2) the date of the filing of a petition for divorce; or (3) any date agreed to by the spouses.

property division: Marital property is divided equally, unless an equal division of marital property would be inequitable or inappropriate in any given case. Marital fault is not a factor for consideration.

alimony: The court has the discretion to award alimony in an amount and duration it deems proper. The court may consider adultery.

child custody: Child custody decisions are made in accordance with the best interests of the child. The court will order joint custody—referred to in Florida as "shared parental responsibility"—unless the court finds that this arrangement would be detrimental to the child. The court will presume that joint custody would be detrimental to the child where either parent has: (1) committed domestic violence; (2) abandoned the child; (3) engaged in conduct toward the child or other children demonstrating that the continuing involvement of the parent in the child's life threatens the life, safety, well-being, or physical, mental, or emotional health of the child or other children; or (4) is incarcerated in a correctional institution and that parent is (a) expected to remain incarcerated for a substantial period of the child's youth; (b) is a violent career criminal, habitual felony offender, sexual predator, or has been convicted of murder or sexual battery; or (c) a court determines that continuing the child's relationship with the incarcerated parent would be detrimental to the child.

child support: Child support is determined according to the income-shares model. The age of majority is eighteen.

Georgia

residency requirement: One spouse must have lived in Georgia for six months immediately prior to the application for divorce.

grounds for divorce: (1) Irretrievable breakdown of the marriage; (2) intermarriage by persons within prohibited degrees of consanguinity; (3) mental incapacity at the time of the marriage; (4) impotency at the time of the marriage; (5) force, menace, duress, or fraud in obtaining the marriage; (6) pregnancy of the wife by a man other than the husband at the time of the marriage, unknown to the husband; (7) adultery; (8) abandonment for one year; (9) conviction for an offense involving moral turpitude, for which the spouse is sentenced to imprisonment for two or more years; (10) alcohol abuse; (11) cruelty; (12) incurable mental illness, provided that the mentally ill spouse has been confined to an institution for the mentally ill or been under continuous treatment for at least two years immediately preceding the commencement of the divorce action; and (13) drug abuse.

marital property: Marital property consists of all property acquired during the marriage. Marital property does not include gifts, inheritances, or property acquired prior to marriage.

property division: Marital property is divided equitably. The court may consider marital fault.

alimony: The court has the discretion to award alimony in an amount and duration it deems proper. The court may consider marital fault. Alimony will not be awarded to a spouse whose adultery or desertion caused the separation of the spouses. Alimony terminates upon the re-marriage of the recipient.

child custody: Child custody decisions are made in accordance with the best interests of the child. The court must take domestic violence into account. The court will allow a child over the age of fourteen to select the custodial parent, provided that the parent he or she selects is suit-able. There is no preference in favor of joint custody.

child support: Child support is determined according to the variable percentage method. The age of majority is eighteen. The court may provide for child support to continue until the child graduates from high school where a child is still in high school at age eighteen, but in no event shall child support continue past age twenty.

Hawaii

residency requirement: The petitioner must have lived in Hawaii for at least three months immediately prior to the application for divorce. A final divorce will only be granted if one spouse has lived in Hawaii for six months immediately prior to the application for divorce.

grounds for divorce: (1) Irretrievable breakdown of the marriage; (2) living separate and apart for a continuous period of two years or more immediately preceding the application for divorce, provided there is no reasonable likelihood that cohabitation will be resumed, and it would not be harsh or oppressive to the respondent or contrary to the public interest to grant a divorce on this basis; (3) living separate and apart under a decree of separation from bed and board, the term of separation has expired, and no reconciliation has occurred; and (4) living separate and apart for two years under a decree of separate mainte-nance, and no reconciliation has occurred.

marital property: Marital property consists of all property owned by both spouses.

property division: Marital property is divided equitably. The court may consider marital fault. In general, property acquired during the mar-riage is divided equally. Property acquired prior to marriage, gifts, and inheritances are generally awarded to the spouse that owns that prop-erty.

alimony: The court has the discretion to award alimony in an amount and duration it deems proper. The court may consider marital fault. Alimony terminates upon the remarriage of the recipient.

child custody: Child custody decisions are made in accordance with the best interests of the child. The court will presume that it is not in a child's best interests to award custody to a parent who has committed domestic violence. There is no preference in favor of joint custody.

child support: Child support is determined according to a variation of the Melson formula. The age of majority is eighteen. The court may extend child support beyond age eighteen if the child is still in high school at age eighteen.

Idaho

residency requirement: The petitioner must have lived in Idaho for six weeks immediately prior to the application for divorce.

grounds for divorce: (1) Irreconcilable differences; (2) living separate and apart for five years; (3) adultery; (4) extreme cruelty; (5) abandonment; (6) willful neglect; (7) alcohol abuse; (8) conviction of a felony; and (9) permanent insanity.

marital property: Marital property consists of all property acquired during the marriage, including income from separate property. Marital property does not include gifts, inheritances, or property acquired prior to marriage. Marital property also does not include property acquired in exchange for separate property.

property division: Marital property is divided substantially equally, unless it would be inequitable or inappropriate to do so given the circumstances of the case. Marital fault is not a factor for consideration.

alimony: The court has the discretion to award alimony in an amount and duration it deems proper. The court may consider marital fault.

child custody: Child custody decisions are made in accordance with the best interests of the child. The court must take domestic violence into account. The court will presume that joint custody is in the best interests of the child.

child support: Child support is calculated according to the income-shares model. The age of majority is eighteen unless the child is still in high school at age eighteen, in which case the age of majority is nineteen.

Illinois

residency requirement: One spouse must have lived in Illinois for ninety days immediately prior to the application for divorce.

grounds for divorce: (1) Living separate and apart for a continuous period in excess of two years, irreconcilable differences have caused the irretrievable breakdown of the marriage, and reconciliation would be impracticable; (2) living separate and apart for a continuous period of six months, irreconcilable differences have caused the irretrievable breakdown of the marriage, reconciliation would be impracticable, and both spouses have filed a written stipulation to that effect with the court; (3) impotence at the time of the marriage and continuing until the time of divorce; (4) one spouse was already married at the time of the marriage; (5) adultery; (6) abandonment for one year; (7) alcohol abuse for two years; (8) drug abuse for two years; (9) attempted murder of the other spouse; (10) extreme and repeated physical and mental cruelty against the other spouse; (11) conviction of a felony or other infamous crime; and (12) infection of the other spouse with a sexually transmitted disease.

marital property: Marital property consists of all property acquired during the marriage, including all vested and unvested retirement benefits and stock options. Marital property does not include gifts, inheritances, or property acquired prior to marriage. Marital property also does not include property acquired in exchange for separate property, or the appreciation of separate property, irrespective of whether the appreciation of separate property was caused by the efforts of either spouse or the contribution of marital property. Marital property also does not include income from separate property, unless that income was the result of the efforts of either spouse. If separate property is commingled with marital property such that it is no longer possible to determine what constitutes separate property and what constitutes marital property, the property will be deemed marital property. The cutoff date for the acquisition of marital property is the date of legal separation, a divorce decree or declaration of invalidity of the marriage.

property division: Marital property is divided equitably, without regard to marital fault. If marital property or marital effort is contributed to separate property, the marital estate is entitled to reimbursement provided that the contribution is traceable and was not a gift. The same holds true in reverse with respect to separate property contributed to marital property. The marital estate will only be reimbursed for marital effort contributed to separate property if the marital effort is significant and results in substantial appreciation of the separate property.

alimony: The court has the discretion to award alimony in an amount and duration it deems proper, without regard to marital fault. Alimony terminates upon the death of either spouse. Alimony also terminates if the recipient remarries or begins cohabiting with someone else.

child custody: Child custody decisions are made in accordance with the best interests of the child. The court must take domestic violence into account. There is no preference in favor of joint custody.

child support: Child support is calculated according to the variable percentage method. The age of majority is eighteen unless the child is still in high school at age eighteen, in which case child support continues until the child graduates from high school or reaches age nineteen, whichever occurs first.

Indiana

residency requirement: One spouse must have lived in Indiana for at least six months immediately prior to the application for divorce.

grounds for divorce: (1) Irretrievable breakdown of the marriage; (2) conviction of a felony; (3) impotence existing at the time of the marriage and continuing until the time of the application for divorce; and (4) incurable insanity continuing for at least two years.

marital property: Marital property consists of all property owned by the spouses.

property division: Marital property is divided equitably. Marital fault is not listed as a factor for consideration. The court shall presume that an equal division of marital property is equitable. In determining whether an unequal division of marital property is appropriate in any given case, the court will consider whether property constitutes a gift or inheritance and whether property was acquired prior to marriage.

alimony: The court has the discretion to award alimony in an amount and duration it deems proper. Marital fault is not listed as a factor for consideration. The court may not award rehabilitative alimony for a period longer than three years.

child custody: Child custody decisions are made in accordance with the best interests of the child. The court must take domestic violence into account. There is no preference in favor of joint custody.

child support: Child support is calculated according to the income-shares model. The age of majority is twenty-one.

Iowa

residency requirement: Unless the respondent is a resident of Iowa and is served by personal service, the petitioner must have lived in Iowa for at least one year immediately prior to the application for divorce.

grounds for divorce: Breakdown of the marriage to the extent that the legitimate objects of matrimony have been destroyed and there remains no reasonable likelihood that the marriage can be saved.

marital property: Marital property consists of all property owned by both spouses. Marital property does not include gifts or inheritances, unless it would be unjust not to include inherited and gifted property as marital property.

property division: Marital property is divided equitably, without regard to marital fault.

alimony: The court has the discretion to award alimony in an amount and duration it deems proper, without regard to marital fault.

child custody: Child custody decisions are made in accordance with the best interests of the child. The court must take domestic violence into account. Iowa favors joint custody. The court may award joint custody over the objection of one or both parents.

child support: Child support is calculated according to the variable percentage model. The age of majority is eighteen. The court may order child support to continue beyond age eighteen if the child is still in high school at age eighteen.

Kansas

residency requirement: One spouse must have been a resident of Kansas for sixty days immediately prior to the application for divorce.

grounds for divorce: (1) Incompatibility; (2) failure to perform a material marital duty or obligation; and (3) incompatibility by reason of mental illness or mental incapacity of one or both spouses, wherein the mentally ill spouse has been confined for mental illness for two years or has been adjudged mentally ill or mentally incapacitated while confined for mental illness.

marital property: Marital property consists of all property owned by both spouses.

property division: Marital property is divided equitably, without regard to marital fault. The court will consider the time, source, and manner of acquisition of marital property in dividing marital property.

alimony: The court has the discretion to award alimony in an amount and duration it deems proper, without regard to marital fault. The court may not award alimony for a period in excess of 121 months.

child custody: Child custody is determined in accordance with the best interests of the child. The court must take domestic violence into account. If the parents have entered into a parenting plan, the court will presume that the custodial arrangement set forth in the parenting plan is in the best interests of the child. There is no preference in favor of joint custody.

child support: Child support is calculated according to the income-shares model. The age of majority is eighteen unless the child is still in high school at age eighteen, in which case child support continues until June 30th of the school year in which the child turns eighteen. The court may extend child support until June 30th of the school year in which the child turns nineteen.

Kentucky

residency requirement: One spouse must have resided in Kentucky for 180 days immediately prior to the application for divorce.

grounds for divorce: Irretrievable breakdown of the marriage.

marital property: Marital property consists of all property acquired during the marriage. Marital property does not include gifts, inheritances, or property acquired prior to marriage. Marital property also does not include property acquired in exchange for separate property. Marital property also does not include the appreciation of separate property or the income from separate property, unless the income or appreciation resulted from the significant efforts of either spouse. The cutoff date for the acquisition of marital property is the date of a decree of legal separation.

property division: Marital property is divided equitably, without regard to marital fault.

alimony: The court has the discretion to award alimony in an amount and duration it deems proper. Marital fault is not listed as a factor for consideration. Alimony terminates upon the death of either spouse or the remarriage of the recipient.

child custody: Child custody is determined in accordance with the best interests of the child. The court must take domestic violence into account to the extent the domestic violence and abuse has affected the child and the child's relationship with both parents. There is no preference in favor of joint custody.

child support: Child support is calculated according to the income-shares model. The age of majority is eighteen unless the child is still in high school at age eighteen, in which case child support continues until the child graduates from high school or reaches age nineteen, whichever occurs first.

Louisiana

residency requirement: One spouse must be domiciled in Louisiana. The court will presume that a spouse is domiciled in Louisiana where that spouse has lived in Louisiana for at least six months immediately prior to the application for divorce.

grounds for divorce: (1) Living separate and apart for 180 days after filing the petition for divorce; (2) living separate and apart for a period of six months or more immediately prior to the application for divorce; (3) adultery; and (4) conviction of a felony with a sentence of death or imprisonment at hard labor.

marital property: Marital property consists of all property acquired during the marriage, and damages awarded for loss or damage to marital property. Marital property does not include gifts, inheritances, or property acquired prior to marriage. Marital property also does not include property acquired in exchange for separate property, or damages awarded for loss or damage to separate property. Marital property includes the income from separate property. Where property is acquired using a combination of marital property and separate property, that property is deemed marital property unless the value of the marital property contributed was inconsequential as compared with the value of the separate property contributed.

property division: Marital property is divided equally. The court may reimburse one spouse for the financial contributions he or she made to the education or training of the other spouse that increased the other spouse's earning power, provided that the contributing spouse did not benefit during the marriage from the other spouse's increased earning power. If marital property is used to acquire, maintain, improve, or pay down debt on separate property, the spouse who does not own the separate property is entitled to a reimbursement of one half of the value that the marital property had at the time that it was used. The same holds true in reverse if separate property is used to acquire, maintain, improve, or pay down debt on marital property. If separate property increases in value as a result of the uncompensated labor or industry of either spouse, the spouse who does not own the separate property is entitled to a reimbursement of one-half of the increase attributed to marital labor.

alimony: The court has the discretion to award alimony in an amount and duration it deems proper, provided that alimony may not exceed one-third of the paying spouse's net income. Alimony may not be awarded to a spouse who is guilty of marital fault. Alimony terminates upon the death of either spouse. Alimony also terminates if the recipient remarries or begins cohabiting with someone else.

child custody: Child custody is determined in accordance with the best interests of the child. The court shall award joint custody unless sole custody is in the child's best interests. If the parents reach agreement with respect to custody, the court shall award custody in accordance with the parents' agreement unless that agreement is not in the best interests of the child.

child support: Child support is calculated according to the income shares model. The age of majority is eighteen unless the child is still in high school at age eighteen, in which case child support continues until the child graduates from high school or reaches age nineteen, whichever occurs first.

Maine

residency requirement: (1) The petitioner must have lived in Maine for six months immediately prior to application for divorce; (2) the petitioner must live in Maine and the spouses must have been married in Maine; (3) the petitioner must live in Maine and the spouses must have lived in Maine while married; or (4) the respondent must live in Maine.

grounds for divorce: (1) Irreconcilable differences; (2) adultery; (3) impotency; (4) extreme cruelty; (5) abandonment for three years prior to the commencement of the action; (6) alcohol or drug abuse; (7) failure to provide for one's spouse even though one has the ability to do so; (8) cruel and abusive treatment; or (9) confinement for mental illness for at least seven consecutive years prior to the commencement of the action.

marital property: Marital property consists of all property acquired during the marriage. Marital property does not include gifts, inheritances, or property acquired prior to marriage. Marital property also does not include the appreciation of separate property, unless the separate property appreciated as a result of the efforts of either spouse during the marriage or the investment of marital property. The cutoff date for the acquisition of marital property is the date of a decree of legal separation.

property division: Marital property is divided equitably. Marital fault is not listed as a factor for consideration.

alimony: The court may award general alimony, rehabilitative alimony, or reimbursement alimony. Marital fault is not listed as a factor for consideration. The court will presume that general alimony should not be awarded if the spouses were married for less than ten years. If the spouses were married for between ten and twenty years, the court will presume that the duration of support should not exceed one-half the length of the marriage. The court may disregard these presumptions if their application would be inequitable or unjust in any given case. Reimbursement support may be awarded to achieve financial equity in exceptional circumstances, such as economic misconduct by a spouse or substantial contributions a spouse made toward the educational or occupational advancement of the other during the marriage. Reimbursement support will only be awarded if the reimbursement issues cannot be addressed through property division. Alimony terminates upon the death of either spouse, unless the court's order specifies otherwise.

child custody: Child custody is determined in accordance with the best interests of the child. The court must take domestic violence into account and how that violence has affected the child emotionally and the safety of the child. If parents have agreed to joint custody, the court will order joint custody unless such an arrangement would not be in the child's best interests.

child support: Child support is calculated according to the income-shares model. The age of majority is eighteen unless the child is still in high school at age eighteen, in which case child support continues until the child graduates from high school or reaches age nineteen, whichever occurs first.

Maryland

residency requirement: One spouse must have lived in Maryland for one year immediately prior to the application for divorce if the grounds for divorce occurred outside of Maryland. There is no residency requirement if the grounds for divorce occurred in Maryland. Where insanity is the ground for divorce, however, one spouse must have lived in Maryland for at least two years immediately prior to the application for divorce.

grounds for divorce: (1) Voluntarily living separate and apart without cohabitation for twelve months immediately prior to the application for divorce, and there is no reasonable prospect of reconciliation; (2) living separate and apart for two years without cohabitation prior to the application for divorce; (3) adultery; (4) abandonment for twelve months, where the abandonment is deliberate and final and there is no reasonable prospect of reconciliation; (5) conviction of a felony or misdemeanor if the respondent has been sentenced to serve at least three years or an indeterminate sentence, and has served twelve months of the sentence prior to the application for divorce; (6) confinement for mental illness for at least three years, and there is no hope of recovery; (7) cruelty, if there is no reasonable prospect of reconciliation; and (8) excessively vicious conduct, if there is no reasonable prospect of reconciliation.

marital property: Marital property consists of all property acquired during the marriage, including pensions and other retirement benefits, and any real estate held jointly by the spouses with rights of survivorship. Marital property does not include gifts, inheritances, or property acquired prior to marriage. Marital property also does not include property acquired in exchange for separate property.

property division: Marital property is divided equitably. The court may consider marital fault.

alimony: The court has the discretion to award alimony in an amount and duration it deems proper. The court may consider marital fault. Marital fault is not an automatic bar to alimony. Alimony terminates upon the death of either spouse, or the remarriage of the recipient.

child custody: Child custody is determined in accordance with the best interests of the child. There is no preference in favor of joint custody.

child support: Child support is calculated according to the income-shares model. The age of majority is eighteen.

Massachusetts

residency requirement: If the grounds for divorce did not occur in Massachusetts, the spouses must have lived in Massachusetts while married and one spouse must have lived in Massachusetts when the grounds for divorce occurred. Alternatively, the petitioner must have lived in Massachusetts for one year immediately prior to the application for divorce. If the grounds for divorce occurred in Massachusetts, it is sufficient simply if the petitioner resides in Massachusetts and intends to remain there permanently.

grounds for divorce: (1) Irretrievable breakdown of the marriage; (2) adultery; (3) impotency; (4) abandonment for one year; (5) alcohol or drug abuse; (6) cruel and abusive treatment; (7) failure to provide for one's spouse even though one has the ability to do so; (8) imprisonment for five years or more.

marital property: Marital property consists of all property owned by both spouses.

property division: Marital property is divided equitably. The court may consider marital fault, except where the ground for divorce is the irretrievable breakdown of the marriage.

alimony: The court has the discretion to award alimony in an amount and duration it deems proper. The court may consider marital fault, except when the ground for divorce is the irretrievable breakdown of the marriage.

child custody: Child custody is determined in accordance with the best interests of the child. There is no preference in favor of joint custody. The court may award joint legal and/or physical custody over one parent's objection. If the parents have reached an agreement with respect to custody, the court will order custody in accordance with that agreement unless the proposed arrangement is not in the best interests of the child.

child support: Child support is calculated according to the income-shares model. The age of majority is eighteen. The court may provide for child support to continue until the age of twenty-three when a child lives with a parent and is dependent upon that parent for support due to enrollment in an educational program.

Michigan

residency requirement: One spouse must have lived in Michigan for 180 days immediately prior to the application for divorce. If the grounds for the divorce occurred outside of Michigan, one spouse must have resided in Michigan for one year immediately prior to the application for divorce.

grounds for divorce: A breakdown of the marriage relationship to the extent that the objects of matrimony have been destroyed and there remains no reasonable likelihood that the marriage can be preserved.

marital property: Marital property consists of all property earned or acquired during the marriage, including vested pensions and retirement benefits. Where just and equitable, marital property also includes unvested pensions and retirement benefits. Marital property does not include gifts, inheritances, or property acquired prior to marriage. The court may divide separate property in addition to marital property if: (a) one spouse's share of marital property is not enough for his or her maintenance; or (b) the spouse who does not own the separate property contributed to the acquisition, improvement, or accumulation of the separate property.

property division: Marital property is divided equitably. The court may consider marital fault.

alimony: The court has the discretion to award alimony in an amount and duration it deems proper. The court may consider marital fault. Alimony terminates upon the recipient's remarriage.

child custody: Child custody is determined in accordance with the best interests of the child. The court must take domestic violence into account. There is no preference in favor of joint custody.

child support: Child support is calculated according to a variation of the income-shares model. The age of majority is eighteen unless the child is still in high school at age eighteen, in which case child support continues until the child graduates from high school or reaches the age of nineteen years and six months, whichever occurs first.

Minnesota

residency requirement: One spouse must have lived in Minnesota for at least 180 days immediately prior to the application for divorce.

grounds for divorce: Irretrievable breakdown of the marriage relationship.

marital property: Marital property consists of all property acquired during the marriage, including vested pensions and retirement benefits. Marital property does not include gifts, inheritances, or property acquired prior to marriage. Marital property also does not include property acquired in exchange for separate property or the appreciation of separate property. Where justice requires it, the court may include up to one-half of separate property as marital property.

property division: Marital property is divided equitably, without regard to marital fault.

alimony: The court has the discretion to award alimony in an amount and duration it deems proper, without regard to marital fault.

child custody: Child custody is calculated in accordance with the best interests of the child. The child must take into account the effect of domestic violence on the child. The court will presume that joint custody is not in the best interests of the child if one parent has committed domestic violence. If either parent requests joint legal custody, the court will presume that joint legal custody is in the child's best interests.

child support: Child support is calculated according to a variation of the variable percentage method. The age of majority is eighteen unless the child is still in high school at age eighteen, in which case child support continues until the child graduates from high school or reaches age twenty, whichever is sooner.

Mississippi

residency requirement: One spouse must have resided in Mississippi for six months immediately prior to the application for divorce.

grounds for divorce: (1) Irreconcilable differences; (2) impotency; (3) adultery; (4) being sentenced to imprisonment; (5) abandonment for one year; (6) alcohol abuse; (7) drug abuse; (8) habitual cruel and inhuman treatment; (9) insanity or idiocy at the time of marriage, if the petitioner did not know of such insanity or idiocy at the time of the marriage; (10) if one spouse was married to someone else at the time of the marriage; (11) if the wife was pregnant with someone else's child at the time of the marriage and the husband did not know of the pregnancy; (12) if the spouses are related together within degrees of kindred between whom marriage is prohibited by law; and (13) confinement for incurable insanity for at least three years immediately prior to the application for divorce.

marital property: Marital property consists of all property acquired during the marriage. Marital property does not include gifts, inheritances, or property acquired prior to marriage.

property division: Marital property is divided equitably. The court may consider marital fault.

alimony: The court has the discretion to award alimony in an amount and duration it deems proper. The court may consider marital fault.

child custody: Child custody is determined in accordance with the best interests of the child. If both parents agree to joint custody, the court will presume that joint custody is in the best interests of the child.

child support: Child support is calculated according to the variable percentage method. The age of majority is twenty-one unless the child graduates from high school and obtains full-time employment prior to age twenty-one.

Missouri

residency requirement: One spouse must have resided in Missouri for ninety days immediately prior to the application for divorce.

grounds for divorce: Irretrievable breakdown of the marriage with no reasonable likelihood that the marriage can be preserved. If one spouse denies under oath that the marriage is irretrievably broken, the petitioner will have to demonstrate that: (1) the respondent has committed adultery and the petitioner finds it intolerable to live with the respondent; (2) the respondent has behaved in such a way that the petitioner cannot reasonably be expected to live with the respondent; (3) the respondent has abandoned the petitioner for a continuous period of at least six months preceding the application for divorce; (4) the spouses have lived separate and apart by mutual consent for a continuous period of twelve months immediately prior to the application for divorce; or (5) the spouses have lived separate and apart for a continuous period of at least twenty-four months immediately prior to the application for divorce.

marital property: Marital property consists of all property acquired during the marriage. Marital property does not include gifts, inheritances, or property acquired prior to marriage. Marital property also does not include property acquired in exchange for separate property or the appreciation of separate property, unless the appreciation of separate property resulted from the efforts of either spouse or the investment of marital property. Separate property does not become marital property simply because it may have become commingled with marital property. The cutoff date for the acquisition of marital property is the date of a decree of legal separation or a decree of divorce.

property division: Marital property is divided equitably. The court may consider marital fault.

alimony: The court has the discretion to award alimony in an amount and duration it deems proper. The court may consider marital fault. Unless the court orders otherwise, alimony terminates upon the death of either spouse or the remarriage of the recipient.

child custody: Child custody is determined in accordance with the best interests of the child. The court must take domestic violence into account. The court may order joint custody over the objection of one parent.

child support: Child support is calculated according to the income-shares model. The age of majority is eighteen. Where the child is still in school at age eighteen, the court may order child support to continue until the child reaches age twenty-one.

Montana

residency requirement: One spouse must have lived in Montana for ninety days immediately prior to the application for divorce.

grounds for divorce: Irretrievable breakdown of the marriage.

marital property: Marital property consists of all property owned by both spouses.

property division: Marital property is divided equitably, without regard to marital fault. When dividing gifts, inheritances, property acquired prior to marriage, property acquired in exchange for the foregoing property, the appreciation of the foregoing property, or property acquired by a spouse after a decree of legal separation, the court shall consider the contributions of the other spouse to the marriage, including the nonmonetary contributions of a homemaker, the extent to which such contributions have facilitated the maintenance of such property, and whether or not the property division serves as an alternative to support arrangements.

alimony: The court has the discretion to award alimony in an amount and duration it deems proper, without regard to marital fault. Unless the court orders otherwise, alimony terminates upon the death of either spouse or the remarriage of the recipient.

child custody: Child custody is determined in accordance with the best interests of the child. The court must take domestic violence into account. There is no preference in favor of joint custody.

child support: Child support is calculated according to a variation of the Melson formula. The age of majority is eighteen unless the child is still in high school at age eighteen, in which case child support continues until the child graduates from high school or reaches age nineteen, whichever is sooner.

Nebraska

residency requirement: One spouse must have resided in Nebraska for one year immediately prior to the application for divorce, unless the spouses were married in Nebraska and one spouse has resided in Nebraska from the date of marriage until the date of the application for divorce.

grounds for divorce: Irretrievable breakdown of the marriage.

marital property: Marital property consists of all property acquired during the marriage. Marital property does not include gifts, inheritances, or property acquired prior to marriage.

property division: Marital property is divided equitably. Marital fault is not listed as a factor for consideration.

alimony: The court has the discretion to award alimony in an amount and duration it deems proper. Marital fault is not listed as a factor for consideration. Unless the court orders otherwise, alimony terminates upon the death of either spouse or the remarriage of the recipient.

child custody: Child custody is determined in accordance with the best interests of the child. The court must take domestic violence into account. The court may order joint custody over the objection of one or both parents.

child support: Child support is calculated according to the income shares model. The age of majority is nineteen.

Nevada

residency requirement: Unless the grounds for divorce occurred in Nevada, one spouse must have lived in Nevada for at least six weeks immediately prior to the application for divorce.

grounds for divorce: (1) Incompatibility; (2) living separate and apart for one year without cohabitation; and (3) insanity existing for two years prior to the application for divorce.

marital property: Marital property consists of all property acquired during the marriage, and all property held jointly by the spouses with rights of survivorship. Marital property does not include gifts, inheritances, property acquired prior to marriage, or property acquired as compensation for personal injury. Marital property also does not include the income from separate property.

property division: Marital property shall be divided equally, unless an equal division would be inequitable or inappropriate given the circumstances of the case. Marital fault is not listed as a factor for consideration. If one spouse contributed separate property to property held jointly by the spouses, the court may order a dollar-for-dollar reimbursement of that spouse's contribution to the extent the contribution can be traced to the acquisition or improvement of property held jointly. The term "contribution" includes a down payment, a payment for the acquisition or improvement of property, and a payment reducing the principal of a loan used to finance the purchase or improvement of property. The term "contribution" does not include a payment of interest on a loan used to finance the purchase or improvement of property, or a payment made for maintenance, insurance, or taxes on property. In determining whether a reimbursement is warranted, the court will consider the intention of the spouses in placing the property in joint names, the length of the marriage, and any other factor that the court considers relevant.

alimony: The court has the discretion to award alimony in an amount and duration it deems proper. Marital fault is not listed as a factor for consideration. Unless the court orders otherwise, alimony terminates upon the death of either spouse or the remarriage of the recipient.

child custody: Child custody is determined in accordance with the best interests of the child. The court must take domestic violence into account. Where both parents agree to joint custody, the court will presume that joint custody is in the best interests of the child.

child support: Child support is calculated according to the variable percentage model. The age of majority is eighteen unless the child is still in high school at the age of eighteen, in which case support continues until the child graduates from high school or reaches age nineteen, whichever occurs first.

New Hampshire

residency requirement: (1) The petitioner must have lived in New Hampshire for one year immediately preceding the application for divorce; (2) the petitioner must live in New Hampshire and the respondent must have been served with divorce papers in New Hampshire; or (3) both spouses must live in New Hampshire at the time of the application for divorce. In addition, the petitioner must have been living in New Hampshire at the time the cause of action for divorce occurred.

grounds for divorce: (1) Irreconcilable differences; (2) impotency; (3) adultery; (4) extreme cruelty; (5) conviction of and imprisonment for a crime punishable with imprisonment for more than one year; (6) if one spouse has treated the other in a manner that seriously injures the other's health or endangers the other's reason; (7) if one spouse has been missing for two or more years and has not been heard from; (8) alcohol abuse for two years; (9) if one spouse has joined any religious sect or society that professes to believe the relation of husband and wife unlawful, and that spouse has refused to cohabit with the other for six months; and (10) abandonment for two years.

marital property: Marital property consists of all property owned by both spouses, including vested and unvested retirement benefits.

property division: Marital property is divided equitably, without regard to marital fault. The court will presume that an equal division of marital property is equitable. The court may consider marital fault if the marital fault caused the breakdown of the marriage and caused substantial physical or mental pain and suffering, or resulted in substantial economic loss to the marital estate or the other spouse. The court may not consider marital fault if the ground for divorce is irreconcilable differences. The court may consider the fact that certain property was acquired prior to marriage or acquired by gift or inheritance in dividing marital property.

alimony: The court has the discretion to award alimony in an amount and duration it deems proper. The court may consider marital fault unless the ground for divorce is irreconcilable differences.

child custody: Child custody is determined in accordance with the best interests of the child. The court must take domestic violence into account. The court will presume that joint legal custody is in the best interests of the child.

child support: Child support is calculated according to the income-shares model. The age of majority is eighteen or the date the child graduates from high school, whichever is later.

New Jersey

residency requirement: One spouse must have lived in New Jersey for at least one year immediately prior to the application for divorce. If the ground for divorce is adultery that took place in New Jersey, it is sufficient if one spouse lived in New Jersey at the time of the adultery and continued to reside in New Jersey until the application for divorce.

grounds for divorce: (1) Living separate and apart for at least eighteen months and there is no reasonable prospect of reconciliation; (2) adultery; (3) extreme cruelty; (4) drug or alcohol abuse for a period of twelve or more consecutive months immediately prior to the application for divorce; (5) confinement for mental illness for twenty-four or more months immediately prior to the application for divorce; (6) imprisonment for eighteen or more consecutive months after marriage, provided that the spouses have not resumed habitation if the respondent has already been released; and (7) deviant sexual conduct voluntarily performed by the respondent and without the consent of the petitioner.

marital property: Marital property consists of all property acquired during the marriage. Marital property does not include gifts, inheritances, or property acquired prior to marriage.

property division: Marital property is divided equitably. Marital fault is not listed as a factor for consideration.

alimony: The court has the discretion to award permanent, rehabilitative, or reimbursement alimony in an amount and duration it deems proper. The court may consider marital fault. Alimony terminates upon the death of the payer spouse and the remarriage of the recipient. In general, rehabilitative alimony will not terminate upon the remarriage of the recipient.

child custody: Child custody is determined in accordance with the best interests of the child. The court must take domestic violence into account. There is no preference in favor of joint custody.

child support: Child support is calculated according to the income-shares model. The age of majority is eighteen. The court may provide for child support to continue past the age of eighteen if the child is still in high school at age eighteen.

New Mexico

residency requirement: One spouse must have lived in New Mexico for at least six months immediately prior to the application for divorce, and must be domiciled in New Mexico. The term "domicile" means that an individual is physically present in New Mexico, has a place of residence in New Mexico, and intends to live in New Mexico permanently or indefinitely.

grounds for divorce: (1) Incompatibility, which exists when, because of discord or conflict of personalities, the legitimate ends of the marriage relationship are destroyed preventing any reasonable expectation of reconciliation; (2) cruel and inhuman treatment; (3) adultery; and (4) abandonment.

marital property: Marital property consists of all property acquired during the marriage. Marital property does not include gifts, inheritances, or property acquired prior to marriage. Marital property also does not include the income from separate property. The cutoff date for the acquisition of marital property is the date of the divorce decree.

property division: Marital property is divided equally.

alimony: The court has the discretion to award permanent, rehabilitative, or reimbursement alimony in an amount and duration it deems proper. Marital fault is not listed as a factor for consideration. Alimony terminates upon death of the recipient.

child custody: Child custody is determined in accordance with the best interests of the child. The court must take domestic violence into account. The court will factor in the child's preference as to custody if the child is over the age of fourteen. The court will presume that joint custody is in the best interests of the child. When the parents agree as to custody, the court will award custody in accordance with the parents' agreement unless the proposed arrangement is not in the best interests of the child.

child support: Child support is calculated according to the income-shares model. The age of majority is eighteen.

New York

residency requirement: (1) One spouse must have lived in New York for two years immediately prior to the application for divorce; (2) the grounds for divorce occurred in New York and both spouses must live in New York at the time of the application for divorce; or (3) one spouse must have lived in New York for one year immediately prior to the application for divorce and (a) the spouses must have been married in New York; (b) the spouses must have resided in New York while married; or (c) the grounds for divorce occurred in New York.

grounds for divorce: (1) Living separate and apart pursuant to a separation agreement, separation decree or judgment of separation for one year; (2) cruel and inhuman treatment that so endangers the physical or mental well-being of the petitioner as to render it unsafe or improper for the petitioner to cohabit with the respondent; (3) abandonment for one year; and (4) adultery.

marital property: Marital property consists of all property acquired during the marriage. Marital property does not include gifts, inheritances, property acquired prior to marriage, or property acquired as compensation for a personal injury. Marital property also does not include property acquired in exchange for separate property or the appreciation of separate property, unless the appreciation resulted from the efforts of the other spouse. The cutoff date for the acquisition of marital property is the date of execution of a separation agreement or the commencement of a matrimonial action.

property division: Marital property is divided equitably. The court will not consider marital fault unless it is so egregious as to shock the conscience.

alimony: The court has the discretion to award permanent, rehabilitative, or reimbursement alimony in an amount and duration it deems proper. The court will not consider marital fault unless it is so egregious as to shock the conscience. Alimony terminates upon death of either spouse or the remarriage of the recipient.

child custody: Child custody is determined in accordance with the best interests of the child. There is no preference in favor of joint custody.

child support: Child support is calculated according to the income-shares model. The age of majority is twenty-one.

North Carolina

residency requirement: One spouse must have lived in North Carolina for at least six months immediately prior to the application for divorce.

grounds for divorce: (1) Living separate and apart for one year; and (2) living separate and apart for three years without cohabitation by reason of one spouse's incurable insanity.

marital property: Marital property consists of all property acquired during the marriage, including all vested and unvested retirement benefits. Marital property does not include gifts, inheritances, or property acquired prior to marriage. Marital property also does not include property acquired in exchange for separate property, the appreciation of separate property, or the income from separate property. Separate property remains separate property even if it is exchanged for property held in the name of both spouses, unless a contrary intention is expressly stated in the conveyance. The cutoff date for the acquisition of marital property is the date of separation of the spouses.

property division: Marital property is divided equally, unless an equal division of marital property would be inequitable. Marital fault is not listed as a factor for consideration. In general, one spouse may not receive more than half of the other spouse's retirement/pension benefits.

alimony: The court has the discretion to award alimony in an amount and duration it deems proper. The court may consider marital fault. The court may not award alimony to a spouse who engaged in an act of illicit sexual behavior during the marriage and prior to the separation. The court shall award alimony to the less well-off spouse if the wealthier spouse engaged in an act of illicit sexual behavior during the marriage and prior to the separation. Where both spouses engaged in illicit sexual behavior, the issue of alimony is left to the discretion of the court. The court will not consider any illicit sexual behavior that was condoned or forgiven by the other spouse. Alimony terminates upon the death of either spouse. Alimony also terminates if the recipient remarries or begins cohabiting with someone else.

child custody: Child custody is determined in accordance with the best interests of the child. The court must take domestic violence into account. The court will consider joint custody upon the request of either spouse.

child support: Child support is determined according to the income-shares model. The age of majority is eighteen. If the child is still in school at age eighteen, the court may extend child support until the child reaches age twenty.

North Dakota

residency requirement: The petitioner must have lived in North Dakota for at least six months immediately prior to the application for divorce, or at least six months prior to the issuance of the divorce decree.

grounds for divorce: (1) Irreconcilable differences; (2) adultery; (3) extreme cruelty; (4) abandonment for one year; (5) failing to provide for one's spouse when one has the ability to do so for one year; (6) drug or alcohol abuse for one year; and (7) conviction of a felony.

marital property: Marital property consists of all property owned by both spouses.

property division: Marital property is divided equitably. The court may consider marital fault.

alimony: The court has the discretion to award alimony in an amount and duration it deems proper. The court may consider marital fault.

child custody: Child custody is determined in accordance with the best interests of the child. The court must take domestic violence into account. In certain cases, the court will presume that it is not in a child's best interests to award custody to a parent who has committed domestic violence. There is no preference in favor of joint custody.

child support: Child support is calculated according to the variable percentage model. The age of majority is nineteen or the child's graduation from high school, whichever occurs first.

Ohio

residency requirement: The petitioner must have lived in Ohio for at least six months immediately prior to the application for divorce.

grounds for divorce: (1) Incompatibility; (2) living separate and apart for one year without cohabitation; (3) abandonment for one year; (4) if either spouse was married to someone else at the time of the marriage; (5) adultery; (6) extreme cruelty; (7) fraudulent contract; (8) failing to support one's spouse even though one has the ability to do so; (9) alcohol abuse; (10) imprisonment at the time of the application for divorce; and (11) procurement of a divorce outside of Ohio, which does not release the other spouse from the obligations of marriage in Ohio.

marital property: Marital property consists of all property acquired during the marriage. Marital property does not include gifts, inheritances, or property acquired prior to marriage. Marital property also does not include compensation for personal injury, except to the extent the compensation is a reimbursement for lost wages or medical or other expenses. Marital property also does not include passive income from and the passive appreciation of separate property. Marital property includes the income and appreciation of separate property when that income or appreciation was due to the efforts of either spouse or the contribution of marital property. Separate property remains separate even if it is commingled with marital property, unless the separate property is not traceable. The cutoff date for the acquisition of marital property is the date of the final hearing in an action for divorce/legal separation or the date of the decree of legal separation, unless the application of those cutoff dates would be inequitable.

property division: Marital property is divided equally, unless an equal division of marital property would be unjust or inappropriate. Marital fault is not listed as a factor for consideration.

alimony: The court has the discretion to award alimony in an amount and duration it deems proper. Marital fault is not listed as a factor for consideration.

child custody: Child custody is determined in accordance with the best interests of the child. The court must take domestic violence into account. If either parent requests joint custody, the court may award joint custody if it is in the best interests of the child. If both parents jointly file a parenting plan, the court shall order custody in accordance with the parenting plan if the proposed arrangement is in the best interests of the child.

child support: Child support is calculated according to the income-shares model. The age of majority is eighteen unless the child is still in high school at age eighteen, in which case child support continues until the child graduates from high school or reaches age nineteen, whichever is sooner.

Oklahoma

residency requirement: One spouse must have lived in Oklahoma for at least six months immediately prior to the application for divorce.

grounds for divorce: (1) Incompatibility; (2) abandonment for one year; (3) adultery; (4) impotency; (5) extreme cruelty; (6) if the wife was pregnant with someone else's child at the time of the marriage; (7) fraudulent contract; (8) alcohol abuse; (9) failing to support one's spouse even though one has the ability to do so; (10) imprisonment for commission of a felony at the time of the application for divorce (11) insanity for five years; and (12) procurement of a final divorce decree in another state, which does not release the other spouse from the obligations of the marriage in Oklahoma.

marital property: Marital property consists of all property acquired during the marriage. Marital property does not include gifts, inheritances, or property acquired prior to marriage. Marital property also does not include property acquired as a compensation for personal injury, except to the extent that such property reimburses for losses incurred by the marital estate, such as lost wages.

property division: Marital property is divided equitably, without regard to marital fault.

alimony: The court has the discretion to award alimony in an amount and duration it deems proper. The court will rarely consider marital fault.

child custody: Child custody is determined in accordance with the best interests of the child. There is no preference in favor of joint custody.

child support: Child support is calculated according to the income-shares model. The age of majority is eighteen, unless the child is still in high school at eighteen, in which case child support continues until the child graduates from high school or reaches age nineteen, whichever occurs first.

Oregon

residency requirement: One spouse must have lived in Oregon for at least six months immediately prior to the application for divorce if the spouses were not married in Oregon or if the grounds for divorce are irreconcilable differences. If the spouses were married in Oregon and the grounds for divorce are not irreconcilable differences, the only requirement is that one spouse lives in Oregon.

grounds for divorce: (1) Irreconcilable differences have caused the irremediable breakdown of the marriage; (2) either spouse was incapable of entering into the marriage contract because he or she had not reached the legal age at the time or otherwise lacked capacity to consent; or (3) the consent of the other spouse to the marriage was obtained by force or duress.

marital property: Marital property consists of all property owned by both spouses.

property division: Marital property is divided equitably, without regard to marital fault.

alimony: The court has the discretion to award general, rehabilitative, or reimbursement alimony in an amount and duration it deems proper, without regard to marital fault.

child custody: Child custody is determined in accordance with the best interests of the child. The court must take domestic violence into account. The court will only order joint custody where both parents agree to joint custody.

child support: Child support is calculated according to the income-shares model. The age of majority is eighteen. The court may extend child support beyond age eighteen if the child is still in high school at age eighteen.

Pennsylvania

residency requirement: One spouse must have lived in Pennsylvania for at least six months immediately prior to the application for divorce.

grounds for divorce: (1) Irretrievable breakdown of the marriage without any prospect of reconciliation if the spouses have lived separate and apart for at least two years; (2) abandonment for one or more years; (3) adultery; (4) if one spouse, by cruel and barbarous treatment, endangered the life or health of the injured and innocent spouse; (5) if one spouse was married to someone else at the time of the marriage; (6) imprisonment for two or more years; (7) indignities so as to render the other spouse's condition intolerable and life burdensome; and (8) confinement for insanity or serious mental illness for at least eighteen months.

marital property: Marital property consists of all property acquired during the marriage. Marital property includes the appreciation of separate property that occurred during the marriage. Marital property does not include gifts, inheritances, property acquired prior to marriage, or any payment received in connection with any cause of action or claim that accrued prior to the marriage or after the date of final separation. Marital property also does not include property acquired in exchange for property acquired prior to marriage. The cutoff date for the acquisition of marital property is the date of the spouses' final separation.

property division: Marital property is divided equitably, without regard to marital fault.

alimony: The court has the discretion to award alimony in an amount and duration it deems proper, without regard to marital fault. Alimony terminates upon the death of either spouse. Alimony may not be awarded if the spouse seeking support begins cohabiting with someone of the opposite sex after the divorce.

child custody: Child custody is determined in accordance with the best interests of the child. The court must take domestic violence into account. There is no preference in favor of joint custody.

child support: Child support is calculated according to the income-shares model. The age of majority is eighteen. The court may order child support to continue beyond the age of eighteen and may also order parents to contribute to the costs of postsecondary education, such as college.

Rhode Island

residency requirement: One spouse must have lived in Rhode Island for at least one year immediately prior to the application for divorce.

grounds for divorce: (1) Irreconcilable differences that have caused the irremediable breakdown of the marriage; (2) living separate and apart for three years; (3) impotency; (4) adultery; (5) extreme cruelty; (6) abandonment for five years (or less in the discretion of the court); (7) alcohol abuse; (8) drug abuse; (9) the husband's failure to support his wife even though he has the ability to do so; and (10) gross behavior and wickedness repugnant to and in violation of the marriage covenant.

marital property: Marital property consists of all property acquired during the marriage. Marital property does not include gifts, inheritances, or property acquired prior to marriage. Marital property includes the appreciation of separate property that resulted from the efforts of either spouse during the marriage. Marital property also includes the income from separate property.

property division: Marital property is divided equitably. The court may consider marital fault.

alimony: The court has the discretion to award alimony in an amount and duration it deems proper. The court may consider marital fault. Alimony terminates upon the remarriage of the recipient.

child custody: Child custody is determined in accordance with the best interests of the child. The court must take domestic violence into account. There is no preference in favor of joint custody.

child support: Child support is calculated according to the income-shares model. The age of majority is eighteen. If the child is still in high school at age eighteen, the court may extend child support until the child reaches age nineteen.

South Carolina

residency requirement: One spouse must have lived in South Carolina for at least one year immediately prior to the application for divorce. If both spouses live in South Carolina, the petitioner must only have lived in South Carolina for three months immediately prior to the application for divorce.

grounds for divorce: (1) Living separate and apart for one year; (2) adultery; (3) desertion for one year; (4) physical cruelty; and (5) alcohol or drug abuse.

marital property: Marital property consists of all property acquired during the marriage. Marital property does not include gifts, inheritances, or property acquired prior to marriage. Marital property also does not include property acquired in exchange for separate property or the appreciation of separate property, except to the extent that the appreciation resulted directly or indirectly from the efforts of the other spouse during the marriage. The cutoff date for the acquisition of marital property is the earliest of: (a) the entry of a temporary alimony order; (b) the formal signing of a written property or marital settlement agreement; or (c) the entry of a permanent order of alimony or a permanent order approving a property or marital settlement agreement.

property division: Marital property is divided equitably. The court may consider marital fault.

alimony: The court has the discretion to award general, rehabilitative, or reimbursement alimony in an amount and duration it deems proper. The court may consider marital fault. A court may not award alimony to a spouse who has committed adultery. Alimony terminates upon the death of either spouse. Alimony also terminates if the recipient remarries or begins cohabiting with someone else.

child custody: Child custody is determined in accordance with the best interests of the child. There is no preference in favor of joint custody.

child support: Child support is calculated according to the income-shares model. The age of majority is eighteen. The court may order child support to continue until age nineteen or the date the child graduates from high school, whichever occurs first.

South Dakota

residency requirement: The petitioner must live in South Dakota at the time of the application for divorce and must continue living in South Dakota until the date of the divorce decree.

grounds for divorce: (1) Irreconcilable differences; (2) adultery; (3) extreme cruelty; (4) abandonment for one year; (4) failure to provide for one's spouse when one has the ability to do so for one year; (5) alcohol abuse for one year; and (6) conviction of a felony.

marital property: Marital property consists of all property owned by both spouses.

property division: Marital property is divided equitably, without regard to marital fault.

alimony: The court has the discretion to award alimony in an amount and duration it deems proper. The court may consider marital fault.

child custody: Child custody is determined in accordance with the best interests of the child. There is no preference in favor of joint custody.

child support: Child support is calculated according to the income-shares model. The age of majority is eighteen, unless the child is still in high school at age eighteen, in which case the age of majority is nineteen.

Tennessee

residency requirement: If the petitioner was not a resident of Tennessee at the time the grounds for divorce occurred, one spouse must have lived in Tennessee for six months.

grounds for divorce: (1) Irreconcilable differences; (2) living separate and apart for two or more years, and there are no minor children of the spouses; (3) impotency at the time of the marriage and continuing until the time of the application for divorce; (4) either spouse knowingly entered into a second marriage while the first marriage was still in effect; (5) adultery; (6) abandonment for one year; (7) conviction of a crime that renders the spouse infamous; (8) being sentenced to imprisonment for conviction of a felony; (9) attempting the life of the other spouse, by poison or any other means showing malice; (10) refusal to move with one's spouse to Tennessee without reasonable cause and being willfully absent from the spouse residing in Tennessee for two years; (11) if the wife was pregnant with someone else's child at the time of the marriage without her husband's knowledge; (12) drug or alcohol abuse arising after the marriage; (13) cruel and inhuman treatment so as to render cohabitation unsafe and improper; (14) indignities so as to render the spouse's position intolerable; and (15) if one spouse has turned the other out of doors without cause and has failed to provide for the other spouse even though he or she has had the ability to do so.

marital property: Marital property consists of all property acquired during the marriage, including vested and unvested retirement benefits and stock options. Marital property does not include gifts, inheritances, or property acquired prior to marriage. Marital property also does not include compensation for a personal injury, such as workers' compensation and social security disability payments, except to the extent that such property compensates for lost wages, medical expenses, and property damage to marital property. Marital property also does not include property acquired in exchange for separate property or the income from and appreciation of separate property. However, marital property includes the income from and appreciation of separate property wherein both spouses substantially contributed to the separate property's preservation and appreciation. The term "substantial contribution" includes the direct or indirect contribution of a spouse as a homemaker, wage earner, parent, or family financial manager. The cutoff date for the acquisition of marital property is the date of the final divorce hearing or the date of an order of legal separation when the court has made a final disposition of property.

property division: Marital property is divided equitably, without regard to marital fault.

alimony: The court has the discretion to award alimony in an amount and duration it deems proper. The court may consider marital fault. Alimony terminates upon the death or remarriage of the recipient. Alimony may also terminate if the recipient begins cohabiting with someone else.

child custody: Child custody is determined in accordance with the best interests of the child. There is no preference in favor of joint custody. If the parents have agreed to joint custody, the court will presume that joint custody is in the best interests of the child.

child support: Child support is determined according to the variable percentage method. The age of majority is eighteen.

Texas

residency requirement: One spouse must have lived in Texas for at least six months immediately prior to the application for divorce.

grounds for divorce: (1) The marriage has become insupportable because of discord or conflict of personalities that destroys the legitimate ends of the marital relationship and prevents any reasonable expectation of reconciliation; (2) living separate and apart without cohabitation for three years; (3) abandonment for one year; (4) adultery; (5) conviction of a felony and imprisonment for over one year; (6) cruel treatment; and (7) confinement for mental illness for three years.

marital property: Marital property consists of all property acquired during the marriage. Marital property does not include gifts, inheritances, or property acquired prior to marriage. Marital property also does not include property acquired as compensation for personal injuries, to the extent that the property does not compensate for losses to the marital estate.

property division: Marital property is divided equitably. The court may consider marital fault.

alimony: The court has the discretion to award alimony in an amount and duration it deems proper, provided that the court may only order maintenance in cases where (1) the marriage lasted for ten years or longer or (2) the spouse from whom alimony is sought committed a family offense. The court may consider marital fault. The court will presume that alimony is not warranted unless the spouse seeking support has exercised diligence in seeking suitable employment or developing the necessary skills to become self-supporting during a period of separation and during the time the divorce dispute is pending. This presumption does not apply to spouses who suffer from an incapacitating physical or mental disability. The court may not order alimony that remains in effect for more than three years after the date of the order, and shall limit the duration of support to the shortest reasonable period that allows the spouse seeking maintenance to meet his or her reasonable needs by obtaining appropriate employment or developing an appropriate skill, unless the ability of that spouse to provide for his or her minimum reasonable needs through employment is substantially or totally diminished because of physical or mental disability, duties as the custodian of an infant or young child, or another compelling impediment to gainful employment. This limitation does not apply to spouses who suffer from an incapacitating physical or mental disability that prevents them from being able to support themselves through appropriate employment. The court may also not order support that exceeds the lesser of (a) $2,500; or (b) 20 percent of the spouse's average monthly gross income. Alimony terminates upon the death of either spouse. Alimony also terminates if the recipient remarries or begins cohabiting with someone else.

child custody: Child custody is determined in accordance with the best interests of the child. The court must take domestic violence into account. The court will not award joint custody in cases involving domestic violence, and the court will presume that it is not in the best interests of a child to award custody to a parent who has committed domestic violence. There is no preference in favor of joint custody.

child support: Child support is determined according to the variable percentage method. The age of majority is eighteen. The court may extend child support beyond age eighteen if the child is still in high school at age eighteen.

Utah

residency requirement: One spouse must have lived in Utah for at least three months immediately prior to the application for divorce.

grounds for divorce: (1) Irreconcilable differences; (2) living separate and apart under a decree of separate maintenance for three years without cohabitation; (3) impotency at the time of marriage; (4) adultery; (5) abandonment for more than one year; (6) failure to provide for one's spouse even though one has the ability to do so; (7) alcohol abuse; (8) conviction for a felony; (9) cruel treatment to the extent of causing bodily injury or great mental distress; and (10) incurable insanity.

marital property: Marital property consists of all property acquired during the marriage. Marital property does not include gifts, inheritances, or property acquired prior to marriage. When justice requires it, the court may also include separate property as marital property.

property division: Marital property is divided equally, unless it would be inequitable to do so under the circumstances of the case. The court may not consider marital fault. Property acquired by gift and inheritance is generally awarded to the spouse who owns the property unless (1) the other spouse contributed to the maintenance, enhancement, or protection of such property; (2) the property was commingled with marital property; or (3) the property was gifted to the other spouse. If one spouse's earning capacity has been greatly enhanced through the efforts of both spouses during the marriage, the court may make a compensating adjustment in dividing marital property.

alimony: The court has the discretion to award alimony in an amount and duration it deems proper. The court may consider marital fault.

Under appropriate circumstances, the court may attempt to equalize the spouses' respective standards of living in awarding support. If one spouse's earning capacity has been greatly enhanced through the efforts of both spouses during the marriage, the court may make a compensating adjustment in awarding support. In determining support in cases of very short-term marriages, the court will generally restore spouses to their pre-marital conditions. Except where extenuating circumstances justify the payment of alimony for a longer period of time, alimony may not be awarded for a period longer than the length of the marriage. Alimony terminates upon the death of either spouse. Alimony also terminates if the recipient remarries or begins living with someone else.

child custody: Child custody is determined in accordance with the best interests of the child. The court must take the parents' moral standards into account. The court will give particular weight to the preference of a child of the age of sixteen years or more. The court may not discriminate against a parent due to a disability. The court may award joint custody when both parents have requested joint custody and joint custody is in the child's best interests.

child support: Child support is calculated according to the income-shares model. The age of majority is eighteen. The court may order support to continue until the child reaches age twenty-one.

Vermont

residency requirement: One spouse must have lived in Vermont for at least six months. A divorce will only be decreed if one spouse has lived in Vermont for one year immediately prior to the date of the final divorce hearing. Temporary absence from Vermont due to illness, employment in another state, service as a member of the armed services, or another legitimate reason shall not affect the six-month or one-year periods.

grounds for divorce: (1) Living separate and apart for six consecutive months and a court finds that resumption of marital relations is not reasonably probable; (2) adultery; (3) being sentenced to imprisonment at hard labor for three years or more and that spouse is actually in prison at the time of the application for divorce; (4) cruel and inhuman treatment of intolerable severity; (5) abandonment or when either spouse has been absent for seven years and has not been heard from during that time; (6) failing to provide for one's spouse even though one has the ability to do so; and (7) incurable insanity.

marital property: Marital property consists of all property owned by both spouses.

property division: Marital property is divided equitably. The court may consider marital fault.

alimony: The court has the discretion to award alimony in an amount and duration it deems proper. Marital fault is not listed as a factor for consideration.

child custody: Child custody is determined in accordance with the best interests of the child. The court must take domestic violence into account. If the parents do not agree to joint custody, the court will award one parent sole custody.

child support: Child support is calculated according to the income-shares model. The age of majority is eighteen. The court may order child support to continue until the child graduates from high school.

Virginia

residency requirement: One spouse must have lived in Virginia for at least six months prior to the application for divorce.

grounds for divorce: (1) Living separate and apart for one year; (2) living separate and apart for six months, wherein the spouses have entered into a separation agreement and there are no minor children of the marriage; (3) adultery, provided that the act occurred within five years of the application for divorce and the spouses did not voluntarily cohabit after knowledge of the adultery; (4) a felony conviction after the marriage resulting in a sentence of imprisonment for more than one year, provided that cohabitation has not been resumed after imprisonment; (5) cruelty, causing reasonable apprehension of bodily hurt, provided that the application for divorce is made within one year of the cruel acts; and (6) abandonment for one year.

marital property: Marital property consists of all property acquired during the marriage, including pensions and retirement benefits, and all property held jointly by the spouses. Marital property does not include gifts, inheritances, or property acquired prior to marriage. Marital property also does not include personal injury and workers' compensation recoveries, except to the extent that the recoveries are attributable to lost wages or medical expenses not covered by health insurance during the marriage. Marital property does not include property acquired in exchange for separate property, provided that the property is maintained as separate property. Marital property also does not include the income from separate property, except to the extent that the income resulted from the efforts of either spouse. Marital property also does not include the appreciation of separate property, except to the extent that the appreciation resulted from the investment of marital property or the significant efforts of either spouse. When marital property and separate property are commingled, resulting in the loss of identity of the contributed property, the contributed property shall be deemed transmuted to the category of property receiving the contribution. When marital property and separate property are commingled into newly acquired property, resulting in the loss of identity of the contributing properties, the commingled property shall be deemed transmuted to marital property. When separate property is retitled to the names of both spouses, the retitled property is deemed transmuted to marital property. To the extent the contributed/retitled property is traceable and was not a gift, however, the contributed/retitled property shall retain its original classification. The cutoff date for the acquisition of marital property is the date of the spouses' final separation.

property division: Marital property is divided equitably. The court may take marital fault into account. The court may not direct payment of more than half of one spouse's pension/retirement benefits to the other spouse.

alimony: The court has the discretion to award alimony in an amount and duration it deems proper. The court may consider marital fault. The court may not award support to a spouse who has committed adultery, unless it would be unjust to deny alimony given the respective degrees of fault during the marriage and the relative economic circumstances of the spouses. Alimony terminates upon the death of either spouse. Alimony also terminates if the recipient remarries or begins with someone else for one year, unless the termination of support would be unconscionable.

child custody: Child custody is calculated in accordance with the best interests of the child. The court must take domestic violence into account. There is no preference in favor of joint custody.

child support: Child support is calculated according to the income-shares model. The age of majority is eighteen unless the child is still in high school at age eighteen, in which case child support continues until the child reaches age nineteen or graduates from high school, whichever occurs first.

Washington

residency requirement: One spouse must live in Washington.

grounds for divorce: Irretrievable breakdown of the marriage.

marital property: Marital property consists of all property acquired during the marriage. Marital property does not include gifts, inheritances, or property acquired prior to marriage. Marital property also does not include income from separate property.

property division: Marital property is divided equitably, without regard to marital fault.

alimony: The court has the discretion to award alimony in an amount and duration it deems proper, without regard to marital fault. Alimony terminates upon the death of either spouse or the remarriage of the recipient.

child custody: Child custody is determined in accordance with the best interests of the child. There is no preference in favor of joint custody.

child support: Child support is calculated according to the income-shares model. The age of majority is eighteen. The court may provide for child support to continue until the child graduates from high school.

West Virginia

residency requirement: If the spouses were married in West Virginia, one spouse must live in West Virginia at the time of the application for divorce. If the spouses were not married in West Virginia, then one spouse must have lived in West Virginia for at least one full year immediately prior to the application for divorce. If adultery is the ground for divorce and the respondent does not reside in West Virginia and cannot be personally served within West Virginia, the petitioner must have lived in West Virginia for at least one year immediately prior to the application for divorce.

grounds for divorce: (1) Irreconcilable differences; (2) living separate and apart for one year; (3) cruel or inhuman treatment, including but not limited to reasonable apprehension of bodily harm, false accusation of adultery or homosexuality, or conduct or treatment that tends to destroy the mental or physical well-being, happiness, and welfare of the other and render continued cohabitation unsafe or unendurable; (4) adultery; (5) conviction for a felony where the conviction is final; (6) confinement for permanent and incurable insanity for three years immediately prior to the application for divorce; (7) drug or alcohol abuse arising after the marriage; (8) abandonment for six months; and (9) abuse or neglect of a child of either or both of the spouses.

marital property: Marital property consists of all property acquired during the marriage. Marital property does not include gifts, inheritances, or property acquired prior to marriage. Marital property also does not include property acquired in exchange for property acquired before the marriage, or any passive appreciation of separate property. Marital property includes the appreciation of separate property that results from the efforts of either spouse during the marriage or the contribution or investment of marital property. The cutoff date for the acquisition of marital property is the final separation of the spouses.

property division: Marital property is divided equally, unless it would be inequitable to do so. The court may not consider marital fault. In dividing gifts and inheritances, the court will give preference to the spouse who received the property. In awarding business interests, the court will give preference to the spouse having the closer involvement, larger ownership interest, or greater dependency upon the business entity for income or other resources. The court will further attempt to award marital property interests in a business in order to protect the business from undue hardship or interference caused by one spouse.

alimony: The court has the discretion to award alimony in an amount and duration it deems proper. The court may consider marital fault.

child custody: Child custody is determined in accordance with the best interests of the child. The court must take domestic violence into account. The court will attempt to accommodate the reasonable custodial preference of a child over the age of fourteen. Wherever possible, the court will allocate custodial responsibility according to the proportion of time each parent spent taking care of the child prior to the parents' separation. Provided that both parents have been exercising a reasonable share of parenting functions for the child, the court shall presume that an award of joint legal custody is in the child's best interests.

child support: Child support is determined according to the income-shares model. The age of majority is eighteen. If the child is still in high school at age eighteen, the court may order child support to continue beyond age eighteen, but in no event beyond age twenty.

Wisconsin

residency requirement: One spouse must have lived in Wisconsin for at least six months immediately prior to the application for divorce.

grounds for divorce: Irretrievable breakdown of the marriage.

marital property: Marital property consists of all property acquired during the marriage. Marital property does not include gifts, inheritances, or property acquired prior to marriage. Marital property also does not include property acquired in exchange for separate property. Wherein justice requires it, the court may also divide separate property in addition to marital property.

property division: The court will divide marital property equally, unless it would be inequitable to do so. The court may not consider marital fault.

alimony: The court has the discretion to award alimony in an amount and duration it deems proper. Marital fault is not listed as a factor for consideration.

child custody: Child custody is determined in accordance with the best interests of the child. The court must take domestic violence into account. The court shall presume that joint legal custody is in the child's best interests. The court will provide for physical custody in a manner that provides both parents meaningful time with the child.

child support: Child support is calculated according to the variable percentage method. The age of majority is eighteen unless the child is still in high school at age eighteen, in which case child support continues until the child graduates from high school or reaches age nineteen, whichever occurs first.

Wyoming

residency requirement: (1) The petitioner must have lived in Wyoming for at least sixty days immediately prior to the application for divorce; or (2) the spouses must have been married in Wyoming and the petitioner must have lived in Wyoming from the date of the marriage until the date of the application for divorce.

grounds for divorce: (1) Irreconcilable differences in the marital relationship; and (2) confinement for incurable insanity for at least two years immediately prior to the application for divorce.

marital property: Marital property consists of all property acquired during the marriage.

property division: Marital property will be divided equitably. The court may consider marital fault.

alimony: The court has the discretion to award alimony in an amount and duration it deems proper. The court may consider marital fault.

child custody: Child custody is determined in accordance with the best interests of the child. The court must take domestic violence into account. There is no preference in favor of joint custody.

child support: Child support is calculated according to the income-shares model. The age of majority is eighteen unless the child is still in high school at age eighteen, in which case child support continues until the child graduates from high school or an equivalent program, but in no event shall child support continue beyond age twenty.

Appendix B

Attorney and Mediator Referral Sources

American Bar Association
541 N. Fairbanks Court
Chicago, Illinois 60611
1-800-285-2221

- Provides a list of reputable lawyer referral services for every state.
- Available online at www.abanet.org/legalservices/lris/directory.html or simply go to www.abanet.org and click on "General Public Resources" and then on "Lawyer Referral Services."

The Best Lawyers in America
129 First Avenue
Aiken, South Carolina 29801
(803)-648-0300

- Provides a list of the best family law lawyers in America based on peer review evaluations by other lawyers; widely regarded as the preeminent referral guide to the legal profession.
- Available online at www.bestlawyers.com.
- The most recent edition of *The Best Lawyers in America* should also be available at your local law library.

Association for Conflict Resolution
1527 New Hampshire Avenue, N.W.
Washington, D.C. 20036
(202)-667-9700

- Provides a list of divorce/family dispute mediators who have met specified training and experience requirements.
- Available online at www.acresolution.org—click on "Referrals and Training."
- When looking online, remember to check the mediator's biography to ensure that he or she is a member of the Family section.

Mediate.com
P.O. Box 5190
Eugene, Oregon 97405
(541)-345-1629

- Will provide you with a list of mediators targeted to your needs and located in your area.
- Contact mediate.com online at www.mediate.com—click on "Mediator Referral" and complete the form that follows.

Appendix C

Suggested Further Reading

Reconciliation

Robert Stephan Cohen, *Reconcilable Differences: 7 Essential Tips to Remaining Together from a Top Matrimonial Lawyer* (Simon & Schuster, 2002).

The Divorce Litigation Process

James T. Friedman, *The Divorce Handbook: Your Basic Guide to Divorce* (Random House, 1999).

The Financial Aspects of Divorce

Violet Woodhouse et al., *Divorce and Money: How to Make the Best Financial Decisions During Divorce* (Nolo, 2002).

Bruce L. Richman, *J.K. Lasser Pro Guide to Tax and Financial Issues in Divorce* (John Wiley, 2002).

Domestic Violence

Dawn Bradley Berry, *The Domestic Violence Sourcebook* (McGraw-Hill, 2000).

Meg Kennedy Dugan and Roger R. Hock, *It's My Life Now: Starting Over After an Abusive Relationship or Domestic Violence* (Routledge, 2000).

Child Custody Disputes

James W. Stewart and Terry Johnston, *The Child Custody Book: How to Protect Your Children and Win Your Case* (Impact, 2000).

Visitation and Shared Parenting

Isolina Ricci, *Mom's House, Dad's House: Making Two Homes for Your Child* (Fireside, 1997).

Brette McWhorter Sember, *The Visitation Handbook: Your Complete Guide to Parenting Apart* (Sphinx, 2002).

Divorce Mediation

Paula James, *The Divorce Mediation Handbook: Everything You Need to Know* (Jossey-Bass, 1997).

Do-it-Yourself Divorces

Daniel Sitarz, *Divorce Yourself: The National No-Fault Divorce Kit* (Nova, 2002).

How to File for Divorce In . . . (Sphinx) (state-specific do-it-yourself divorce kits).

Glossary

abandonment: When one spouse leaves the other for a specified period of time.

abuse of discretion: A significant mistake made by a trial court. "Abuse of discretion" is the standard generally applied by an appellate court when reconsidering a trial court's decision.

adultery: Voluntary sexual relations with someone other than one's spouse.

alienation of affections: The term used to describe a child's changed feelings toward one parent as a result of the other parent's efforts to badmouth that parent or otherwise negatively affect the child's relationship with that parent.

alimony: A sum of money paid by one spouse to another, to provide for that spouse's needs after the couple has separated or divorced.

allegations: In the context of divorce litigation, allegations are claims made by one spouse against the other in legal papers.

annulment: A legal action canceling the marriage. Annulment is available only where the conditions for a valid marriage were not met. For example, most states will annul a marriage if either spouse was married to somebody else at the time of the marriage (bigamy).

answer: In the context of divorce litigation, an answer is the legal document filed by the respondent in response to a petition for divorce.

appeal: A request that a higher court review a legal decision.

appellate court: A higher court that reviews the decisions of trial courts.

appreciation: An increase in value.

basis: The original cost of an asset. An asset's basis is used to determine the capital gains due upon the asset's sale.

capital gains: The difference between the original purchase price of an asset and its sale price. Individuals must generally pay taxes on capital gains.

case law: In the context of divorce litigation, case law consists of decisions issued by judges in divorce disputes. Judges in the same state must generally follow previous decisions—or case law—in cases involving the same issues and similar facts.

closely held corporation: A corporation in which the shares are held by a very small number of individuals, often just the members of one family.

cohabitation: Living with someone in a marriage-like relationship.

commingling: Mixing separate property with marital property.

community property: In the context of a divorce, community property is the property that a court will divide between spouses. Community property consists of all property acquired during the marriage, subject to certain exceptions.

complaint: In the context of divorce litigation, a complaint is the petition for divorce. The complaint will set forth the facts of the case and the allegations against the other spouse.

condonation: A defense to a fault-based divorce where the petitioner had already forgiven or overlooked the respondent's marital fault—for example, by reconciling after the respondent committed adultery.

contempt of court: When an individual violates a court order—such as an order to pay child support. As a penalty for contempt of court, the court may impose fines or jail time.

contested divorce: A divorce dispute in which the spouses cannot agree on one or more issues.

custodial parent: The parent with whom the child resides most of the time.

decree: In the context of a divorce, a decree is the judge's order officially dissolving the marriage.

de facto custody: When one parent moves out of the marital home, leaving the children behind with the other parent, the parent with whom the children reside is considered to have de facto custody.

defendant: In the context of divorce litigation, the defendant is the individual who did not file for divorce but instead must respond to his or her spouse's petition for divorce.

defense: A defense prevents someone from being held responsible for the conduct at issue. For example, a defense to a claim of adultery is that the other spouse forgave the adulterous spouse for his or her behavior.

deposition: The testimony of a witness taken out of court, under oath.

dischargeable: When an individual files for bankruptcy, he or she no longer has to pay certain debts and obligations. These debts and obligations are considered dischargeable in bankruptcy.

discovery: The process whereby both sides learn the relevant facts of the case. Discovery usually consists of requests for documents and witness depositions.

dissipation: Wasting marital property—for example, buying expensive gifts for lovers using marital property.

divorce statutes: The laws that set forth the rules on property division, alimony, custody, and child support.

domicile: The state in which an individual lives in and has an intention to remain in permanently.

duress: Wrongful pressure to force someone to do something against his or her will.

elective share: The share of an estate that a spouse is automatically entitled to receive, irrespective of the provisions of a will.

emancipation: Emancipation occurs when a child has become free from parental control or support. A child can become emancipated by getting married, becoming self-supporting, or abandoning the parental home.

equitable distribution: The process of dividing marital property between spouses according to what is just and appropriate in any given case.

equitable distribution factors: The factors that courts take into account when arriving at an equitable distribution of marital property.

expectancy: Property that one expects to receive in the future but one has no vested right to receive, such as an expected inheritance.

felony: A very serious crime, punishable by a term in state or federal prison.

fraudulent transfers: In the context of divorce litigation, fraudulent transfers are gifts or bargain sales made with the tacit understanding that the property will be returned after the divorce is final.

gross income: Gross income is the total amount of income that an individual earns, without any adjustments for taxes or other expenses.

grounds: In the context of divorce litigation, grounds are the legal basis—or reasons—for the divorce.

hold harmless clause: A provision in an agreement whereby one person agrees to accept full responsibility for a joint obligation, such as credit card debt, and to protect the other person from any liability in connection with that obligation.

impotency: Physical inability to engage in sexual intercourse.

imputing income: When an individual is voluntarily underemployed— for example, a surgeon who leaves his $200,000-a-year position to work as a teacher at $20,000 a year—a court may treat that individual as earning what he or she could be earning, rather than what he or she is actually earning, for the purposes of alimony and child support. In other words, a court may impute a higher income to that individual.

in loco parentis: When someone other than a child's natural parents acts as a parent to the child, that individual is considered to stand in loco parentis to the child.

joint custody: An arrangement whereby both parents share custody of the child. Joint custody generally means joint legal custody and joint physical custody. In joint legal custody, both parents have equal rights to make important decisions concerning the child. In joint physical custody, the child resides with each parent for an equal or approximately equal amount of time.

lien: A lien is an official claim against property in connection with a debt. When a lien is placed on property, it is generally difficult to sell or otherwise dispose of that property until the lien is cleared.

liquid assets: Assets that can be readily accessed for cash, such as publicly traded stock.

maintenance: Alimony, or spousal support.

majority: The age at which a child is considered an adult.

marital estate: The term used to describe the entire pot of marital property.

marital home: The home in which a couple lives together while married.

marital property: The property that a court will divide between spouses in a divorce. In most states, marital property consists of all property acquired during the marriage, subject to certain exceptions.

marital tort: An action brought by one spouse against the other for wrongdoing, such as intentional physical abuse committed during the marriage.

misdemeanor: A far less serious crime than a felony. Punishment for misdemeanors generally consists of a very limited time in jail and/or a fine.

net income: Net income is the total amount of income that an individual earns, minus taxes and other expenses. In general, monthly net income is the amount of money that an individual has available to spend each month.

nullify: To invalidate.

parental alienation syndrome: See "alienation of affections."

personal jurisdiction: The authority of a court to make decisions that bind an individual. A court will only have personal jurisdiction over an individual if he or she has had some contact with the state in which the court sits.

petition: In the context of divorce litigation, a petition is the document by which one spouse seeks a divorce. A petition is also known as a complaint.

petitioner: In the context of divorce litigation, the petitioner is the spouse who files for divorce. A petitioner is also known as a plaintiff.

plaintiff: In the context of divorce litigation, the plaintiff is the spouse who files for divorce. A plaintiff is also known as a petitioner.

precedent: Prior judicial decisions involving the same legal issues.

prenuptial agreement: A contract signed prior to marriage that specifies each spouse's rights in the event of death or divorce.

primary caretaker: The parent who takes care of the child's needs on a day-to-day basis.

probate: The process by which courts administer the estates of the deceased.

QDRO: A QDRO, or Qualified Domestic Relations Order, is a document through which a court can divide retirement benefits between spouses on an as-and-when-paid basis.

reconciliation: A defense to a fault-based divorce wherein the spouse filing for divorce has already forgiven the other spouse for the conduct at issue.

recrimination: A defense to a fault-based divorce in which the spouse filing for divorce is also guilty of some kind of marital fault. For example, a respondent might defend an adultery-based divorce by arguing that the petitioner was also guilty of adultery.

rehabilitative alimony: Spousal support that is paid for a short period of time to enable the financially dependent spouse to acquire the education and job skills necessary to become self-sufficient.

reimbursement alimony: A sum of money paid by one spouse to the other to compensate that spouse in special circumstances, such as when one spouse contributed toward the other's education or training.

separate property: The property that a court cannot divide between spouses in a divorce. In many states, separate property consists of property acquired before marriage, gifts, and inheritances.

sole custody: An arrangement whereby only one parent has custody of the child. Sole custody generally includes both sole legal custody and sole physical custody. Sole legal custody means that only one parent has the right to make important decisions concerning the child. Sole physical custody means that a child resides primarily with one parent.

split custody: A custodial arrangement in which one parent has sole custody of one child, and the other parent has sole custody of another child.

spousal support: Alimony, or maintenance.

tax-deductible: Tax-deductible expenses are subtracted from income for the purposes of calculating taxes. In general, the more tax deductions you can claim, the lower your tax bill will be.

title: Legal ownership of property. For example, the person whose name is on a deed to real estate has title to that property.

transmutation: The process by which separate property becomes marital property, or vice versa.

trial court: In the context of divorce litigation, a trial court is the court that hears your divorce dispute.

uncontested divorce: A divorce in which the couple has no dispute on any legal or factual issue.

visitation: The time that the non-custodial parent spends with the child on a regular basis.

Bibliography

Browne, Marlene M., *The Divorce Process: Empowerment Through Knowledge* (1st Books Library, 2001).

Curtis, Lynn, "Valuation of Stock Options in Dividing Marital Property Upon Dissolution," *Journal of the American Academy of Matrimonial Lawyers,* Volume 15, 1998.

Heywood, John (editor), *California Family Law Practice and Procedure* (Matthew Bender, 2002).

——— (editor), *Valuation and Distribution of Marital Property* (Matthew Bender, 2002).

Leski, Dennis (editor), *Child Custody and Visitation Law and Practice* (Matthew Bender, 2002).

——— (editor), *Modern Child Custody Practice* (Matthew Bender, 2002).

Parley, Louis I., and Alexander Lindey, *Lindey and Parley on Separation Agreements and Antenuptial Contracts* (2nd Edition, Matthew Bender, 2002).

Raggio, Grier H., and Michael Stutman, *How to Divorce in New York: Negotiating Your Divorce Settlement Without Tears or Trial* (St. Martin's/ Griffin, 1997).

Rutkin, Arnold H., *Family Law and Practice* (Matthew Bender, 2002).

Sitarz, Daniel, *Divorce Yourself: The National No-Fault Divorce Kit,* (5th Edition, Nova, 2002).

White, Helga, "Professional Goodwill: Is It a Settled Question or Is There 'Value' in Discussing It," *Journal of the American Academy of Matrimonial Lawyers,* Volume 15, 1998.

Index